Developing a Keyword Extractor and Document Classifier:

Emerging Research and Opportunities

Dimple Valayil Paul
Department of Computer Science, Dnyanprassarak Mandal's College and Research Centre, Goa University, Goa, India

A volume in the Advances in Data Mining and Database Management (ADMDM) Book Series

Published in the United States of America by
    IGI Global
    Engineering Science Reference (an imprint of IGI Global)
    701 E. Chocolate Avenue
    Hershey PA, USA 17033
    Tel: 717-533-8845
    Fax: 717-533-8661
    E-mail: cust@igi-global.com
    Web site: http://www.igi-global.com

Library of Congress Cataloging-in-Publication Data

Names: Paul, Dimple Valayil, 1976- author.
Title: Developing a keyword extractor and document classifier : emerging
  research and opportunities / by Dimple Valayil Paul.
Description: Hershey, PA : Information Science Reference, [2021] | Includes
  bibliographical references and index. | Summary: "This book presents a
  system for information retrieval using stemming, keyword extraction, and
  categorization"-- Provided by publisher.
Identifiers: LCCN 2020009699 (print) | LCCN 2020009700 (ebook) | ISBN
  9781799837725 (hardcover) | ISBN 9781799856078 (paperback) | ISBN
  9781799837732 (ebook)
Subjects: LCSH: Examinations--Design and construction. | Educational tests
  and measurements--Technological innovations. |
  Classification--Technological innovations. | Text data mining.
Classification: LCC LB3060.65 .P38 2021 (print) | LCC LB3060.65 (ebook) |
  DDC 371.26/1--dc23
LC record available at https://lccn.loc.gov/2020009699
LC ebook record available at https://lccn.loc.gov/2020009700

This book is published in the IGI Global book series Advances in Data Mining and Database Management (ADMDM) (ISSN: 2327-1981; eISSN: 2327-199X)

British Cataloguing in Publication Data
A Cataloguing in Publication record for this book is available from the British Library.

Advances in Data Mining and Database Management (ADMDM) Book Series

ISSN:2327-1981
EISSN:2327-199X

Editor-in-Chief: David Taniar, Monash University, Australia

MISSION

With the large amounts of information available to organizations in today's digital world, there is a need for continual research surrounding emerging methods and tools for collecting, analyzing, and storing data.

The **Advances in Data Mining & Database Management (ADMDM)** series aims to bring together research in information retrieval, data analysis, data warehousing, and related areas in order to become an ideal resource for those working and studying in these fields. IT professionals, software engineers, academicians and upper-level students will find titles within the ADMDM book series particularly useful for staying up-to-date on emerging research, theories, and applications in the fields of data mining and database management.

COVERAGE

- Decision Support Systems
- Database Security
- Factor Analysis
- Profiling Practices
- Data Mining
- Educational Data Mining
- Heterogeneous and Distributed Databases
- Association Rule Learning
- Predictive Analysis
- Data Quality

IGI Global is currently accepting manuscripts for publication within this series. To submit a proposal for a volume in this series, please contact our Acquisition Editors at Acquisitions@igi-global.com or visit: http://www.igi-global.com/publish/.

Titles in this Series

For a list of additional titles in this series, please visit:
http://www.igi-global.com/book-series/advances-data-mining-database-management/37146

Multidisciplinary Functions of Blockchain Technology in AI and IoT Applications
Niaz Chowdhury (The Open University, Milton Keynes, UK) and Ganesh Chandra Deka
(Ministry of Skill Development and Entrepreneurship, New Delhi, India)
Engineering Science Reference • © 2021 • 255pp • H/C (ISBN: 9781799858768) • US
$245.00

Handbook of Research on Engineering, Business, and Healthcare Applications of Data Science and Analytics
Bhushan Patil (Independent Researcher, India) and Manisha Vohra (Independent Researcher, India)
Engineering Science Reference • © 2021 • 583pp • H/C (ISBN: 9781799830535) • US
$345.00

Advanced Deep Learning Applications in Big Data Analytics
Hadj Ahmed Bouarara (Tahar Moulay University of Saida, Algeria)
Engineering Science Reference • © 2021 • 351pp • H/C (ISBN: 9781799827917) • US
$245.00

Opportunities and Challenges for Blockchain Technology in Autonomous Vehicles
Amit Kumar Tyagi (Vellore Institute of Technolgy, Chennai, India) Gillala Rekha (K. L. University, India) and N. Sreenath (Pondicherry Engineering College, India)
Engineering Science Reference • © 2021 • 316pp • H/C (ISBN: 9781799832959) • US
$245.00

Cross-Industry Use of Blockchain Technology and Opportunities for the Future
Idongesit Williams (Aalborg University, Denmark)
Engineering Science Reference • © 2020 • 228pp • H/C (ISBN: 9781799836322) • US
$225.00

701 East Chocolate Avenue, Hershey, PA 17033, USA
Tel: 717-533-8845 x100 • Fax: 717-533-8661
E-Mail: cust@igi-global.com • www.igi-global.com

Based test Paper Models, Type IV focuses on Syllabus Coverage Evaluation in Test Paper Models and Type V is on Answer Evaluation of Short Descriptive Questions.

The work performed under each of these five different types of problems is briefly described below -

Type I: The Test Paper Template Generation process is modeled here as a multi-constraint optimization problem. By using the search technique of evolutionary programming and the concept of levels of educational taxonomy three different algorithms have been designed and implemented to generate test paper templates.

Type II: It includes a new approach for constructing the question similarity matrix and using this matrix for Grouping of Similar Questions from a Question Bank using Partition Based Clustering. This approach has resulted in reducing the best case time complexity $O(n \times (n-1)/2 \log n)$ of hierarchical clustering approach to $O(n \times (n-1)/2)$.

Type III: Multi-Objective optimization algorithms are also found efficient for Question Selection in Template Based Test Paper Models. Question selection plays a key role in test paper generation systems. The multi-constraint optimization problem of Question Selection has been solved using Evolutionary Approach, Elitist Evolutionary approach and Elitist Differential Evolution Approach. Even though Evolutionary Approach and Elitist Evolutionary Approach of Question Selection successfully terminate with near optimal solutions, they encountered significant runtime delay during the subsequent stages of iterative population generation. Hence an enhanced evolutionary approach with a better convergence known as Elitist Multi-Objective Differential Evolution has been experimented.

Type IV: A modularized syllabus containing weightages assigned to different modules of a subject are very useful to both teaching as well as to the student community. In the current educational scenario, criteria like Bloom's taxonomy, learning outcomes, etc. have been used for evaluating the syllabus coverage of a test paper. But we have not come across any work that focuses on unit-weightages for computing the syllabus coverage. Hence in this work we have addressed the problem of evaluating the syllabus-coverage of an examination test paper by analyzing the questions on different criteria. Cosine Similarity Measure is initially experimented to compute the similarity matrix of question content and syllabus content. The similarity matrix is used as a guideline in clustering the module-wise questions, matching its weightage against Syllabus File and evaluating the syllabus coverage of the test paper. But due to the limitation of cosine which represent the terms as bags of words, the underlying sequential information provided by the ordering of the words is typically lost. In order to overcome this limitation, we extended the work by incorporating Word Order Similarity metric which computes similarity matrix of question content and syllabus content on the basis of word order similarity measure.

Type V: The descriptive examination test paper when compared to objective test paper acts as a better aid in continuous assessment for testing the progress of a student under various cognitive levels at different stages of learning. Unfortunately, assessment of descriptive answers is found to be tedious and time consuming by instructors. The manual descriptive answer paper evaluation system at undergraduate level commonly uses the master key or the question solution key. Solution key for every question are prepared by the instructor or paper-setter who frames the examination test paper. The points in the solution key are collected from the specified text book and are used as a baseline in evaluating the student answer. Even though there are few attempts in automation or semi-automation of descriptive answer paper evaluation, none of them focuses on finding the co-occurrence match of multiple words in student answer content as well as in the question solution key content. Therefore, an attempt has been made to address the problem of automatic evaluation of descriptive answer using vector-based similarity matrix with order-based word-to-word syntactic similarity measure. The experimental results prove that this approach is promising for application in automatic evaluation of descriptive answer paper.

Majority of the algorithms implemented as part of this book are integrated and a web-based tool named Test Paper Generation System (TPGS), has been developed as a prototype so that this book becomes useful to the immediate stakeholders namely the paper-setters /course- instructors and feedback can be obtained to continue further research for CBOES. A brief description of QPGS tool with screenshots is presented as one among the chapter of this book.

Introduction

Examinations are inseparable components of educational program because they are the well accepted parameters to ascertain the level of excellence of learners. They are subsystem in a wider set of evaluation which measures qualitative as well as quantitative aspects of learners. Examinations assist in regular assessment of learner's capability, provide regular feedback to learners and determine the effectiveness of teaching by monitoring learner's progress. Written examination is a conventional yet a universal tool to evaluate learner's performance in an educational area. They are identified to be cost-effective means of assessing a large number of learners. Written examinations provide a mechanism by which instructors and institutions assure uniformity in the assessment process. Written examinations are preferred usually over oral examinations in terms of their objectivity, impartiality and expenditure in conducting examinations for a large number of learners.

The existing manual approach of conducting written examination is a very lengthy procedure and needs the instructor to put in a substantial effort and devote quality time in the conduct of the same. It is considered by majority as an extremely tedious and stressful activity. Each examination is conducted with a pre-defined test paper that has to be answered within the specified time period. The test paper usually has a complex structure and consists of descriptive type as well as objective type of questions. Test papers generally are based on paper format specifications viz. blue print and differ from one another in terms of marks allocation, completion time, module weightage, number of questions, question types, level of difficulty, etc.

There are many Online Examination Systems (OES) that deal with objective type of questions and allow various users of the system to set the test paper, to answer the test paper and to grade the answer paper. While formulating the questions for a test paper, there are many theories that provide frameworks on levels of thinking which have serious impact on framing good questions. Bloom's taxonomy is commonly cited as a tool to use different cognitive levels in selecting the questions (Cognitive is used to comprise activities such as remembering and recalling knowledge, thinking, problem-solving and creating). Cognitive domain contains those objectives which deal with recall or recognition of knowledge and the development of intellectual abilities and skills. It is the domain in which most of the work in curriculum development has taken place and where the clearest definitions of objectives have been phrased as descriptions of student behavior. The idea of Bloom's classification system was framed at an informal meeting of college examiners who attended the 1948 American Psychological Association Convention in Boston. During this meeting, interest was articulated in a theoretical framework which could be used to enable communication among examiners. Subsequently, there was agreement that such a theoretical framework might best be attained through a system of classifying the goals of the educational process, as educational objectives deliver the basis for building curricula and test, and characterize the starting point for much of our educational research. Educational researcher Benjamin Bloom and colleagues have suggested six different cognitive stages in learning such as knowledge (know), understanding(under), application(appl), analysis(anal), synthesis(synth) and evaluation(eval) (Bloom, B.S., et.al 1956). Details of verbs and question examples that represent intellectual activity at each level of Bloom's taxonomy can be found in (Yeh, L. C. & LIN, S. P. 2003; Khairuddin, N. N. & Hashim, K. 2008). Curriculum builders discover that the taxonomy helps them to specify objectives so that it becomes easier to design learning experiences and formulate evaluation devices. Cognitive processing levels for a test paper template are decided on the basis of the taxonomy that is selected by the paper-setter for each examination. Though there exist many such systems which allow conducting online examination, very few of them deal with descriptive type of questions. The approaches used for objective test paper generation cannot be directly applied for setting a descriptive test paper.

Considering the document classification domain, the main problems which prevent fast and high-quality document processing in electronic document management systems are insufficient and unstructured information, information redundancy and presence of great deal of undesirable user information. The human factor has a significant impact on the efficiency of document search. An average user is not aware of the advance option of a query language and uses simply typical queries. Development of a specialized software toolkit intended for information systems and electronic document management systems can be effective solution of tasks listed above. Such toolkit should be based on the means and methods of Automatic Keyword Extraction and Text classification.

Hence this research work is devoted to analyze, design and implement algorithms for test paper modeling, keyword extraction from student submissions and document classification of student textual documents that can be used for descriptive as well as objective type questions. The concepts of multi-objective optimization algorithms and partition-based grouping/clustering algorithms have formed the basis for this research work.

RELATED WORK

Optimization consists of a search for one or multiple feasible solutions corresponding to the optimal values of one or multiple objectives of a problem (Papadimitriou C. H. & Steiglitz, K. 1982; Bernhard, K. & Vygen, J. 2001). The feasible solution or optimal solution satisfies possible constraints inherent in the problem. In single-objective optimization, it is possible to determine between any given pair of solutions if one is better than the other. As a result, we usually obtain a single optimal solution. However, in multi-objective optimization there is no straight forward method to determine if a solution is better than the other. Hence, multi-objective constraint based combinatorial optimization as compared to single objective optimization is generalized as the optimization of more than one objective simultaneously. Since multiple objectives usually conflict with each other, the result of a Multi-Objective Optimization Problem (MOOP) (Ehrgott, M. & Gandibleux, X. 2002) is usually not a single solution but a set of solutions. These solutions represent the best compromises between different objectives. This is done in such a way that the objective functions associated with the problem are minimized, or maximized, taking into account a set of requirements that constrain the potential possible solutions. The central characteristic of the constrained component is that not all solutions inside the search space are feasible. Furthermore, in Combinatorial Optimization Problems (COPs), the set of feasible solutions has a finite number of alternatives. Multi-objective COPs with constraints have been a potential research area for the last few decades due to the many criteria and combinatorial nature of many real-life problems (Neumann, F. & Witt, C. 2010; Zhi, F.L., Ji, S & Jia, L. 2010). Thus, the importance of dealing with these kinds of problems lies in finding novel techniques which are able to solve them in an effective and efficient way so as to bring about significant savings in resources as well as considerable savings in time. Thus, the importance of dealing with these kinds of problems lies in finding novel techniques which are able to solve them in an effective and efficient way so as to bring about significant savings in resources as well as considerable savings in time. Grouping or clustering is the most common form of unsupervised learning and is particularly useful in many applications such as automatic categorization of documents, duplicate content detection, search optimization, building taxonomy of documents, etc (Halkidi,M, Batistakis, Y. & Vazirgiannis, M. 2002; Xu, R. &Wunsch, D. 2005). Document clustering has been studied for many decades but still is far from an insignificant and solved problem as it includes many challenges as below-

1. Choosing suitable features of the documents for clustering.
2. Finding an appropriate (dis)similarity measure between documents.
3. Selecting a proper clustering method utilizing the above (dis)similarity measure.
4. Implementing the clustering algorithm using an efficient and effective method that makes it feasible in terms of required memory and CPU resources.
5. Finding ways of assessing the quality of the performed clustering.

Document clustering algorithms commonly use four major steps such as pattern recognition, pattern proximity determination, grouping and output evaluation. Pattern recognition identifies the number of patterns and features contained in the query specification. Pattern proximity determines the best similarity formula to be used in the clustering algorithm. Grouping is an iterative process which applies the similarity formula, computes the pair-wise similarity of each document with the rest of the documents and generates new clusters of documents based on the specified threshold value. Output evaluation is generally carried out using f-measure. F-measure combines two different retrieval measures such as precision and recall into one measure. Precision is defined as the measure of relevant versus non-relevant items returned. In terms of document clustering, precision is the measure of high similarity of documents in the cluster versus low similarity with documents in other clusters. Recall is defined as the measure of relevant documents retrieved versus relevant documents not retrieved. In terms of document clustering, recall is used to measure the lack of documents in other clusters whose individual similarity to documents in another cluster is high (Ekblaw, A.R. 2012). In addition to the four steps described above, most document clustering methods also perform several pre-processing steps including stop words removal, stemming and normalization on the document set. Each document is represented by a vector of frequencies of remaining terms within the document. Some document clustering algorithms employ an extra pre-processing step that divides the actual term frequency by the overall frequency of the term in the entire document set. The idea is that if a term is too common across different documents, it has little discriminating power (Mooi, E. & Sarstedt, M. 2011).

Data Mining also popularly referred to as Knowledge Discovery in Databases (KDD), is the automated or convenient extraction of patterns representing knowledge implicitly stored in large databases, data warehouses and other massive information repositories. Data mining refers to extracting or mining knowledge from large amounts of data. Text data mining concerns the application of data mining (knowledge discovery in databases, KDD) to unstructured textual data (Susan P. I 2009).

Data Mining can be loosely described as looking for patterns in data and Text Mining is about looking for patterns in text. However, the superficial similarity between the two conceals real differences. Data Mining can be more fully characterized as the extraction of implicit, previously unknown, and potentially useful information from data (Gregory P-S, Chabane D., Lise G., 2006). The information is implicit in the input data: it is hidden, unknown, and could hardly be extracted without recourse to automatic techniques of data mining.

With Text Mining, however, the information to be extracted is clearly and explicitly stated in the text. Most authors go to great pains to make sure that they express themselves clearly and unambiguously and, from a human point of view, the only sense in which it is "previously unknown" is that human resource restrictions make it infeasible for people to read the text themselves (Fan, W., Linda & Rich, Stephanie & Zhang, Zhongju. 2006). The problem, of course, is that the information is not couched in a manner that is amenable to automatic processing. Text Mining strives to bring it out of the text in a form that is suitable for consumption by computers directly, with no need for a human intermediary. Another requirement that is common to both Data and Text Mining is that the information extracted should be "potentially useful." In one sense, this means actionable—capable of providing a basis for actions to be taken automatically. In the case of Data Mining, this notion can be expressed in a relatively domain independent way: Actionable patterns are ones that allow non-trivial predictions to be made on new data from the same source. Performance can be measured by counting successes and failures, statistical techniques can be applied to compare different data mining methods on the same problem, and so on.

However, in many Text Mining situations it is far harder to characterize what "actionable" means in a way that is independent of the particular domain at hand. In many data mining applications, "potentially useful" is given a different interpretation: the key for success is that the information extracted must be comprehensible in that it helps to explain the data (Burney, Atika & Akbar, Ali & Sultan, Ahmer 2009).This is necessary whenever the result is intended for human consumption rather than (or as well as) a basis for automatic action. This criterion is less applicable to Text Mining because, unlike data mining, the input itself is comprehensible.

Automatic Text Mining techniques have a long way to go before they rival the ability of people, even without any special domain knowledge, to clean information from large document collections. Knowledge Discovery in Text (KDT) and Text Mining are mostly automated techniques that aim to discover high level information in huge amount of textual data and present it to the potential user (analyst, decision-maker, etc). KDT is the non-trivial process of identifying valid, novel, potentially useful, and ultimately understandable patterns in unstructured textual data. Text Mining is a step in the KDT process consisting of particular data mining and Natural Language Processing (NLP) algorithms that under some acceptable computational efficiency limitations produce a particular enumeration of patterns over a set of unstructured textual data. Text Mining uses unstructured textual information and examines it in attempt to discover the structure and implicit meanings "hidden" within the text. Text Mining is considered to be an exciting research area that tries to solve the information overload problem by using techniques from data mining, machine learning, NLP, Information Retrieval (IR) and knowledge management (Witten, Ian & Don, Katherine & Dewsnip, Michael & Tablan, Valentin. 2004).

Text Mining can also be defined as the application of algorithms and methods from the fields of machine learning and statistics to texts with the goal of finding useful patterns. Natural language processing, Data mining and Machine learning techniques work together to automatically discover patterns at the extracted information and the metadata that have been derived from the documents. Text Mining has been receiving attention in many areas such as Security applications, Biomedical applications, Academics and Software applications. Research and development departments of major companies, including IBM and Microsoft are researching Text Mining techniques and developing programs to further automate the mining and analysis processes. Text mining software is also being researched by different companies working in the area of search and indexing in general as a way to improve their results.

Keyword extraction of text mining is a classification task: each word phrase in a document is either a keyword or not, and the problem is to correctly classify a phrase into one of these two categories. Keyword Extraction is an entirely different method for inferring keyword's metadata. Here, all the words that occur in the document are listed and information retrieval heuristics are used to select those that seem to characterize it best. Most keywords are noun phrases, and syntactic techniques may be used to identify these and ensure that the set of candidates contains only noun phrases. Most machine learning and Text Mining techniques are adapted towards the analysis of text collections. Texts are composed of words or phrases and have an inherent sequential structure. Such a text can be viewed as a sequence of words, stop words, punctuation marks, parentheses and keywords where each keyword has an associated frequency. The basic problem in analyzing such a text collection is to find keywords, i.e., sequences of words occurring frequently close to each other. Keywords are used as attributes for mining rules or as a basis for measuring the similarity of new (unclassified) documents with existing (classified) ones. Focus is on the problem of extracting keywords from text's collection in order to use them as attributes for text classification. Keywords or search terms could be defined as sequences of adjacent words within a text window (e.g. Two or more successive words of the text / a sentence) forming a meaningful, descriptive phrase related to the content of the text document. Keywords provide a semantic metadata that summarize and characterize documents. Since Keywords summarize documents very concisely, they can be used as a low-cost measure of similarity between documents, making it possible to group documents by measuring overlap between the Keywords to which they are assigned to.

Text classification techniques have been well developed in the past twenty years. With the availability of many text classification methods, empirical evaluation is important to provide guidance for method selection in applications. Due to the subjectivity in the class concept definition, analytical assessment of text classifier is hard. When classifying a document, no information is used except for the document's content itself. Some tasks constrain documents to a single category, whereas in others each document may have many categories. Sometimes category labeling is probabilistic rather than deterministic, or the objective is to rank the categories by their estimated relevance to a particular document.

We have used a preprocessing step in our document classifier. Our classifier takes as input a text document, finds the set of keywords of the document and then classifies it using the predefined weights stored for different keywords in each class. We have assumed that the subject expert of a class gives all the keywords and weights for all keywords of a class. A keyword having more importance in a class is given a higher weight for that class and may be given a lower or a different weight in another class. In order to classify a given document we find the cumulative weight of all the keywords of that document in all the predefined classes considering the weights of these keywords in each class, which contain these keywords. The document is assigned to that class which has the highest cumulative weight for the keywords of that document. In case of restriction on maximum number of documents that can be assigned to a class, the class is assigned considering the cumulative weights of all classes in descending order for the different classes. In case of restriction on maximum number of documents that can be assigned to a class, the class is assigned considering the cumulative weights of all classes in descending order for different classes.

MOTIVATION

As the emphasis on continuous assessment is gaining significance and the number of courses offered by educational institutions is increasing day by day along with an increase in the number of students enrolling for the courses, there is a need to have a change in the manual test paper setting system adopted in most of the academic institutions. The change is essential as the manual test paper composition system is encountering a major limitation of unproductive utilization of time and resources. In order to overcome the limitation, it is necessary to design and implement a set of algorithms for test paper modeling. The auto generated dynamic model can greatly improve-

1. Adaptability
2. Save time and expenditure
3. Avoid repetition of questions
4. Create variants or versions of a particular question or the whole test paper
5. Carry out syllabus coverage evaluation of test paper
6. Perform answer evaluation of a test paper
7. Maintain quality of test paper with respect to weightage of units/modules
8. Check Proportion of each type of question and
9. Evaluate Proportion of coverage of cognitive learning domain, etc.

Current existing automatic paper generation systems can be classified under three main categories, namely, random-algorithm-based system (Anthony, M. M. 2007), backtracking system and intelligent information optimization system. However, first two systems cannot satisfy the instructor specified multiple requirements simultaneously (Fujiwara, H. and Shimono, T. 1983; Li, Y. &Tang, J. (2012). In order to overcome the limitations of the first two automatic paper generation systems, the third system using intelligent information optimization has been widely studied by many researchers (Liu, D., Wang, J & Zheng, L. 2013; Meng, Y., et.al 2012). According to their investigation, this problem requires solving many other sub-problems and majority of them are based on Multi-Objective Combinatorial Optimization (MOCO) (Ehrgott, M. & Gandibleux, X. 2002). MOCO has the characteristic that no unique solution exists but a set of mathematically equally good solutions can be identified. It explores a finite search space of feasible solutions and finds the optimal ones that balance multiple objectives (often conflicting) simultaneously. Constrained problems, either single or multi-objective, are difficult tasks to be modeled and solved by conventional mathematical techniques (Beheshti, Z., Mariyam, S. & Shamsuddin, H. 2013). As such, an important area of research is in the area of novel meta-heuristics (Gandomi, A. H. et.al 2013; Yang, X. S. 2013) that can efficiently solve such problems. In the last few decades, nature-inspired meta-heuristics have become an effective and efficient alternative to solve single-objective and multi-objective Constraint Optimization Problem (COP). All meta-heuristic algorithms use some trade-off between local search and global exploration. Hence, the main motivation for this research work has been to design and implement a set of multi-objective meta-heuristic optimization algorithms that can be used to automate the manual test paper generation system.

Text Mining is about inferring structure from sequences representing natural language text, and may be defined as the process of analyzing text to extract information that is useful for particular purposes often called "metadata". Compared with the kind of data stored in databases, text is unstructured, amorphous, and contains information at many different levels. Despite the fact that the problems are difficult to define clearly, interest in Text Mining is burgeoning because it is perceived to have enormous potential practical utility.

CONTRIBUTIONS

The main contributions of this research work are as under-

1. Design and implementation of multi-constraint optimization algorithms for Test paper Template (QPT) Generation. Three different template generation approaches namely evolutionary approach, pareto-optimal evolutionary approach and bi-proportional scaling approach, have been implemented and their performance study carried out.

2. Design and implementation of partition-based clustering algorithm for repeated question identification via matrix representation.

3. Design and implementation of multi-constraint algorithm for question selection: The question selection process from a question bank has been modeled as a multi-constraint problem and solved using three different approaches namely evolutionary approach, elitist evolutionary approach and elitist differential evolution approach.

4. Design and implementation of grouping algorithm using two different syntactic similarity measures for syllabus coverage evaluation of a test paper.

5. Design and implementation of grouping algorithm using similarity matrix for short descriptive answer evaluation.

All these algorithms for test paper modeling have been published and also integrated in a prototype model which is developed as a general-purpose software tool that can be used in experimentation of effectiveness of the multi-objective algorithms designed as part of this research work and to promote further research in this area.

SIGNIFICANCE OF THE STUDY

The results of this study will prove useful to-

1. Provide future directions to other researchers who are interested in carrying out research study on automation of test paper modeling.

2. Assist universities and other learning institutions to standardize quality of test paper formulation as well as answer paper assessment, by accepting well defined parameters such as: blueprint for test paper pattern, educational taxonomies with its cognitive levels for student skill assessment, subject-wise question bank for automatic question selection, subject-wise syllabus having module-wise topics along with module-wise weightages for evaluating syllabus coverage of test paper and question-paper-wise question solution key for evaluating answer paper.

3. Facilitate automatic generation of qualitative test paper satisfying subject's syllabus module coverage constraint, taxonomy's cognitive level coverage constraint, time constraint, type of question constraint, question conflict constraint, etc. and there-by provide a benchmark for future research.

BOOK OUTLINE

This book is presented in seven chapters. The first chapter has presented the introductory concepts, related work, motivation, contributions and significance of the research study which is followed by outline of the book. Chapter 2 presents multi-objective optimization algorithms for template generation and investigates the significance of these algorithms in dynamic test paper template formulation. To be more precise, the chapter initially identifies significance of multi-constraint evolutionary approach for Test paper Template (QPT) generation. Further the chapter continues with highlights on advantages of pareto-optimal evolutionary approach based templates over evolutionary approach based templates. Finally the chapter concludes with discussion on efficiency of an incremental template generation algorithm which has been designed using bi-proportional matrix scaling approach. Chapter 3 introduces grouping algorithm for question clustering via matrix representation methods. The theme of this chapter lies in designing partition-based grouping algorithm with a similarity matrix for question cluster formulation. Performance evaluation has been carried out by finding precision, recall and f-measure scores for the datasets used in the study. Chapter 4 presents the design and use of multi-constraint optimization algorithm for question selection in template based Test paper Model (QPM). The evolutionary approach, elitist evolutionary approach as well as the elitist differential evolution approach based QPMs are designed for performing an intelligent question selection from the pre-defined question bank. The previously generated templates as well as the previously formulated question clusters are used as input for the multi-constraint question selection problem. Chapter 5 highlights an enhanced partition-based grouping algorithm for syllabus coverage evaluation of a QPM. Chapter 6 presents details of the modeling of answer paper evaluation problem and the usage of partition-based grouping algorithm for answer evaluation of short descriptive questions of a QPM. Chapter 7 concludes the book by summarizing the research and with a discussion on how future research can handle the issues raised in this research study. The QPGS software tool developed as a byproduct of this research, along with the screenshots presenting the functionalities of different algorithms designed and implemented during the research work has been placed as Appendix A at the end of this book.

REFERENCES

Anthony, M. M. (2007). *Random question sequencing in computer-based testing (CBT) assessments and its effect on individual student performance* (Master's Dissertation). University of Pretoria.

Beheshti, Z., Mariyam, S. & Shamsuddin, H. (2013). A Review of Population-based Meta-heuristic Algorithms. *International Journal of Advances in Soft Computing and its Application, 5*(1), 1-35.

Bernhard, K., & Vygen, J. (2001). *Combinatorial optimization: Theory and Algorithms (Algorithms and Combinatorics)* (3rd ed.). Springer.

Bloom, B. S., Engelhart, M. D., Furs, E. J., Hill, W. H., & Krath-wohl, D. R. (1956). *Taxonomy of educational objectives: The classification of educational goals, Handbook I: Cognitive domain*. David McKay Company.

Burney, A., Akbar, A., & Sultan, z. (2009). *Knowledge Discovery using Text Mining: A Programmable Implementation on Information Extraction and Categorization*. Academic Press.

Ehrgott, M., & Gandibleux, X. (2002). Multiobjective Combinatorial Optimization-Theory, Methodology, and Applications. *Multiple Criteria Optimization: State of the Art Annotated Bibliographic Surveys International Series in Operations Research Management Science, 52*, 369–444.

Ekblaw, A. R. (2012). Feasibility and effectiveness: Comparing document clustering algorithms from a user's perspective. *Journal of Information Science*, 1–20.

Fan, W., Wallace, L., Rich, S., & Zhang, Z. (2006). Tapping the Power of Text Mining. *Communications of the ACM, 49*(9), 76–82. doi:10.1145/1151030.1151032

Fujiwara, H., & Shimono, T. (1983). On the Acceleration of Test Generation Algorithms. *IEEE Transactions on Computers Archive, 32*(12), 1137-1144.

Gandomi, A. H., Yang, X. S., Talatahari, S., & Alavi, A. H. (2013). *Meta-heuristics in Modeling and Optimization, Metaheuristic Applications in Structures and Infrastructures* (1st ed.). Elsevier.

Gregory, P.-S., Chabane, D., & Lise, G. (2006). What are the grand challenges for data mining? *SIGKDD Explorations*, *8*(2), 70–77. doi:10.1145/1233321.1233330

Halkidi, M., Batistakis, Y., & Vazirgiannis, M. (2002). Cluster Validity Methods: Part II. *SIGMOD Record*, *31*(3), 19–27. doi:10.1145/601858.601862

Imberman. (2009). *Effective use of the KDD Process and Data Mining for Computer Performance Professionals* (Thesis). College of Staten Island.

Khairuddin, N. N., & Hashim, K. (2008). Application of Bloom's Taxonomy in Software Engineering Assessments. *Proceedings of the 8th WSEAS International Conference on Applied Computer Science*, 66-69.

Li, Y., & Tang, J. (2012). The Research of Examination Paper Generation Based on Index System Metrics and Multi-Objective Strategy. *Journal of Software Engineering and Applications*, *5*(8), 634–638. doi:10.4236/jsea.2012.58073

Liu, D., Wang, J., & Zheng, L. (2013). Automatic Test Paper Generation Based on Ant Colony Algorithm. *Journal of Software*, *8*(10), 2600–2606. doi:10.4304/jsw.8.10.2600-2606

Meng, Y., Jin, L. S. C. F. H., & Chen, Q. (2012). The Research on the Automatic Generation of Concept Weights and Optimal Composition for Test Item in E-learning System. *Proceedings of 2nd International Conference on Materials, Mechatronics and Automation, LNIT, 15*, 46-52.

Mooi, E., & Sarstedt, M. (2011). *Cluster Analysis, A Concise Guide to Market Research*. Springer-Verlag. doi:10.1007/978-3-642-12541-6

Neumann, F., & Witt, C. (2010). *Bio-inspired Computation in Combinatorial Optimization - Algorithms and Their Computational Complexity, Natural Computing Series*. Springer.

Papadimitriou, C. H., & Steiglitz, K. (1982). *Combinatorial Optimization: Algorithms and Complexity*. Prentice-Hall.

Pukelsheim, F. (2014). Bi-proportional Matrix Scaling and the Iterative Proportional Fitting Procedure. *Proceedings of Annals of Operation Research*, 269-283.

Witten, I., Don, K., Dewsnip, M., & Tablan, V. (2004). Text mining in a digital library. *International Journal on Digital Libraries*, *4*(1), 1–4. doi:10.100700799-003-0066-4

Xu, R., & Wunsch, D. II. (2005). Survey of clustering algorithms. *IEEE Transactions on Neural Networks*, *16*(3), 645–678. doi:10.1109/TNN.2005.845141 PMID:15940994

Yang, X. S. (2013). Optimization and Metaheuristic Algorithms in Engineering. In *Metaheuristics in Water, Geotechnical and Transport Engineering* (pp. 1–23). Elsevier. doi:10.1016/B978-0-12-398296-4.00001-5

Yeh, L. C., & Lin, S. P. (2003). The research of Bloom's taxonomy for educational objects. *The Journal of Educational Research*, *105*, 94–106.

Zhi, F. L., Ji, S., & Jia, L. (2010). Strategy and Applied Research of Multi-Constrained Model of Automatic Test Paper Based on Genetic Algorithm. *Applied Mechanics and Materials*, *37-38*, 1223–1230. doi:10.4028/www.scientific.net/AMM.37-38.1223

Chapter 1
Dynamic Template Generation

ABSTRACT

A test blueprint/test template, also known as the table of specifications, represents the structure of a test. It has been highly recommended in assessment textbook to carry out the preparation of a test with a test blueprint. This chapter focuses on modeling a dynamic test paper template using multi-objective optimization algorithm and makes use of the template in dynamic generation of examination test paper. Multi-objective optimization-based models are realistic models for many complex optimization problems. Modeling a dynamic test paper template, similar to many real-life problems, includes solving multiple conflicting objectives satisfying the template specifications.

TERMINOLOGY USED

The general terminology used in this chapter is brie y discussed in Table 1.

The Test paper Template (TPT) shown in Table 2 is a systematic design plan which lays out exactly how the test paper gets created.

The TPT with maximum marks (TM), distribution of unit/module weights $(u_1, u_2..., u_m)$, distribution of cognitive levels weights $(l_1, l_2..., l_n)$, etc. so suggested in the QPT Format in Table 3 above is expected to ensure that-

1. The weight given to each unit/module, $(u_1, u_2..., u_m)$ in a test paper is appropriate, so that the important modules are not neglected.

DOI: 10.4018/978-1-7998-3772-5.ch001

Table 1. Terminology used for dynamic template generation

Term	Meaning
Course	Course is a Degree/Diploma program offered at a university. Example: 1. Bachelor of Science (Computer Science)-B.Sc (Comp.Sc.) 2. Bachelor of Computer Application -BCA
Subject	S is a subject/paper offered in different semesters of a course. Example: Software Engineering (SE) in 6th Semester and Information Technology (IT) in 1st Semester of B.Sc(Comp. Sc).
Modules/ Units	For each subject, there is a prescribed syllabus having different modules/units. A set of related topics is grouped as one unit/module. Each module is allotted a particular weightage. Example: Module on Software Requirement in SE subject has weightage of 30% in the 6th semester of B.Sc (Comp. Sc).
Educational Taxonomy	A classification system of educational objectives based on level of student understanding necessary for achievement or mastery. Example- Benjamin Bloom, Solo etc.
m, n, TM	m, n, TM are the Instructor specified number of modules, number of levels and total marks respectively for generating a dynamic QPT.
Module (p_i)	p_i is the ith module specified by Instructor for QPT, $p=<p_1...,p_m>$
Taxonomy Level (q_j)	q_j is the jth level specified by Instructor for QPT, $q=<q_1,...,q_n>$
Module Weight (u_i)	u_i is the weight assigned to the ith module in the QPT
Level Weight (l_j)	l_j is the weight assigned to the jth level in the QPT
Module-Level-Weight (x_{ij})	x_{ij} is the weight assigned to the ith module of j^h level in the QPT
Question Paper Template (QPT) of maximum marks TM	QPT is an m×n matrix with rows representing Modules p_i (i= 1 to m), columns representing Educational Taxonomy Levels q_j (j= 1 to n), cells representing i^{th} module of j^h level x_{ij} such that $$\sum_{i=1}^{m} u_i = \sum_{j=1}^{n} l_j = TM$$
m`, n`, tm	m`, n`, tm are the Instructor specified number of modules, number of levels and total marks respectively for generating a scaled QPT.
Scaled Module-Level-Weight ($x`_{vw}$)	$x`_{vw}$ is the scaled weight assigned to the vth module of wth level.
Scaled Module Weight ($u`_v$)	$u`_v$ is the scaled weight assigned to the vth module
Scaled Level Weight ($l`_w$)	$l`_w$ is the scaled weight assigned to the wth level
Scaled QPT (qpt) of maximum marks tm	qpt is an m`×n` matrix generated from QPT by scaling its rows with respect to m` modules and scaling its columns with respect to n` levels such that $$\sum_{v=1}^{m`} = u`_v = \sum_{w=1}^{n`} l`_w = tm$$

2. The weightage of cognitive skills, (l_1, l_2..., ln) tested are appropriate. For example, there are sufficient questions requiring application and understanding of logical reasoning.

Table 2. Test paper template (TPT) format

Unit/Level	level 1	level 2	level 3	...	level n	Unit Weight
unit1	x_{11}	x_{12}	x_{13}	...	x_{1n}	u_1
unit2	x_{21}	x_{21}	x_{23}	...	x_{2n}	u_2
...	...	...	...	...	...	...
unit m	x_{m1}	x_{m2}	x_{m3}	...	x_{mn}	u_m
Level Weight	l_1	l_2	l_3	...	l_n	TM

3. Weight of modules and weight of cognitive skills are proportionately adjusted for generating templates that are used for different test papers with varying total marks, TM.
4. Test paper satisfies both time and marks constraints
5. Test paper takes into account of different difficulty levels.
6. Weight allotted to a cell of a template also known as module-level-weight, $x_{11}..., x_{mn}$ is the proportionate weightage assigned to the particular level under a module of a template.

In order to incorporate all the above requirements of a template, it is necessary to design an algorithm for dynamic template generation and use it for generation of test paper that has proper weightage allotted to subject content, cognitive learning domain, type of question, total marks, etc. and can be used for generation of several test papers almost without repetition depending on the paper-setter's choice. The number of unique test papers (without any overlap) that can be prepared for the given subject using a generated template (Suskie, L. 2009) depends on the quality and size of the Question Bank (QB) (Hwang, G.J., Lin, B.M.T.& Lin, T.L. 2006). The quality of a QB is decided on the basis of the type of questions, such as questions of 1 mark, 2 marks, 5 marks, etc. that exist in the QB for each unit under different cognitive levels of an Educational Taxonomy (Krathwohl, D. R. 2002).

RELATED WORK

Two main methods have been proposed by researchers for solving Multi-Objective Optimization Problems (MOOP) namely 1) conventional or classical method and 2) meta-heuristic algorithms. The classical methods commonly use a single random solution, updated at each of the iteration with a deterministic procedure to find the optimal solution. Hence, classical methods are able to generate one optimal solution at the end of the iterative procedure. On the other hand, meta-heuristic algorithms are based on a population of solutions which will hopefully lead to a number of optimal solutions at every generation. The population based meta-heuristics algorithms collect ideas and features present in nature or in our environment and use it for implementing them as search algorithms using a stochastic procedure. Search mechanisms of meta-heuristics have the capability to explore large and complex search spaces while finding one or more optimal solutions (Zitzler, E. and Deb. 2008). The features found in nature represented as an algorithm through these methods generally use a substantial number of operators and parameters which must be appropriately set. There is no unique/standard definition of meta-heuristics in the literature. However, the recent trend is to name all stochastic algorithms with randomization and global exploration as meta-heuristic. Randomization provides a good way to move away from local search to the search on the global scale. Therefore, almost all meta-heuristic algorithms are usually suitable for global optimization. Meta-heuristic can be an effective way to use, by trial and error, to produce acceptable solutions to a complex problem in a reasonably practical time. The complexity of the problem of interest makes it impractical to search every possible solution or combination and therefore, the goal is to find good and feasible solutions in a satisfactory time period. There is no guarantee that the optimum solution can be found. Also, we are unable to predict whether an algorithm will work and if it does work, there is no reason that explains why it works. The idea is to have a competent and practical algorithm which will work majority of the time and will be able to produce qualitatively good solutions (Gandomi, A. et.al 2013). Among the quality solutions found, it can be expected that some of them are nearly-optimal or optimal, though there is no guarantee for such optimality to occur always. Hence, meta-heuristic algorithms have been successfully applied to find solutions for many complex real-world optimization problems. Meta-heuristic algorithms can be classified into different categories based on the source of inspiration from nature. The main category is the biologically-inspired algorithms, which generally use biological evolution and/or collective behavior of animals as their model. Science is an added inspiration for meta-heuristic algorithms. These algorithms are generally inspired by physics and chemistry. Furthermore, art-inspired algorithms have been successful for global optimization. These are generally inspired by the creative behavior of artists such as musicians and architects. Social behavior is an additional source of inspiration and the socially inspired algorithm simulate social manners to solve optimization problems. Even though there are dissimilar sources of inspiration for meta-heuristic optimization algorithms, they also have similarities in their structures. Therefore, they can also be classified into two main categories: 1) evolutionary algorithms and 2) swarm algorithms. Evolutionary algorithm generally uses an iterative procedure based on a biological evolution progress to solve optimization problems, whereas swarm-intelligence-based algorithms use the collective behavior of animals such as birds, insects or fishes (Holland, J. H. 1975). Three main types of evolutionary algorithms have been evolved during the last few years: Genetic Algorithms (GA) mainly developed by J.H. Holland (Holland, J. H. 1975)., Evolutionary Strategies (ES) developed by Ingo Rechenberg (Fogel, D.B. 1994), and Evolutionary Programming (EP) by D.B Fogel (Fogel, D.B. 1995). Each of these Evolutionary Algorithms uses different representations of data, different operators working on them and different implementations. They are, however, inspired by the same principles of natural biological evolution. Similar to evolutionary algorithms, three main types of swarm algorithm have also been evolved during the last few years: Particle Swarm Optimization (PSO) developed by Kennedy and Eberhart (Kennedy, J. and Eberhart, R. C. 1995), Ant Colony Optimization (ACO) developed by Dorigo (Karaboga, D. 2005). and Artificial Bee Colony (ABC) Algorithm developed by Karaboga (Karaboga, D. 2005). Each of these Swarm Algorithms deals with collective behaviors of animals that result from the local interactions of individual components with each other as well as with their environment. Finding an optimal solution to an optimization problem is often a challenging task, and depends on the choice and the correct use of the right algorithm. The choice of an algorithm may depend on the type of problem, the available set of algorithms, computational resources and time constraint. For large-scale, nonlinear and global optimization problems, there is often no standard guideline for algorithm choice and in many cases, there are no efficient exact algorithms (Holland, J. H. 1975).Therefore, depending on the number of multiple conflicting objectives that need to get satisfied as well as on the complexity of the search space, it is necessary to choose efficient and effective search and optimization mechanisms from the available population based, biologically inspired meta-heuristic Evolutionary Algorithms and Swarm Algorithms that solve the problem by applying reasonable time and space constraints.

The automated objective test sheet generation model has undergone many changes over a period of time and also has incorporated efficient algorithms such as Evolutionary Algorithms (Zhi, F.L., Ji, S.& Jia, L. 2010; Lin, et.al

2012; Peipei, G.,et.al 2012; Hu. J. et.al 2011; Huang, M.,et.al 2009; Liu, S.W. 2010; Ho, T. F.,et.al 2009; Lirong, X. & Jianwei, S. 2010; Liu, Y.et.al 2008) and Swarm Algorithms (Bloom, B.S.,1956; Ming, L., Jin-gang, M. & Jing, Z. 2009; DASCALU, M. 2011; Yin, P. Y., Chang, K. C. & Hwang, G. J. 2006) for generation of single test sheet or multiple test sheet sets that meet multiple assessment criteria. Both these algorithms were similar in terms of their search and optimization, and were found successful in composition of near-optimal multiple objective test sheets. As a matter of choice, we proceeded with the pioneer algorithm among them; Evolutionary Algorithm (EA), for the generation of automated descriptive test paper model. EAs typically, have a set (population) of solution candidates (individuals), which we try to gradually improve. Improvements may be generated by applying different variation operators, most notably mutation and crossover, to certain individuals. The quality of solutions is measured by a so-called fitness function or objective function. Mutation means a new individual is generated by slightly altering a single parent individual, whereas crossover operator generates a new individual by recombining information from two parents. Most Evolutionary Algorithms used in practice consider either one or both of these operators. Based on the fitness value of individuals, a selection procedure removes some individuals from the population. The cycle of variation and selection is repeated until a solution of sufficient fitness is found. The strength of this general approach is that each component can be adapted to the particular problem under consideration. This adaptation can be guided by an experimental evaluation of the actual behavior of the algorithm or by previously obtained experience. Also, not every Evolutionary Algorithm (EA) needs to have all components described above (Coello-Coello, C.,et.al. 2007; Deb, K. 2001). Since a population of solution candidates gets processed in each of the iteration, the outcome of EA can also be a population of feasible solutions. If an optimization problem includes a single objective, EA population members are expected to converge to a single optimum solution satisfying the given objective. On the other hand, if a problem includes multi-objectives, EA population members are expected to converge to a set of optimum solutions satisfying multiple objectives. Solution to multi-objective problems consists of sets of tradeoffs between objectives. Multiple optimal solutions exist because no one solution can be optimal for multiple conflicting objectives. If none of the two solutions, of multi-objective problem that are compared dominates each other, these solutions are called non-dominated solutions, pareto-optimal solutions or trade-off solutions. The set of all pareto-optimal solutions is called the pareto-optimal set (pareto-front). Since such solutions are not dominant on each other and there exists no other solution in the entire search space which dominates any of these solutions, such solutions are of utmost importance in a MOOP. Hence, Evolutionary MOOP consists of determining all solutions to the MOOP problem that are optimal in the pareto sense (Deb, K. and Gupta. 2005; Thiele, L. and Zitzler, E.1999).

EVOLUTIONARY APPROACH FOR TEST PAPER TEMPLATE GENERATION

Over the last few years, many diverse evolutionary algorithms have been introduced for solving constrained optimization problems. However, due to the variability of problem characteristics, no single algorithm performs consistently over a range of problems. Evolutionary approach applies genetically inspired operators such as selection and mutation to populations of potential solutions in an iterative fashion, creating new populations while searching for an optimum solution. Selection is in charge of applying the fitness function and choosing candidate solutions satisfying these fitness conditions, while recombination (mutation) results in maintaining diversity among solutions. The best value of mutation rate is problem-specific. This value also depends on the size of the population as well as the nature and implementation of the algorithm. However, there is no single best mutation rate for most of the real-world evolutionary optimization problems (Srinivas, M. and Patnaik, M. 1994). Despite its randomized nature, evolutionary approach takes advantage of the old knowledge held in a parent population to generate new solutions with improved knowledge. Evolutionary Approach monitors quality of test paper based on a wide range of paper-setter requirements such as the average degree of difficulty, kinds of questions, selection of modules, selection of cognitive levels, etc. In order to incorporate the above requirements, we have applied the well-established concept of Educational Taxonomies along with evolutionary approach. The methodology adopted consists of the following main steps-

Step1-Select Units or Modules of a Subject: Examination is conducted for a subject of a course having pre-defined university specified syllabus file with unit-wise/module-wise contents. It is necessary to mention whether the test paper template is designed for all units or modules of a subject or selected unit of a subject

Step2-Decide Cognitive Processing Levels: Paper-setters always attempt to include questions that measure higher levels of cognitive processing. This is not a good approach to evaluate performance of students at different levels of learning such as Excellent, Good, Average, etc. It should be the goal of the paper-setter to ensure that their questions have cognitive characteristics testing the understanding, problem-solving, critical thinking, analysis, synthesis, evaluation and interpretation rather than just declarative knowledge.

Step3- Design Test Paper Template: The template specification as represented in Table.2.3 gives the flexibility for constructing many qualitatively good examination test papers using the same template. The template defines scope of the paper with respect to syllabus contents and content of skills being measured by the examination. We have generated templates with three major difficulty levels such as High, Medium and Low. High difficulty templates have high distribution of marks across higher/difficult levels of taxonomy. Medium difficulty templates have proportionate distribution of marks across all levels of taxonomy and low difficulty templates have low distribution of marks across higher/difficult levels of taxonomy. The test paper template so generated is then used for dynamic generation of a test paper. The quality of the test paper will depend on the quality of questions framed by paper-setters and populated in the QB. Multiple test paper generation is considered as a requirement in the current university-based examination system. This requirement is important as the generated test papers can be used at different times due to the discrepancy in the conduct of an examination or failure of students at the regular examination or occurrence of any other unexpected events. The test paper generation from the template is outside the scope of this chapter.

Steps for Applying Evolutionary Approach in Template Generation-

Step1-Generate Population: Population consists of P (paper-setter input) different test paper templates which are either generated initially or at successive iterations. A template is formed by randomly assigning integer-valued module-level-weight to each cell of a template in such a way that it satisfies unit weightage and level weightage.

Step2-Calculate Fitness: Calculate fitness score of each template. The details of Fitness calculation are explained in Subsection 1.3.1

Step3-Selection: Apply selection operation to the generated population. It is carried out based on the criteria that the set of templates with fitness value in the range of 0.5-1.0 are to be identified and selected.

Step4-Mutation: Among the selected templates, identify the ones that can be mutated to increase their fitness value. Perform mutation on these identified templates by altering the module-level weight of a set of cells and accordingly adjusting the rest of the cell values.

Step5-Termination: Repeat step 1 to step 4 for the paper-setter specified number of iterations or until near optimal/optimal solution is found (whichever is earlier).

Problem Statement

Let TM be the total marks allotted for the question paper. Let m be the number of units selected by Paper Setter and n be the number of taxonomy levels selected. Let $U=<u_1, u_2,...,u_m>$ be the vector of unit weights where u_i is the weight assigned to the ith unit, and, $L=<l_1,l_2,...,l_n>$ be the vector of level weights where l_j is the weight assigned to the jth level.

Let $X=<x_{11}, x_{12}, x_{ij},...,x_{mn}>$ be the set of module-level-weights where x_{ij} is the module-level-weight assigned to the jth level of ith unit.

For a unit i, $\sum_{j=1}^{n} x_{ij}=u_i$, and

For a level j, $\sum_{i=1}^{m} x_{ij}=l_i$

The problem is to assign module-level-weights, $X=<x_{11}, x_{12}, x_{ij},...,x_{mn}>$, so as to get the optimum value for the fitness function (F). Let w_1 be the percentage of importance assigned to unit coverage and let w_2 be the percentage of importance assigned to taxonomy level coverage. The problem can be mathematically stated as follows:

Maximize F =

$$\frac{((w_1 \times \sum_{i=1}^{m}(1-(\sum_{j=1}^{n}|(x_{ij} \times TM)/u_i-l_j|/TM))/m)}{w_1+w_2} \\ +((w_2 \times \sum_{j=1}^{m}(1-(\sum_{i=1}^{n}|(x_{ij} \times TM)/l_i-u_j|/TM))/n)$$ (1)

subject to the constraints

$$\sum_{j=1}^{n} x_{ij} = u_j,$$

$$\sum_{i=1}^{m} x_{ij} = l_i,$$

$$x_{ij} > 0$$

In order to define fitness, we have defined the following terms-

The term Weakness was initially coined to indicate that it is not the fittest value and it is improved as it goes through iterative process.

1. The Weakness of a Unit (WU_i): For a unit i, $X_i = <x_{i1}, x_{i2}, \ldots, x_{in}>$ and $X_i \in X$. Before calculating WU_i, normalize X_i to obtain $X_i = <x_{i1}, \ldots, x_{in}>$ such that $x_{ij} = x_{ij} \times TM / u_i$.

$$WU_i = \left(\sum_{j=1}^{n} | x_{ij} - l_j | \right) / TM \qquad (2)$$

2. The Fitness of a Unit (F_{unit}):

$$F_{unit} = \sum_{i=1}^{m} (1 - WU_i) / m \qquad (3)$$

3. **The Weakness of a Level (WL_j):** For a level j, $X_j = <x_{1j}, x_{2j}, \ldots, x_{mj}>$ and $X_j \in X$. Before calculating WL_j, normalize X_j to obtain $X_j = <x_{1j}, \ldots, x_{1m}>$ such that $x_{ij} = x_{ij} \times TM / l_j$.

$$WL_j = \left(\sum_{i=1}^{m} | x_{ij} - u_i | \right) / TM \qquad (4)$$

4. The Fitness of a Level (F_{level}):

$$F_{level} = \sum_{j=1}^{n} (1 - WL_j) / n \qquad (5)$$

10

5.   The Overall Fitness (F), of the Template:

$$\mathbf{F} = (w_1 \times \sum_{i=1}^{m} \mathbf{F_{unit}} + w_2 \times \sum_{j=1}^{n} \mathbf{F_{level}}) / (w_1 + w_2) \tag{6}$$

Algorithm Design

Evolutionary QPT generation has been carried out by Evolutionary QPT Generation Algorithm presented as Algorithm 1

Algorithm 1 Evolutionary QPT Generation Algorithm

Procedure *Evolutionary QPT Generation (U, L, w₁,w₂,TM)*

  Input: U, L, w₁,w₂,TM

  U=<u₁, u₂,..., uₘ> : Instructor specified modules for template generation

  L = <l₁, l₂,...,lₙ> : Instructor specified levels for template generation

  w₁: percentage of importance assigned to module coverage

  w₂: percentage of importance assigned to module coverage

  TM: Instructor specified total marks for QPT

  Output: QPT, Pareto-optimal Evolutionary Approach based QPT

  //Assign module-level-weights for QPT

  for each uᵢ in U (i=1 to m) do

  for each lⱼ in L (j=1 to n) do

  Random selection (xᵢⱼ) for $\sum_{j=1}^{n} x_{ij}=u_i, \sum_{i=1}^{m} x_{ij}=l_i$

  //Normalize xᵢⱼ for Unit-Fitness-Constraints

  for each uᵢ in U (i=1 to m) do

  for each lⱼ in L (j=1 to n) do

    xᵢⱼ=xᵢⱼ ×TM/u

  //Evaluate-Unit-Fitness-Constraints

  for i=1 to m do

    $\mathbf{WU_i} = (\sum_{j=1}^{n} | x_{ij} - l_j |) / TM$

    $\mathbf{F_{unit}} = \sum_{i=1}^{m} (1 - WU_i)/m$

  end for

  //Normalize xᵢⱼ for Level-Fitness-Constraints

  for each uᵢ in U (i=1 to m) do

  for each lⱼ in L (j=1 to n) do

    $x_{ij}=x_{ij} \times TM/l_j$

  //Evaluate-Level-Fitness-Constraints

  for j=1 to n do

    $\mathbf{WL_j} = (\sum_{i=1}^{m} |x_{ij} - u_i|) / TM$

    $\mathbf{F_{level}} = \sum_{j=1}^{n} (1 - WL_j)/n$

  end for

  //Evaluate-Overall-Fitness-of-Template

  $\mathbf{F} = (w_1 \times \sum_{i=1}^{m} \mathbf{F_{unit}} + w_2 \times \sum_{j=1}^{n} \mathbf{F_{level}}) / (w_1 + w_2)$

  end procedure

Experimental Results

Experimental study was conducted using the syllabus prescribed for Software Engineering (SE) offered in the third year of the three year bachelor's degree course of computer science (B.Sc Computer Science) at Goa University. Bloom's taxonomy with six levels such as Knowledge, Understanding, Application, Analysis, Synthesis and Evaluation were considered as cognitive processing levels.

1. **Sample Input Screen:** Paper-setter is given the flexibility to choose some/all units of a subject and also all/some learning objectives of the specified subject. Test paper template for different examinations such as in-semester (20 marks), end-semester (80 marks), practical (50 marks), etc. can be generated. Provision is also made to prepare test paper template on different difficulty levels such as Low, Medium and High. Figure 1 below shows the sample input screen for test paper template generation.

Figure 1. Input screen for test paper template generation

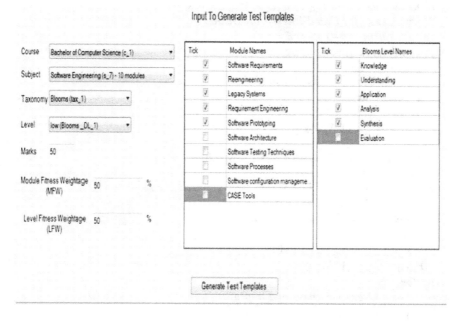

2. **Results Obtained:** Figure 2 and Figure 3 below show sample screen shots of the iterative stages of SE test paper template generation. It is generated by accepting the following modules of SE syllabus as well as the following levels of Bloom's taxonomy, respectively, as input.

a. First five modules, namely, Software Requirement, Re-engineering, Legacy Systems, Requirement Engineering and Software Prototyping of SE syllabus, 2) First five levels of Bloom's taxonomy namely Knowledge, Understanding, Application, Analysis and Synthesis, respectively.

Figure 2. Iterative stages of test paper template generation

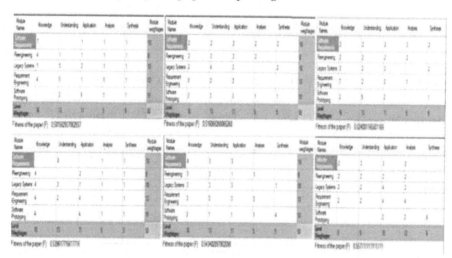

Table.3 displays the experimental results obtained after iteratively generating SE templates with 5 units and 5 levels as input. The population size P was set to 10, mutation rate was assigned as 0.5 and the number of iterations was set to 100. The number of templates generated in the worst case for this input could be 10×100=1000. The results indicate that the algorithm terminated with an optimal solution at the 82nd iteration.

Table 4 below shows experimental results obtained after iteratively generating SE templates with 8 units and 6 levels as input. The population size P was set to 10, mutation rate was assigned as 0.5 and the number of iterations was set to 100. The results indicate that optimal solution is not achieved even after 100 iterations. Hence, the algorithm terminates after 100 iterations in this case.

Figure 3. Iterative stages of test paper template generation (with im- proved fitness)

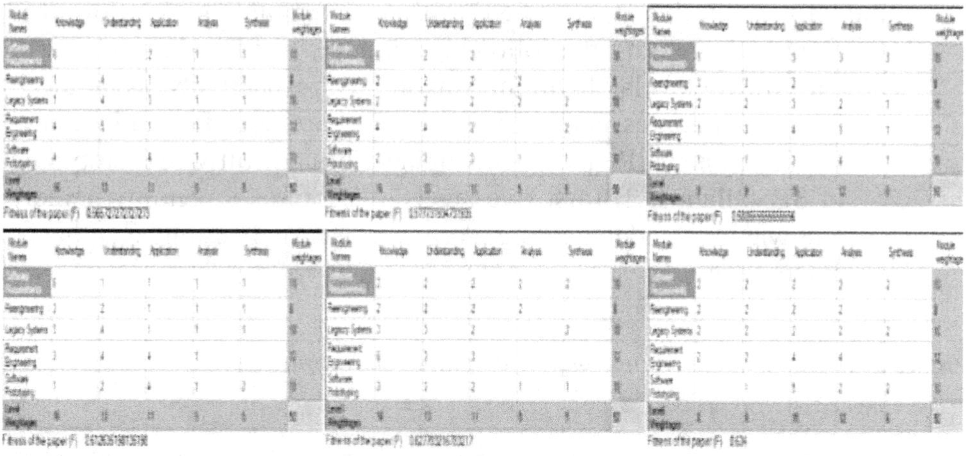

Table 3. Computed fitness of SE Template with 5 units and 5 levels

Template No	Iteration No	Fitness	Template No	Iteration No	Fitness
$i_{1,1}$	1	0.5031	$i_{28,1}$	28	0.6913
$i_{1,2}$	1	0.5064	$i_{28,2}$	28	0.7003
$i_{1,3}$	1	0.5099	.	.	.
$i_{1,4}$	1	0.5104	$i_{52,1}$	52	0.7588
$i_{1,5}$	1	0.5159	$i_{52,2}$	52	0.7588
$i_{1,6}$	1	0.5206	.	.	.
$i_{1,7}$	1	0.5279	$i_{64,1}$	64	0.7204
$i_{1,8}$	1	0.5315	$i_{64,2}$	64	0.7399
$i_{1,9}$	1	0.5397	.	.	.
$i_{1,10}$	1	0.5434	$i_{70,1}$	70	0.7802
$i_{2,1}$	2	0.5498	.	.	.
$i_{2,2}$	2	0.5568	$i_{77,1}$	79	0.8802
.	.	.	$i_{77,2}$	79	0.8905
$i_{3,1}$	3	0.5922			
.	.	.	$i_{82,1}$	82	0.9617
$i_{4,1}$	4	0.6047	$i_{82,2}$	82	0.9902
.	.	.			

Table 4. Computed fitness of SE Template with 8 units and 6 levels

Template No	Iteration No	Fitness	Template No	Iteration No	Fitness
$i_{1,1}$	1	0.5001	$i_{28,1}$	28	0.5703
$i_{1,2}$	1	0.5012	$i_{28,2}$	28	0.5716
$i_{1,3}$	1	0.5034	.	.	.
$i_{1,4}$	1	0.5075	$i_{52,1}$	52	0.6102
$i_{1,5}$	1	0.5093	$i_{52,2}$	52	0.6113
$i_{1,6}$	1	0.5108	.	.	.
$i_{1,7}$	1	0.5127	$i_{64,1}$	64	0.6313
$i_{1,8}$	1	0.5135	$i_{64,2}$	64	0.6326
$i_{1,9}$	1	0.5149	.	.	.
$i_{1,10}$	1	0.5198	$i_{70,1}$	70	0.6741
$i_{2,1}$	2	0.5202	$i_{70,2}$	70	0.6758
$i_{2,2}$	2	0.5209	.	.	.
.	.	.	$i_{77,1}$	79	0.7005
$i_{3,1}$	3	0.5223	$i_{77,2}$	79	0.7011
.	.	.	.	.	.
$i_{4,1}$	4	0.5291	$i_{100,9}$	100	0.7318
.	.	.			

Summary

This work focused on a new approach for dynamic Test paper generation by using test paper templates that are obtained using Evolutionary Algorithm. The main advantage of this new approach is the application strengths of Evolutionary Approach for dynamic test paper generation. We have carried out experimental study of Evolutionary Algorithm with a population size of 10 with its mutation probability of 0.5 which successfully explored the search space and optimally generated dynamic templates.

Complexity of Evolutionary Algorithm has been generally determined in terms of the relationship between the search space and the difficulty in finding a solution. The search space in our multi-objective evolutionary approach-based optimization problem of dynamic template generation is discrete and two-dimensional; that is, a solution in the search space is represented by two different types of components such as the selected units of the syllabus and the selected levels of Bloom's taxonomy. Hence, complexity of this template generation algorithm is found to be proportional to the number of units and the number of levels selected for a template.

PARETO-OPTIMALEVOLUTIONARY APPROACH FOR TEST PAPER TEMPLATE GENERATION

The adaptability of evolutionary approach was best used for QPT generation in Section 2.3. Even though Evolutionary Algorithm (EAs) designed in Section 2.3 have been successfully implemented for test paper generation, they are found not efficient with respect to time for meeting multi-constraints specified by an instructor for generating multiple QPTs for different types of test papers. The evolutionary approach-based test paper templates of section 3 had a major disadvantage that it used randomized approach for assigning module-level weights. Even though it generated population of test paper templates iteratively, many of them were not adequate in terms of its fitness. During the iterative population generation, significant runtime delay was observed. This is due to the wastage of time in searching a set of random module-level-weights that satisfied both module weights and level weights. Also, EAs never guaranteed the generation of the instructor specified number of templates even after running it for the instructor specified number of iterations. In order to overcome the limitation of EAs, an enhanced EA using pareto-optimal solution has been designed. This algorithm is found to generate multiple optimal Test paper Templates (QPTs) in lesser time satisfying instructor specified multi-constraints. Pareto-optimality based Multi-Objective Evolutionary Algorithm (MOEA) generates optimal trade-off solutions also known as pareto-optimal set of QPTs. As a notion in pareto-optimal MOEA, the instructor/paper-setter has been provided with a set of pareto-optimal QPT solutions, which are not dominated by any other QPT solutions. Each of these designed QPTs can act as a standard in generating a test paper by performing an intelligent search of questions based on the designed QPT.

Goals of MOEA Implemented for Pareto-Optimality: Two goals have been taken into account while designing pareto-approach based MOEA for multiple QPT generation, which are listed below -

GUIDING THE SEARCH TOWARDS PARETO SET

Keeping a Diverse Set of Non-Dominated Solutions

The first goal is mainly related to assigning scalar fitness values in the presence of multiple objectives. Scalar fitness assignment is carried out by transforming multi-objective problem into a mono-objective problem (Guang, C.2010). The second goal concerns generation of diverse candidate solutions. In contrast to single-objective optimization, where objective function and fitness function is directly and easily related, in multi-objective optimization fitness assignment and selection have to take into account all the different objectives. Among the different fitness assignment strategies, the most commonly used are those based on aggregation (Talbi, E.G. 2009; Caramia, M. and Olmo, D. 2008). This approach, which mimics the weighted-sum method, aggregates the objectives into a single parameterized objective function. The parameters of this function are systematically varied during the optimization run in order to find a set of non-dominated solutions instead of a single trade-off solution. In our MOEA, we apply the weighted sum method to optimize the two objectives such as: the percentage of coverage assigned to module weights and also the percentage of importance assigned to taxonomy level weights. Our aggregate function applies two different weights independently to these objectives and generates a single parameterized objective function equivalent to these two objectives. The methodology adopted is the same as the one used in evolutionary approach.

STEPS FOR EVOLUTIONARY APPROACH IN TEMPLATE GENERATION-

Step1-Generate Population of QPT: Q different test paper templates as specified by instructor/paper- setter are either generated initially or at successive iterations to form a population. The set of templates of the initial population is formed by calculating the module-level-weights of each cell by using the formula: $x_{mn} = (u_m \times l_n) / TM$ and adjusting them to its nearest integer values.

Step2-Calculate Fitness of QPT: Calculate fitness of QPTs using the Fitness Function. Details of Fitness (F) calculation is explained in section 4.1

Step3-Selection: Apply selection operation to the generated QPTs. It is carried out based on the criteria that the set of QPTs with fitness value in the range of 0.8-1.0, is to be identified and selected.

Step4-Mutation: Among the selected QPTs, identify the ones that can be mutated to increase its fitness value. Perform mutation on these identified templates by altering the module-level weight of any cell and accordingly adjusting the rest of the cell values.

Step5-Termination: Step 1 till step 4 are repeated iteratively until an optimum number of solutions is found or the instructor specified number of iterations is completed (whichever is earlier).

PROBLEM DESCRIPTION

Input for QPT Generation

1. TM = Total marks allotted for designing QPTs.
2. $U=U=<u_1, u_2..., u_m>$, the vector of selected unit/module weights where u_i is the weight assigned to the ith unit.
3. $L=<l_1, l_2..., l_n>$, the vector of selected cognitive level weights of educational taxonomy where lj is the weight assigned to the jth cognitive level.

Problem Statement

The problem is to assign module-level-weights, $X=<x_{11}..., x_{mn}>$, so as to get the optimum value for the Fitness Function (F). Let w1 be the percentage of importance assigned to module coverage and let w2 be the percentage of importance assigned to taxonomy level coverage. In order to define fitness, we have defined the following terms-

Similar to the use of the term Weakness in evolutionary approach, in earlier section, the term Weakness in this approach was also initially coined to indicate that it is not the fittest value and it is improved as it goes through iterative process.

1. The Weakness of a Unit (WU_i):

For a unit i, $\mathbf{WU}_{i} = \sum_{j=1}^{n} x_{ij}$ (7)

2. The Fitness of a Unit (F_{unit}):

$$\mathbf{F_{unit}} = \sum_{i=1}^{n} WUi/TM \tag{8}$$

3. The Weakness of a Level (WLj):

18

For a level j, $\mathbf{WL_j} = \sum_{i=1}^{m} x_{ij}$ (9)

4. The Fitness of a Level (F_{level}):

$\mathbf{F_{level}} = WL_j/TM$ (10)

5. The Overall Fitness(F), of the Template:

$$\mathbf{F} = (\mathbf{w_1} \times \sum_{i=1}^{m} \mathbf{F_{unit}} + \mathbf{w_2} \times \sum_{j=1}^{n} \mathbf{F_{level}}) / (\mathbf{w_1} + \mathbf{w_2})$$ (11)

Algorithm Design

Pareto-optimal QPT generation has been carried out by pareto-optimal QPT Generation Algorithm presented as Algorithm 2

Algorithm 2 Pareto-optimal Evolutionary QPT Generation Algorithm
  Procedure *Pareto-optimal QPT Generation (U, L, w₁,w₂,TM)*
  Input: U, L, w₁,w₂,TM
  U=<u₁, u₂,..., uₘ> : Instructor specified modules for template generation
  L= <l₁, l₂,...,lₙ> : Instructor specified levels for template generation
  w₁ : percentage of importance assigned to module coverage
  w₂ : percentage of importance assigned to module coverage
  TM: Instructor specified total marks for QPT
  Output: QPT, Pareto-optimal Evolutionary Approach based QPT
  // Assign module-level-weights for QPT
  for each uᵢ in U (i=1 to m) do
  for each lⱼ in L (j=1 to n) do
    $x_{ij} \leftarrow (u_i \times l_j)/TM$
  //Evaluate-Unit-Fitness-Constraints
  for i=1 to m do
    $\mathbf{WU_i} = \sum_{j=1}^{n} x_{ij}$
    $\mathbf{F_{unit}} = WU_i/TM$
  end for
  //Evaluate-Level-Fitness-Constraints
  for j=1 to n do
    $\mathbf{WL_j} = \sum_{i=1}^{m} x_{ij}$
    $\mathbf{F_{level}} = WL_j/TM$
  end for
  //Evaluate-Overall-Fitness-of-Template
    $\mathbf{F} = (\mathbf{w_1} \times \sum_{i=1}^{m} \mathbf{F_{unit}} + \mathbf{w_2} \times \sum_{j=1}^{n} \mathbf{F_{level}}) / (\mathbf{w_1} + \mathbf{w_2})$
  end procedure

Experimental Results

Using the Goa University examination test papers and the cognitive levels of Bloom's taxonomy, multiple QPT's were generated for the subject of Software Engineering (SE) offered at the third year of the three year bachelor's degree course of computer science (B.Sc Computer Science).

Input Data

1.   Total marks= 50
2.   Selected module weights =05, 15, 15, 15
3.   Selected level weights = 15,15,05,15
4.   Population size=10
5.   Mutation rate=0.2
6.   Paper-setter Specified Number of iterations=50
7.   percentage of importance assigned to module coverage=0.50
8.   percentage of importance assigned to taxonomy level coverage =0.50
9.   Expected number of QPTs=3

Results Obtained

SE pareto-optimal QPT1 of Table.5, SE Pareto-optimal QPT2 of Table.6 and SE pareto-optimal QPT3 of Table.7 below shows the three different samples of generated QPT's for SE. Generation of these QPT's were successful within 50 iterations.

Table 5. SE Pareto-optimal QPT1

Module /level	know	under	appl	anal	module weight
Software Architecture	2	1	1	1	05
Software Test. Tech.	4	5	1	5	15
Software Process	5	4	1	5	15
S Software Conf. Mgmt.	4	5	2	4	15
level weight	15	15	5	15	50

Table 6. SE Pareto-optimal QPT2

Module /level	know	under	appl	anal	module weight
Software Architecture	1	2	1	1	05
Software Test. Tech.	5	4	2	4	15
Software Process	4	5	1	5	15
S Software Conf. Mgmt.	5	4	1	5	15
level weight	15	15	5	15	50

Table 7. SE Pareto-optimal QPT3

Module /level	know	under	appl	anal	module weight
Software Architecture	1	1	1	2	05
Software Test. Tech.	5	5	1	4	15
Software Process	5	5	1	4	15
Software Conf. Mgmt.	4	4	2	5	15
level weight	15	15	5	15	50

Performance Analysis of QPT Generation

Table 8 shows the experimental results obtained after iteratively generating the instructor specified number of SE QPTs (3 in this case). Performance comparison of the solutions of pareto-optimal based evolutionary approach is carried out with the solutions of evolutionary approach of section 3. Results indicate that the pareto-optimal based evolutionary algorithm has achieved optimal QPTs at the 40th iteration, whereas the evolutionary algorithm failed to generate optimal QPT solutions even after 50 iterations.

Summary

A new approach for generating multiple set of test papers using QPTs has been discussed. The main advantage of pareto-optimal based evolutionary algorithm as compared to our previously designed evolutionary algorithm of section 1.3 is that the runtime delay of the previous approach is significantly reduced by avoiding randomized approach for population generation. We have carried out the experimental study of pareto-optimal evolutionary algorithm with a

Table 8. Performance analysis of evolutionary algorithm and pareto-optimal algorithm

Evolutionary Algorithm			Pareto-Optimal Evolutionary Algorithm			Evolutionary Algorithm			Pareto-Optimal Evolutionary Algorithm		
Template No	Iteration No	Fitness	Template No	Iteration No	Fitness	Template No	Iteration No	Fitness	Template No	Iteration No	Fitness
$t_{1,1}$	1	0.5001	$t_{1,1}$	1	0.7045	$t_{28,1}$	28	0.6603	$t_{28,1}$	28	0.8717
$t_{1,2}$	1	0.5212	$t_{1,2}$	1	0.7066	$t_{28,2}$	28	0.6686	$t_{28,2}$	28	0.8726
$t_{1,3}$	1	0.5334	$t_{1,3}$	1	0.7077	.	.	.	.	.	.
$t_{1,4}$	1	0.5475	$t_{1,4}$	1	0.7079	$t_{32,1}$	32	0.6872	$t_{32,1}$	32	0.9109
$t_{1,5}$	1	0.5511	$t_{1,5}$	1	0.7093	$t_{32,2}$	32	0.6893	$t_{32,2}$	32	0.9113
$t_{1,6}$	1	0.5613	$t_{1,6}$	1	0.7108	.	.	.	.	.	.
$t_{1,7}$	1	0.5733	$t_{1,7}$	1	0.7127	$t_{34,1}$	34	0.6911	$t_{34,1}$	34	0.9313
$t_{1,8}$	1	0.5812	$t_{1,8}$	1	0.7149	$t_{34,2}$	34	0.6936	$t_{34,2}$	34	0.9326
$t_{1,9}$	1	0.5884	$t_{1,9}$	1	0.7158	.	.	.	.	.	.
$t_{1,10}$	1	0.6094	$t_{1,10}$	1	0.7198	$t_{40,1}$	40	0.7198	$t_{40,1}$	40	0.9971
$t_{2,1}$	2	0.6104	$t_{2,1}$	2	0.7202	$t_{40,2}$	40	0.7205	$t_{40,2}$	40	0.9988
$i_{2,2}$	2	0.6183	$i_{2,2}$	2	0.7209	$t_{40,2}$	40	0.7232	$t_{40,2}$	40	0.9997
.	.	.	.	.	.	$t_{45,1}$	45	0.7311	$t_{45,1}$	45	terminate
$t_{3,1}$	3	0.6275	$t_{3,1}$	3	0.8223	$t_{45,2}$	45	0.7365	$t_{45,2}$	45	terminate
.	.	.	.	.	.	.	.	.	.	.	.
$t_{4,1}$	4	0.6364	$t_{4,1}$	4	0.8291	$t_{50,9}$	50	0.7399	$t_{50,9}$	50	terminate
.	.		.	.							

population size of 10 with its mutation probability of 0.2 which successfully explored the search space and optimally generated multiple sets of dynamic templates. This new approach is important in situations where instructors wish to generate multiple set of test papers in a subject for the same examination. Examinations such as in-semester, end-semester etc., forces the proportionate coverage of modules and cognitive levels. Using multiple QPTs, there are lesser probabilities of similar questions getting automatically extracted during the question selection process. Complexity of pareto- optimal evolutionary approach has been generally determined in terms of the relationship between the search space and the difficulty in finding a solution. The search space in our multi-objective pareto-optimal evolutionary approach-based optimization problem of dynamic template generation is discrete and two-dimensional; that is, a solution in the search space is represented by two different types of components such as the selected units of the syllabus and the selected levels of Bloom's taxonomy. Hence, complexity of this template generation algorithm is found to be proportional to the number of units and the number of levels specified for QPT generation.

BI-PROPORTIONAL SCALING METHOD FOR TEST PAPER TEMPLATE GENERATION

The dynamic templates generated by the previously discussed two different evolutionary approaches of section 1.3 and section 1.4 were successful in providing the flexibility for constructing many qualitatively sound examination test papers using the same template. But, the iterative process of generation of population of QPTs using basic evolutionary algorithm of section 1.3 encountered significant run-time delays, and also had no guarantee of finding optimal solutions in a finite amount of time. On the other hand, pareto-optimal based evolutionary algorithm of section 1.4 has been able to reduce the run-time delay, but still was unable to always guarantee the generation of optimal solutions within the user specified number of iterations. In order to overcome these limitations, we have introduced a matrix balancing technique that automatically scales and balances all entries of the QPT. The Bi-proportional matrix balancing technique performs iterative scaling and proportional fitting of the QPT to satisfy the instructor specified number of modules of the subject, instructor specified number of levels of taxonomy and instructor specified marks requirement of each examination.

The mathematical foundation and wide spread application of matrix scaling problem has attracted researchers from multiple disciplines to use it in various applications. Estimating the entries of a large matrix to satisfy a set of prior consistency requirements is a problem that frequently occurs in economics, transportation, statistics, regional science, operation research and other areas (Schneider, M. and Zenios, S. 1990; Ga ke, N. and Pukelsheim, F. 2008; Speed, T. P. 2005). There are several scaling problems, each with different consistency requirements and therefore the definition of a scaled matrix is problem dependent (Mesnard, L. D. 2002; Lahr, M. and Mesnard L. 2004). In general, matrix scaling is considered as a mathematical scaling procedure which can be used to ensure that a matrix of data is adjusted so that the scaled matrix agrees with the original row and column constraints. The original matrix values are gradually adjusted through repeated iterations to fit it to user input row and column constraints. To solve a problem using matrix scaling procedure, we need to identify the marginal tables and the seed cells. The procedure alternates between fitting the rows and fitting the columns of the seed cells to the identified marginal table entries. Result of the fitting process is a scaled matrix with corresponding set of estimated cells probabilities or cell means (Fienberg, S. E. and Meyer, M. M. 2004). An L1-error function is normally incorporated in matrix scaling problems for measuring the distance between current row and column sums and target row and column marginal entries. The procedure converges to bi-proportional fit if and only if the L1-error tends to zero. In case of non-convergence, a separate procedure to handle error points (+e and -e) needs to be considered (Pukelsheim, F. 2014; Oelbermann, K-F. 2013). The seed cell entries can be of continuous variant or of discrete variant types (Oelbermann, K-F. 2013). In the continuous variant, non-negative real numbers are permitted where as in the discrete variant, non-negative integers are considered. Matrix scaling procedure with discrete variant is found appropriate for QPT scaling. The procedure alternates between fitting the modules and also fitting the cognitive levels and converges with a bi- proportionally scaled and balanced QPT. Cognitive processing levels of a QPT are decided on the basis of the taxonomy that is selected for each examination. The scaled QPT so generated is then used for framing a test paper by performing an intelligent selection of questions.

Problem Statement

Given a QPT for subject S of maximum marks TM as shown in Table 3 represented as m × n matrix where m is the number of units/modules such that p={p_1, p_2,...,p_m}, n is the number of levels such that q={q_1, q_2,...,q_n} and each cell x_{ij} representing the weight assigned to the ith module for the ith taxonomy level, the problem is to dynamically generate a scaled qpt for the instructor input number of modules m', instructor input number of levels n' and instructor input total marks tm.

Bi-Proportional Matrix Scaling for Dynamic QPT Generation

The main modules for scaled QPT generation using bi-proportional matrix scaling procedure are shown in Figure.4.

Figure 4. Scaled QPT Generation using Bi-proportional Matrix Scaling Method

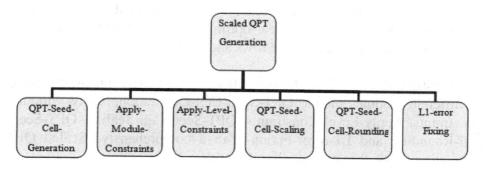

The brief details of modules of Scaled QPT generation are presented in different steps below:

Step1-QPT-Seed-Cell-Generation: Extracts QPT module-level- weights corresponding to instructor input m' modules and n' levels and represents the extracted module-level-weights as Seed-Cells.

Step2-Apply-Module-Constraints: Extracts QPT module weights corresponding to instructor input m' modules, normalizes the module weights with respect to instructor input tm (total marks) and represents the normalized module weights as scaled-module-weights.

Step3-Apply-Level-Constraints: Extracts QPT level weights corresponding to instructor input n' levels, normalizes the level weights with respect to instructor input tm (total marks) and represent the normalized level weights as scaled-level-weights.

Step4-QPT-Seed-Cell-Scaling: Iteratively scale the rows and columns of Seed-Cells to t them to the scaled-module-weights and scaled-level-weights until the Seed-Cells meet the imposed module, level and total marks constraints and outputs the scaled matrix as qpt.

Step5-QPT-Seed-Cell-Rounding: It applies closest integer rounding rule on qpt.

Step6-L1-error-Fixing: The L1-error encountered during rounding procedure is identified by counting along the rows and columns of qpt and verifying how many of them are not yet adjusted to the row totals and column totals respectively. If L1-error encountered is zero, then the generated output is considered as an optimal dynamic qpt. In all the other cases, the generated output is a near-optimal qpt. L1-error con- verges by proportionately adjusting the rows and columns with +e and -e errors.

Algorithm Design Scaled QPT generation has been carried out by processing six different modules such as QPT-Seed-Cell-Generation, Apply- Module-Constraints, Apply-Level-Constraints, QPT-Seed-Cell-Scaling, QPT-Seed-Cell-Rounding and L1-error-Fixing with a comprehensive Scaled QPT Generation Algorithm presented as Algorithm 3.

Algorithm 3 Scaled QPT Generation using Bi-proportional Matrix Scaling Method

Procedure *Scaled QPT Generation (p, q, tm)*

Input: *QPT, p, q, tm*

QPT: *Instructor specified Question Paper Template*

$p = <p_1, p_2,..., p_m>$: *Instructor specified modules for scaling*

$q = <q_1, q_2,..., q_n>$: *Instructor specified levels for scaling*

tm: *Instructor specified total marks for scaled QPT*

Output: *qpt, Scaled QPT*

//*QPT-Seed-Cell-Generation*

for each p_v in p (v=1 to m') **do**

    for each q_w in q (w=1 to n') **do** $x'_{vw} \leftarrow x_{ij}$;

    //*Apply-Module-Constraints*

//*Extract module-weights corresponding to m' modules*

for v=1 to m' **do** $u'_v \leftarrow \sum_{w=1}^{n'} (x'_{vw})$;

//*Normalize module-weights with respect to tm total marks*

for v=1 to m' **do** $u'_v \leftarrow (u'_v / \sum_{v=1}^{m'} u'_v) \times tm$;

// *Apply-Level-Constraints*

//*Extract level-weights corresponding to n levels*

for w=1 to n' **do** $l'_w \leftarrow \sum_{v=1}^{m'} (x'_{vw})$;

//*Normalize level-weights with respect to tm total marks*

for w=1 to n' **do** $l'_w \leftarrow (l'_w / \sum_{w=1}^{n'} l'_w) \times tm$

    //*QPT-Seed-Cells-Scaling*

flag_sum_mw=false;

flag_sum_lw=false;

While (flag_sum_mw = false || flag_sum_lw =false) **do**

//*Check whether Seed-Cell satisfies imposed module constraints*

    for v = 1 to m' **do** sum_mw $\leftarrow \sum_{w=1}^{n'} x'_{vw}$;

    if $u'_v \neq$ sum_mw **then** exit for

      else if v=m' then

      flag_sum_mw=true;

    end if

    end for

    //*Check whether Seed-Cell satisfies imposed level constraints*

    for w= 1 to n' **do** sum_lw $\leftarrow \sum_{v=1}^{m'} x'_{vw}$;

    if l'w $\neq$ sum_lw **then** exit for

      else if w=n' then

      flag_sum_lw=true;

    end if

end for

// *perform iterative alternate scaling of seed-row and seed-column in order to fit them to scaled-   module-weights and scaled-level-weight respectively*

if (flag_sum_tw = false || flag_sum_lw =false) **then**

// **Seed-row-scaling**

  for v= 1 to m' **do**

    for w= 1 to n' **do** $x'_{vw} \leftarrow (x'_{vw} / \sum_{w=1}^{n'} x'_{vw}) \times u'_v$

// **Seed-column-scaling**

  for v= 1 to m' **do**

for w= 1 to n' **do** $x'_{vw} \leftarrow (x'_{vw} / \sum_{v=1}^{m'} x'_{vw}) \times l'_w$

end if

 end while

Call **QPT-Seed-Cell-Rounding**

Call **L1-error-Fixing**

return qpt // *a scaled QPT*

end procedure

Experimental Results

Experimental study was carried out using the following case study. We have considered Bloom's taxonomy for this study. Experimental data used for the case study are as follows:

1. S= Software Engineering (SE), a subject offered at the third year of the three year bachelor's degree course of computer science (B.Sc Computer Science) at Goa University.
2. m=8; m'=6
3. n=6; n'=4
4. p= {legacy systems, requirement engineering, software prototyping, software architecture, software testing techniques, software processes, software configuration management, CASE tools}; p'= {legacy systems, software prototyping, software architecture, software testing techniques, software configuration management, CASE tools}
5. q={knowledge(know), understanding(under), application(appl), analysis(anal), synthesis(synth), evaluation(eval)}; q'= {understanding, analysis, synthesis, evaluation}
6. QPT= SEQPT, an end semester QPT of SE for maximum marks, TM= 100 is shown in Table.9; tm=60.

Table 9. SE test paper template (SEQPT)

Module/Level	know	under	appl	anal	synth	eval	Cumulative-Module-Weight
Legacy Systems	1	4	1	1	6	2	15
Requirement Eng.	1	6	2	2	2	2	15
Software Prot.	1	2	2	1	2	2	10
Software Arch.	1	1	1	4	2	6	15
Soft. Test. Tech.	1	1	2	2	2	2	10
4Software Process.	1	1	2	2	2	2	10
Soft. Conf. Mgmt.	1	2	6	2	2	2	15
CASE tools	4	1	1	1	1	2	10
Cumulative- Level-Weight	11	18	17	15	19	20	100

Sequence of Steps Carried out for Scaled SEQPT Generation is as Below

Step1-SEQPT-Seed-Cell-Generation: SEQPT seed cells are formulated by extracting SEQPT module-level-weights corresponding to six selected modules and four selected levels. SEQPT-Seed-Cells formulated are represented in Table.10.

Table 10. SEQPT-seed-cells

4	1	6	2
2	1	2	2
1	4	2	6
1	2	2	2
2	2	2	2
1	1	1	2

Step2-Apply-Module-Constraints: SEQPT scaled-module-weights are generated by normalizing the module weights of modules such as legacy systems, software prototyping, software architecture, software testing techniques, software configuration management and CASE tools with respect to 60 marks. SE-scaled-module-weights, SE-mw generated is shown in Table.11.

Table 11. SEQPT-scaled-module-weights

Module	SE-mw
Legacy Systems	15
Software prot.	7
Software Arch.	16
Soft. Test. Tech.	8
Soft. Conf. Mgmt.	8
CASE tools	6
Total Marks	60

Step3-Apply-Level-Constraints: SEQPT scaled-level-weights are generated by normalizing the level weights of levels such as understanding, analysis, synthesis and evaluation with respect to 60 marks. SE-scaled- level-weights, SE-lw generated are represented in Table.12.

Table 12: SEQPT-Scaled-Level-Weights

Level	Under	anal	synth	eval	Total Marks
SE-lw	13	12	17	18	60

Step4-SEQPT-Seed-Cell-Scaling: SEQPTs iterate alternate scaling starts by merging the SE-Seed-Cells with SE-mw and SE-lw. Initial stage of SE-Seed-Cell scaling is shown in Table.13 below.

Table 13. Initial stage of SEQPT-seed-cell-scaling

Start	13	12	17	18
15	4	1	6	2
7	2	1	2	2
16	1	4	2	6
8	1	2	2	2
8	2	2	2	2
6	1	1	1	2

SEQPTs iterative scaling continues until the scaled SEQPT, SEqpt fulfills SE-mw and SE-lw. Iterative stages of SE-Seed-Cell-Scaling are represented in Table.14. SEQPT iterative alternate bi-proportional scaling terminates at the end of fourth iteration.

Step5-QPT-Seed-Cell-Rounding: Table.15 represents the scaled and rounded integer values of SE-Seed-Cells at the end of fourth iteration.

Step6-L1-error-Fixing: The near optimal SE-Seed-Cells of Table.16 get proportionately adjusted with +1 and -1 L1-error. The SE-Seed-Cells generated after fixing L1-error are shown in Table.16. The resulting optimal SE-qpt is shown Table. 17.

Table 14. Iterative stages of SEQPT-seed-cell-scaling

Row Adjustment					Column Adjustment				
Iteration 1									
	12.19	12.56	16.87	18.38		13	12	17	18
15	4.62	1.15	6.92	2.31	15.26	4.92	1.10	6.98	2.26
7	2.00	1.00	2.00	2.00	7.06	2.13	0.96	2.02	1.96
16	1.23	4.92	2.46	7.38	15.73	1.31	4.70	2.48	7.23
8	1.14	2.29	2.29	2.29	7.94	1.22	2.18	2.30	2.24
8	2.00	2.00	2.00	2.00	8.02	2.13	1.91	2.02	1.96
6	1.20	1.20	1.20	2.40	5.99	1.28	1.15	1.21	2.35
Iteration 2									
	12.93	12.07	16.92	18.09		13	12	17	18
15	4.84	1.08	6.86	2.22	15.04	4.87	1.08	6.89	2.21
7	2.11	0.95	2.00	1.94	7.01	2.13	0.94	2.01	1.93
16	1.34	4.78	2.52	7.36	15.96	1.34	4.76	2.54	7.32
8	1.23	2.20	2.32	2.25	7.99	1.23	2.19	2.33	2.24
8	2.13	1.91	2.01	1.95	8.00	2.14	1.90	2.02	1.95
6	1.28	1.15	1.21	2.36	6.00	1.29	1.14	1.22	2.34
Iteration 3									
	12.99	12.01	16.99	18.01		13	12	17	18
15	4.85	1.07	6.87	2.20	15.01	4.86	1.07	6.87	2.20
7	2.12	0.94	2.00	1.93	7.00	2.13	0.94	2.01	1.93
16	1.35	4.77	2.54	7.34	15.99	1.35	4.77	2.54	7.34
8	1.24	2.19	2.33	2.25	8.00	1.24	2.19	2.33	2.24
8	2.14	1.90	2.02	1.94	8.00	2.14	1.89	2.02	1.94
6	1.29	1.14	1.22	2.35	6.00	1.29	1.14	1.22	2.34
Iteration 4									
	13.00	12.00	17.00	18.00		13	12	17	18
15	4.85	1.07	6.87	2.20	15	4.85	1.07	6.87	2.20
7	2.13	0.94	2.01	1.93	7	2.13	0.94	2.01	1.93
16	1.35	4.77	2.54	7.34	16	1.35	4.77	2.55	7.34
8	1.24	2.19	2.33	2.24	8	1.24	2.19	2.33	2.24
8	2.14	1.89	2.02	1.94	8	2.14	1.89	2.02	1.94
6	1.29	1.14	1.22	2.35	6	1.29	1.14	1.22	2.34

Table 15. Scaled and rounded seed-cell-scaling

	13	12	17	18
15	5	1	7	2
7	2	1	2	2
16	1	5	3	7
8	1	2	2	2
8	2	2	2	2
6	1	1	1	2

Table 16. SE-Seed-Cells after L1-error Fixing

	13	12	17	18
15	5	1	7	2
7	2	1	2	2
16	1	5	3	7
8	2	2	2	2
8	2	2	2	2
6	1	1	1	3

Table 17. Scaled SEqpt

Module/Level	Under	anal	synth	eval	Cumulative-Module-Weight
Legacy Systems	5	1	7	2	15
Software prot.	2	1	2	2	7
Software Arch.	1	5	3	7	16
Soft. Test. Tech.	2	2	2	2	8
Soft. Conf. Mgmt.	2	2	2	2	8
CASE tools	1	1	1	3	6
Cumulative-Level -Weight	13	12	17	18	**60**

Summary

This work focused on an incremental approach for dynamic test paper generation by using bi-proportional matrix scaling method. The main advantage of this approach is that it performs automatic scaling and balancing of all entries of the QPT by carrying out iterative scaling and proportional fitting procedure.

The procedure alternates between fitting the modules and also fitting the cognitive levels and converges with a bi-proportionally scaled and balanced QPT. Bi-proportional matrix scaling has been found successful in generating a scaled QPT with lesser computational resources. An L1-error function is normally incorporated in matrix scaling problems for measuring the distance between current row and column sums and target row and column marginal entries. The procedure converges to bi-proportional fit if and only if the L1-error tends to zero. We have used matrix scaling with discrete variant which iteratively scales the QPT, assigns integer valued marks (integer round up operation) under different levels of a module, x L1-error by proportionately adjusting the candidate rows and columns with +1 and -1 values respectively and generates a bi-proportionally scaled and balanced QPT. The dynamic QPT so generated can drastically reduce the time and e ort of the user while ensuring test paper quality also.

CONCLUSION

Reforms in the educational system emphasize more on continuous assessment. Continuous assessment requires the generation of dynamic test papers for different examinations. Automatically generating dynamic QPT, satisfying instructors specified number of modules and instructor specified number of taxonomy levels, has been found to be very important in situations where novice instructors wish to formulate test papers for different examinations. The evolutionary approach of section 1.3 has been able to generate population of QPTs, but encountered significant run-time delay during the iterative population generation. Alternatively, pareto-optimal based evolutionary algorithm of section 1.3 has been able to reduce run-time delay, but still was unable to always guarantee generation of optimal solutions within user specified number of iterations. In order to overcome these limitations, bi-proportional matrix balancing technique has been designed and implemented. The bi- proportional matrix balancing technique performs iterative scaling and proportional fitting of the QPT to satisfy the instructor specified number of modules of subject, instructor specified number of levels of taxonomy and Instructor specified marks requirement of each examination. The best advantage of bi-proportional scaling technique is that it avoids re-execution of computationally expensive multi-objective evolutionary algorithms for generating different variants of the successfully generated evolutionary approach based optimal template. Finally, our experimental analysis concludes that evolutionary approach and pareto-optimal evolutionary approach are efficient in generating new and different types of templates, whereas matrix scaling procedure is suitable for re-generating different variants of an existing evolutionary algorithm based QPT with lesser computational resources.

REFERENCES

Bloom, B.S., Engelhart, M. D., Furs, E. J., Hill, W. H., & Krathwohl, D. R. (1956). Taxonomy of educational objectives: The classification of educational goals. In *Handbook I: Cognitive domain*. New York: David McKay Company.

Caramia, M., & Olmo, D. (2008). Multi-Objective Management in freight Logistics, Increasing Capacity, Service Level Safety with Optimization Algorithms. In Multi-Objective Optimization. Springer.

Coello-Coello, C., Lamont, G. B., & Veldhuizen, D. A. V. (2007). *Evolutionary Algorithms for Solving Multi-Objective Problems* (2nd ed.). Springer.

Dascalu, M. (2011). Application of Particle Swarm Optimization to Formative E-Assessment in Project Management, Informatica. *Economic Journal (London), 15*(1), 48–61.

Deb, K. (2001). *Multi-Objective Optimization Using Evolutionary Algorithm*. John Wiley Sons, Inc.

Deb, K., & Gupta, H. (2005). Searching for Robust Pareto-Optimal Solutions in Multi-Objective Optimization Evolutionary Multi-Criterion Optimization. *LNCS, 3410*, 150-164.

Fienberg, S. E., & Meyer, M. M. (2004). *Iterative proportional fitting, Encyclopedia of Statistical Sciences* (2nd ed.). John Wiley.

Fogel, D. B. (1994). Applying Evolutionary Programming to Selected Control Problems. *Computers & Mathematics with Applications (Oxford, England), 27*(11), 89–104. doi:10.1016/0898-1221(94)90100-7

Fogel, D. B. (1995). A Comparison of Evolutionary Programming and Genetic Algorithms on selected Constrained Optimization Problems. *Simulation, 64*(6), 397–404. doi:10.1177/003754979506400605

Gake, N., & Pukelsheim, F. (2008). Divisor methods for proportional representation systems: An optimization approach to vector and matrix apportionment problems. *Mathematical Social Sciences, 56*(2), 166-184.

Gandomi, A., Yang, H., Talatahari, X. S. S., & Alavi, A. H. (2013). *Metaheuristics in Modeling and Optimization, Metaheuristic Applications in Structures and Infrastructures* (1st ed.). Elsevier.

Guang, C., Yuxiao, D., Wanlin, G., & Lina, Y. (2010). A implementation of an automatic examination paper generation system. *Mathematical and Computer Modelling, 51*(11-12), 1339–1342. doi:10.1016/j.mcm.2009.11.010

Ho, T. F., Yin, P. Y., Hwang, G. J., Shyu, S. J., & Yean, Y. N. (2009). Multi-Objective parallel test-sheet composition using enhanced particle swarm optimization. *Journal of Educational Technology & Society, 12*(4), 193–206.

Holland, J. H. (1975). *Adaption in Natural and Artificial Systems: An Introductory Analysis with Applications to Biology, Control and Artificial Systems*. University Press of Michigan.

Hu, J., Sun, Y., & Xu, Q. (2011). The Genetic Algorithm in the Test Paper Generation. *Web Information Systems and Mining, 6987*, 109–113. doi:10.1007/978-3-642-23971-7_16

Huang, M., Tang, L., & Liang, X. (2009). Research on Intelligent Test Paper Generation Based on Improved Genetic Algorithm. *Proceedings of IEEE Chinese Control and Decision Conference (CCDC),* 1884-1886. 10.1109/CCDC.2009.5191822

Hwang, G. J., Chu, H. C., & Lin, J. Y. (2008). An innovative parallel test sheet composition approach to meet multiple assessment criteria for national tests. *Computers & Education, 51*(3), 1058–1072. doi:10.1016/j.compedu.2007.10.006

Hwang, G. J., Lin, B. M. T., & Lin, T. L. (2006). An Effective Approach for Test- Sheet Composition from Large-Scale Item Banks. *Computers & Education, 46*(2), 122–139. doi:10.1016/j.compedu.2003.11.004

Karaboga, D. (2005). An Idea Based On Honey Bee Swarm For Numerical Optimization. Technical Report-TR06, Erciyes University, Engineering Faculty, Computer Engineering Department.

Kennedy, J., & Eberhart, R. C. (1995). Particle swarm optimization. *Proceedings of IEEE International Conference on Neural Networks (ICNN)*, *4*, 1942-1948. 10.1109/ICNN.1995.488968

Krathwohl, D. R. (2002). A revision of Bloom's taxonomy: An overview. *Theory into Practice, 41*(4), 212–219. doi:10.120715430421tip4104_2

Lahr, M., & Mesnard, L. (2004). Bi-proportional techniques in input-output analysis: Table updating and structural analysis. *Economic Systems Research, 16*(2), 115–134. doi:10.1080/0953531042000219259

Lin, H. Y., Su, J. M., & Tseng, S. S. (2012). An adaptive test sheet generation mechanism using genetic algorithm. *Mathematical Problems in Engineering, 2012*, 1–18. doi:10.1155/2012/820190

Lirong, X., & Jianwei, S. (2010). Notice of Retraction Automatic Generating Test Paper System Based on Genetic Algorithm. *Proceedings of Second IEEE International Workshop on Education Technology and Computer Science (ETCS)*, 272-275.

Liu, S. W. (2010). Fengying, Strategy and Realization of Auto-generating Exam Paper Based on Genetic Algorithm. *Proceedings of IEEE International Conference on Artificial Intelligence and Computational Intelligence (AICI)*, 2478-482.

Liu, Y., Wang, Y., Du, Y., & Zhang, J. (2008). Multi-object intellectual test paper assembling based on adaptive operator genetic algorithm. *Computer Applications (Nottingham)*, (no. S1), 22–24.

Mesnard, L. D. (2002). Normalizing bi-proportional methods. *The Annals of Regional Science, 36*(1), 139–144. doi:10.1007001680100070

Ming, L., Jin-gang, M., & Jing, Z. (2009). Automatic generating test paper strategy based on improved particle swarm optimization. *Proceedings of IEEE International Symposium on IT in Medicine and Education (ITIME)*, 711-715.

Oelbermann, K.-F. (2013). *Alternate Scaling algorithm for bi-proportional divisor methods*. Preprint Nr. 04/2013, Institute for Mathematics, University of Augsburg. https://www.math.uni-augsburg.de/

Peipei, G., Niu, Z., Chen, X., & Chen, W. (2012). A test sheet generating algorithm based on intelligent genetic algorithm and hierarchical planning. *Proceedings of SPIE 8334, Fourth International Conference on Digital Image Processing (ICDIP)*.

Pukelsheim, F. (2012). *An L1-analysis of the Iterative Proportional Fitting procedure*. Preprint Nr. 2/2012, University of Augsburg. https://www.math. uni-augsburg.de/

Pukelsheim, F. (2014). Bi-proportional Matrix Scaling and the Iterative Proportional Fitting Procedure. *Proceedings of Annals of Operation Research*, 269-283.

Schneider, M., & Zenios, S. (1990). A comparative study of algorithms for matrix balancing. *Operations Research, 38*(3), 439–455. doi:10.1287/ opre.38.3.439

Speed, T. P. (2005). *Iterative Proportional Fitting, Encyclopedia of Bio-statistics*. Wiley Online Library.

Srinivas, M., & Patnaik, M. (1994). Adaptive Probabilities of Crossover and Mutation in Genetic Algorithms. *IEEE Transactions on Systems Man and Cybernetics, 24*(4), 656–667. doi:10.1109/21.286385

Suskie, L. (2009). *Assessing student learning: A common sense guide* (2nd ed.). Jossey-Bass.

Talbi, E. G. (2009). *Metaheurisitics: From Design to Implementation*. Wiley. doi:10.1002/9780470496916

Thiele, L., & Zitzler, E. (1999). Multiobjective evolutionary algorithms: A comparative case study and the strength of pareto approach. *IEEE Transactions on Evolutionary Computation, 3*(4), 257–271. doi:10.1109/4235.797969

Yin, P. Y., Chang, K. C., & Hwang, G. J. (2006). Particle swarm optimization approach to composing serial test sheets for multiple assessment criteria. *Journal of Educational Technology & Society, 9*(3), 3–15.

Zhi, F. L., Ji, S., & Jia, L. (2010). Strategy and Applied Research of Multi-Constrained Model of Automatic Test Paper Based on Genetic Al- gorithm. *Applied Mechanics and Materials, 37-38*, 1223–1230. doi:10.4028/www. scientific.net/AMM.37-38.1223

Zitzler, E., & Deb. (2008). Evolutionary Multi-Objective Optimization. *Proceedings of Genetic and Evolutionary Computation Conference - GECCO*, 2467-2486.

Chapter 2

Grouping of Questions From a Question Bank Using Partition-Based Clustering

ABSTRACT

During automatic test paper generation, it is necessary to detect percentage of similarity among questions and thereby avoid repetition of questions. In order to detect repeated questions, the authors have designed and implemented a similarity matrix-based grouping algorithm. Grouping algorithms are widely used in multidisciplinary fields such as data mining, image analysis, and bioinformatics. This chapter proposes the use of grouping strategy-based partition algorithm for clustering the questions in a question bank. It includes a new approach for computing the question similarity matrix and use of the matrix in clustering the questions. The grouping algorithm extracts n module-wise questions, compute $n \times n$ similarity matrix by performing $n \times (n-1)/2$ pair-wise question vector comparisons, and uses the matrix in formulating question clusters. Grouping algorithm has been found efficient in reducing the best-case time complexity, $O(n \times (n-1)/2 \log n)$ of hierarchical approach to $O(n \times (n-1)/2)$.

DOI: 10.4018/978-1-7998-3772-5.ch002

TERMINOLOGY USED

The terminology used is presented in the table below -

Table 1. Terminology used for question clustering

Term	Meaning
Subject (S)	S is a subject/paper offered in different semesters of a course.
Modules/Units	For each subject, there is a university pre-scribed syllabus which consists of different modules/units.
Question Bank (QB)	QB is a database which stores module wise questions with its details such as question- no, question-content, question-type, question- marks and question-answer-time
Q	Q is the total number of questions stored under a module
t_i	t_i refers to the total number of questions in which term i appears
$freq_{ij}$	$freq_{ij}$ is the frequency of term i in question j
maximum frequency ($max\,freq_{ij}$)	$max\,freq_{ij}$ is the maximum frequency of a term in question j
term frequency (tf_{ij})	tf_{ij} refers to the importance of a term i in question j. It is calculated using the formula: $tf_{ij} = freq_{ij}/max\,freq_{ij}$
Inverse Document Frequency (idf_i)	idf_i refers to the discriminating power of term i and is calculated as: $idf_i = log_2\,(Q/t_i)$
tf-idf weighting (Wij)	It is a weighting scheme to determine weight of a term in a question. It is calculated using the formula: $W_{ij} = tf_{ij} \times idf_i$
Question-Term-Set, T_i (question q_i)	A set of terms extracted from each question by performing its tokenization, stop word removal, taxonomy verb removal and stemming
Theshold, δ	User input threshold value to find the similarity

2. 2 PARTITION-BASED GROUPING ALGORITHMS FOR QUESTION CLUSTER FORMULATION

The similarity matrix computation has been carried out by using matrix representation of vectors which is a natural extension of existing Vector Space Model (VSM) (Jing, L., Ng, M. K.& Huang, J. Z. 2010; Turney, P. D., Pantel, P. 2010; Wong, S. K. M. and Raghavan, V.V. 1984). VSM is a popular information retrieval system implementation which facilitates representation of a set of documents as vectors in term space. Similarity matrix generates its entries by computing similarity of each pair of questions based on different similarity measure.The partition-based grouping algorithm is an alternative to the most widely used Agglomerative Hierarchical Clustering approach (Huang, A. 2008; Fung, B.C.M, Wang K.& M. Ester. 2003; K. Gowda, C. and Krishna, G. 1978). The Agglomerative Hierarchical clustering starts with a similarity matrix and generates clusters by iteratively merging two questions that are most similar in each of the iteration (Beeferman, D. and Berger, A. 2000; Fisher, D. 1996). The iterative stages are continued until the desired numbers of clusters are found or only one cluster remains. Our partition-based grouping algorithm also starts with a similarity matrix but avoids the iterative stages of hierarchical clustering. It is achieved by formulating disjoint clusters of similar questions in parallel with the generation of each row of the similarity matrix. Hence, the best case time complexity, O ($n\times$ (n-1)/2 log n) of hierarchical clustering can be reduced to O (n $\times$ (n-1)/2) by introducing grouping algorithm. The methodology adopted for finding similarity between module-wise/ unit-wise questions in a QB consists of the following four steps -

Step1-Question Bank Pre-processing
Step2- Question Similarity Matrix Computation
Step3-Generation of Question Clusters
Step4-Evaluating Question Clusters

A brief description of these steps is as follows –

Step1- Question Bank Pre-Processing

The pre-processing of questions is carried out using the following four sub-steps-

Tokenization: Each question is treated as a collection of strings (or bag of words), which are then partitioned into a list of terms.

Filtering Stop Words: Stop words are frequently occurring, in- significant words within the question content and are eliminated.

Filtering Taxonomy Verbs: The Bloom's taxonomy verbs (Yeh, L. C. and LIN, S. P. 2003; Srinivas, M. and Patnaik, M. 1994; Khairuddin, N. N. and Hashim, K. 2008) within the question content are identified and eliminated.

Stemming Words: Stemming is a heuristic process of cutting o the ends of terms for getting the correct root form of the term. There are various word stemmers (Chris, D. P. 1994). available for English text and the most commonly used Porter Stemmer is considered.

Normalization: The idea behind normalization is to convert all terms which mean the same, but are written in different forms (e.g. CPU and C.P.U) to the same form. We are using the following techniques for performing normalization- 1) Lowercase the terms 2) Remove special characters

Step2- Question Similarity Matrix Computation

Similarity matrix computation is performed by considering the matrix representation of vectors. Matrix representation of module-wise questions of a QB considers each question as a vector of terms. Similarity matrix of a set of questions in a QB is a two-dimensional matrix representing the pair-wise similarity of module-wise questions. Pair-wise similarity computation can be performed on different similarity measures. We have used cosine similarity and Jaccard similarity coefficient to assign a similarity score to each pair of compared questions. Jaccard similarity coefficient has been referred either as jaccard coefficient or as jaccard similarity henceforth in the remaining part of this chapter. The cosine function uses angular measure while jaccard uses association coefficient. Cosine similarity is a measure of similarity between two vectors by measuring the cosine of the angle between them. Cosine of the angle is 1.0 for identical vectors and is in the range of 0.0 to 1.0 for non-similar or partially similar vectors. Cosine similarity remains as the most popular measure because of its simple interpretation, easy computation and document length exclusion (Nguyen, D. T. and Chan, C. K. 2012; Subhashini, R. and Kumar, V. J. S. 2010). The term weight score of cosine are calculated according to tf-idf weighting method (Aizawa, A. 2000; Soucy P. 2005). tf-idf is the most commonly used scheme to assign weights to individual terms based on their importance in a collection of module-wise questions. Each weight score is calculated as a product of tf and idf. Higher values of idf correspond to terms which characterize a question more distinctly than others. Description of tf-idf calculation is given in Table. 3.1. jaccard coefficient (Nivattanakul, S. et.al,2013) is a statistical measure for comparing the similarity and diversity of documents. The jaccard similarity can be used, when interested in finding binary differences between two or more documents. It is popularly used in research investigations which focus on the presence/absence between several objects. The jaccard similarity coefficient ranges between 0 and 1. It is 1 when two question vectors are identical and zero when they are disjoint.

The cosine similarity of two question vectors say q_1 and q_2 is calculated by performing the dot product of each questions' term vectors. The calculation of cosine similarity is performed using the following formula:

$$\text{Similarity } (q_1, q_2) = \cos \theta = \frac{(q1, q2)}{(|q1|, |q2|)}. \tag{1}$$

where '.' denotes the dot product between vectors q_1 and q_2. $|q_1|$ and $|q_2|$ are the euclidean norm of q_1 *and* q_2 vectors. The above formula can be expanded in the following manner.

$$\cos \theta = \frac{\sum_{i=1}^{n} wi, q1 \times wi, q2}{qrt(\sum_{i=1}^{n} wi * wi, q1) \times sqrt(\sum_{i=1}^{n} wi * wi, q2)} \tag{2}$$

Jaccard similarity measure compares the sum weight of shared terms to the sum weight of terms that are present in either of the two questions but are not the shared terms. The jaccard similarity calculation is carried out using the following formula:

$$\text{Similarity } (q_1, q_2) = J (q_1, q_2) = \frac{q1 \cap q2}{(q1 \cup q2) - (q1 \cap q2)} \tag{3}$$

Step3- Generating Question Clusters

The grouping algorithm for clustering is a kind of partitioning algorithm (Chali, Y. and Noureddine, S. 2005; Wang, Z. 2011). It considers words of question vectors, applies cosine similarity and jaccard similarity measures and computes question-similarity-matrix. During the process of computation of each row of the question-similarity-matrix, the grouping algorithm does parallel generation of question clusters by selecting the set of questions satisfying the input similarity threshold value, say δ, in a row-wise manner. Result of comparison is used as a standard in formulating similar question clusters. Hence, it does not require initial specification of the number of clusters as well as the iterative stages of cluster formulation. Accordingly, there is no additional time and space requirement for generating the clusters.

A sample of a similarity matrix with the computed pair-wise similarity of questions say x and y denoted as sm_{xy} is represented in Table.3.2 below. The computation of similarity of n questions is carried out by calculating similarity of $n \times (n-1)/2$ pairs of question vectors.

Table 2. Similarity matrix representation for question to question match

	Q_1	Q_2	Q_3	Q_4	Q_5	Q_6	Q_7	...	Q_n
Q_1		sm_{12}	sm_{13}	sm_{14}	sm_{15}	sm_{16}	sm_{17}	...	sm_{1n}
Q_2			sm_{23}	sm_{24}	sm_{25}	sm_{26}	sm_{27}	...	sm_{2n}
Q_3				sm_{34}	sm_{35}	sm_{36}	sm_{37}	...	sm_{3n}
Q_4					sm_{45}	sm_{46}	sm_{47}	...	sm_{4n}
Q_5						sm_{56}	sm_{57}	...	sm_{5n}
Q_6							sm_{67}	...	sm_{6n}
Q_7								...	sm_{7n}
...	...	...	...	...	...	...	...	...	...
Q_n								...	sm_{nn}

Step4- Evaluating Question Clusters

Precision, Recall and F-measure have been used as the metrics to evaluate the accuracy of predictions and the coverage of accurate pairs of comparisons while formulating question clusters. They are computed as:

Precision (P) =

$$\frac{\text{number of relevant question-to-question matches retrieved by the tool}}{\text{total number of question-to-question matches reterieved by the tool}}$$

$$(4)$$

Recall (R) =

$$\frac{\text{number of relevant question-to-question matches retrieved by the tool}}{\text{total number of question-to-question matches given by the instructor}}$$

$$(5)$$

F-measure $= \dfrac{(2 \times P \times R)}{P + R}$

$$(6)$$

PROBLEM STATEMENT

Given a Question Bank for Subject S, QB(S)=$\{qb_1, qb2_1, ..., qb_N\}$ where qb_i =$\{q_{i1}, q_{i2}, ..., qi_{ni}\}$ is the question bank for module i of subject S con- sisting of n_i questions and N=the set of modules under subject S, the problem is to find clusters $C_{i1}, C_{i2}, ...$ of similar questions in qb_i. A question q_{ij} is said to be similar to q_{ik} of module i if similarity $(qst_i, unt_j) >= \delta$ where δ is the user input threshold value to find the similarity. The similarity $(qst_i, unt_j) >= \delta$ function could use any of the similarity measure available. We have used Cosine Similarity and Jaccard Coefficient to perform the experimental study. However, the disadvantage of this model is that equivalent, but not exactly same words are often missed out in matching.

The main modules of this algorithm are shown in Figure.1 below.

Figure 1. Main modules of question cluster formulation

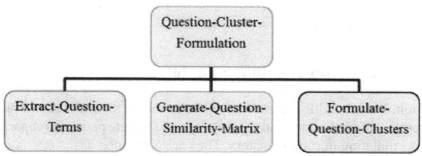

The brief details of modules are presented below-

1. Extract-Question-Terms: Input q_{ij} (j=1 to n_i) and for each q_{ij} it extracts terms t_{ijs} (s=1 to n_{ij}).
2. Extract-Question-Terms: Input q_{ij} (j=1 to n_i) and for each q_{ij} it extracts terms t_{ijs} (s=1 to n_{ij}).
3. Generate-Question-Similarity-Matrix: Input terms t_i s (s=1 to n_{ij}) for all qij (j=1 to n_i).
4. For each pair of questions q_{ij} and q_{ik}, compute similarity (q_{ij}, q_{ik}) for k=j+1 to n_i and represent it as Question-Similarity-Matrix.
5. Formulate-Question-Clusters: Use Question-Similarity-Matrix and find clusters of similar questions satisfying similarity $(q_{ij}, q_{ik}) >= \delta$.

Algorithm Details

Question Cluster Formulation using Partition-based Clustering Algorithm (QCFPCA)

{// start of QCFPCA for (i = 1 to n_i) // for each question of module do
{
Call Term Extraction (qb_i)
Call Question Cluster Formulation (T_i, δ)
}
} //end of QCFPCA

Procedure *Term Extraction* (qb_i)

Input: qb_i -{$q_{i1}, q_{i2}, ..., q_{ini}$}: *question bank for module i of subject S consisting of n_i questions*
Output: T_i= {$t_{i1}[\ ], t_{i2}[\ ] t_{i3}[\ ], ..., t_{ini}[\ ]$}: *extracted terms of questions,* {$q_{i1}, q_{i2}, ..., q_{ini}$}
T_i= {}
for j=1 to n_i do
  extract terms from q_{ij} and store it in array $t_{ij}[\ ]$
  remove stop-words from $t_{ij}[\ ]$
  remove taxonomy verbs from $t_{ij}[\ ]$
  extract stem of each term in $t_{ij}[\ ]$
  T_i _ T_i U $t_{ij}[\ ]$
end for
return T_i= {$t_{i1}[\ ], t_{i2}[\ ] t_{i3}[\ ], ..., t_{ini}[\ ]$}
end procedure

Procedure *Question Cluster Formulation (Ti, ∂)*

Input: T_i ∂
T_i= {$t_{i1}[\ ], t_{i2}[\ ] t_{i3}[\ ], ..., t_{ini}[\ ]$}: *where, t_{is}= {$t_{is1}, t_{is2}, ..., t_{isk}$} for s=1 to n_{i}, n_i ={$q_{i1}, q_{i2}, ..., q_{ini}$}*
∂: *user input threshold value to find similarity*
Output: *k clusters $C_{i1}, C_{i2}, ..., C_{ik}$ where C_{ij} consist of question q'_{ij} belongs to qb_i*
//Initialization
p=0 ; //counter for new cluster formation
cluster_set= [ ];
//Similar-Question-Cluster-Formulation
for j=1 to n_i do
  If q_{ij} not in cluster_set then
    p=p+1;
    C_{ip}*=New-Cluster (q_{ij}, p)*
    cluster_set= cluster_set + q_{ij}
    for k= (j+1) to n_i do
      //Similarity-Matrix-Computation
      if similarity (q_{ij}, q_{ik}) >=∂ then
        add q_{ik} to cluster k
        cluster_set= cluster_set + qik
      end if
    end for
  end if
end for
return k clusters $C_{i1}, C_{i2}, ..., C_{ik}$ where C_{ij} consist of question q'_{ij} belongs to qb_i
end procedure

EXPERIMENTAL RESULTS

Implementation of the algorithm has been done using Microsoft Visual Basic .NET as Front-End Tool and SQL Server as Back End Tool on a 2 GHz processor with 1GB RAM.

Dataset Used

1. S= Software Engineering (SE), a subject offered at the third year of the three year bachelor's degree course of computer science (B.Sc Computer Science) at Goa University.
2. QB(S) =qb_{10}, where *qb10* refers to a module named reengineering
3. $qb_{10} = \{q_{148}, q_{149}..., q_{474}\}$
4. δ=0.60
5. A snapshot of the set of questions { $q_{148}, q_{149},...,q_{474}$} with its ex- tracted list of terms {reengine,busi, process, reengine}, {neat, diagram, bpr, model}, {note, software, reengine}, {neat, diagram, software, process, model} etc, for qb_{10} is displayed in Figure2. Extraction of the set of terms corresponding to qb_{10} is carried out by performing five different sub-steps of QB pre-processing such as tokenization, filtering stop words, filtering taxonomy verbs, stemming words and normalization.

Results Obtained

Figure. 3 below shows sample screen shot of the Question-Similarity- Matrix computation for qb10 by using cosine similarity and jaccard similarity coefficient. Figure 4 represents the process of generation of question clusters. Each question q_{ij} of module qb_{10} in the Question- Similarity-Matrix sequentially gets compared with q_{ik} question in the matrix based on the similarity measure, similarity (qst_i, unt_j)>= δ. If a question does not find its match with any of the generated question clusters, it formulates a New-Cluster (), identifies other similar questions and appends them to the new cluster. Figure. 5 displays the comparative analysis of the question clusters formulated with cosine similarity and jaccard similarity coefficient.

Figure 2. Extracted list of terms under re-engineering module of SE subject

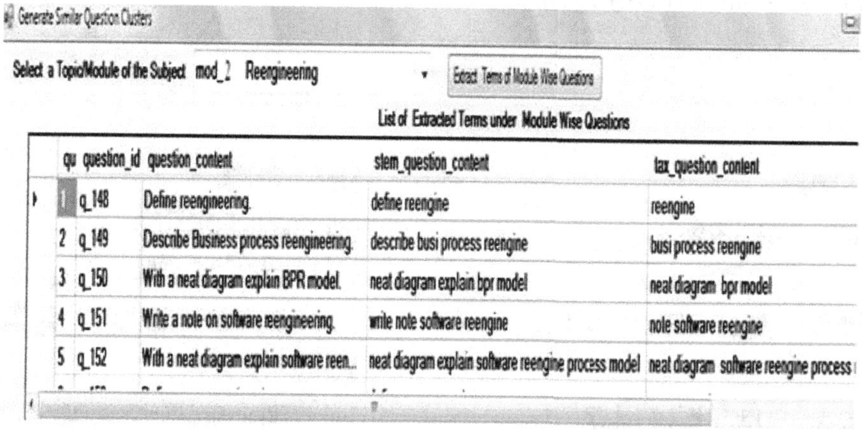

Figure 3. Sample screenshot of the similarity matrix of re-engineering module using cosine and jaccard similarity coefficient

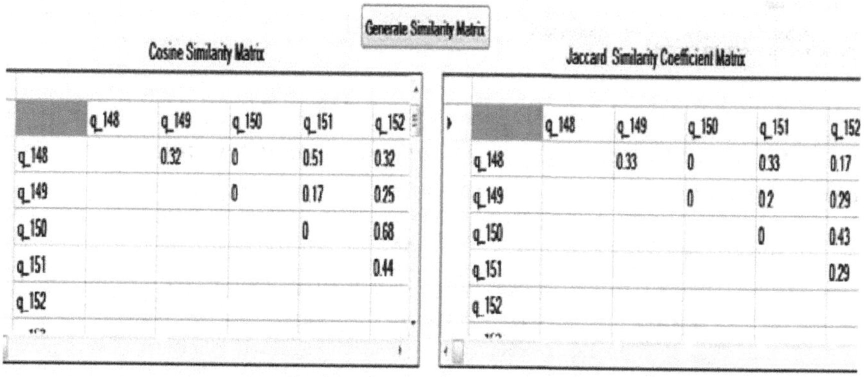

Performance Evaluation

The Precision, Recall and F-measure values are computed to compare the performance of cosine similarity with jaccard coefficient while formulating question clusters for the questions in QB of SE. Table.3 below shows the results of performance evaluation carried out by considering the question clusters formulated using four modules of SE namely reengineering, legacy systems, software testing techniques and software configuration management. Results indicate that cosine similarity outperforms jaccard in clustering questions.

Figure 4. Extracted groups of similar questions using cosine similarity coefficient and jaccard similarity coefficient

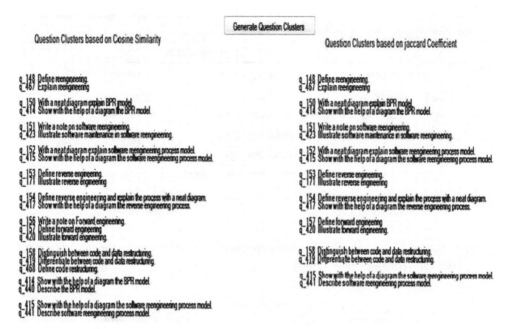

Figure 5. Generated clusters of questions using cosine similarity and jaccard similarity coefficient

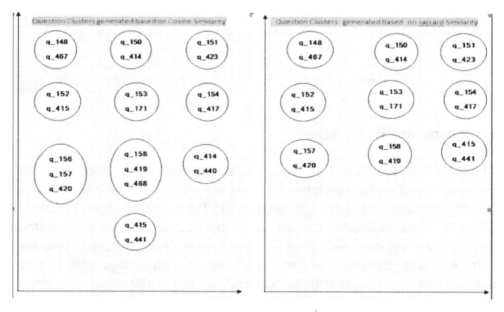

Table 3. Performance evaluation of SE question clusters

Module- of-the-subject	Cosine Precision	Cosine Recall	Cosine F-measure	Jaccard Precision	Jaccard Recall	Jaccard F-measure
mod-2	0.78	0.82	0.80	0.75	0.79	0.76
mod-3	0.78	0.81	0.79	0.73	0.78	0.74
mod-7	0.77	0.82	0.79	0.72	0.77	0.74
mod-9	0.76	0.82	0.78	0.71	0.76	0.73

CONCLUSION

This work focused on a new approach for formulating question clusters by performing n × (n-1)/2 pair-wise question vector comparisons. Similarity matrix computation was carried out using cosine similarity and jaccard similarity coefficient. Results obtained indicate that cosine similarity outperforms jaccard coefficient in formulating question clusters. Generated question clusters are significant in situations where novice instructors wish to formulate different sets of test papers for the same examination.

REFERENCES

Aizawa, A. (2000). The feature quantity: an information-theoretic perspective of tf idf-like measures. *Proceedings of the 23rd ACM SIGIR conference on research and development in information retrieval*, 104-111. 10.1145/345508.345556

Beeferman, D., & Berger, A. (2000). Agglomerative clustering of a search engine query log. *Proceedings of the sixth ACM SIGKDD international conference on Knowledge discovery and data mining*, 407-416. 10.1145/347090.347176

Chali, Y., & Noureddine, S. (2005). Document Clustering with Grouping and Chaining Algorithms, IJCNLP. *LNCS, 3651*, 280–291.

Chris, D. P. (1994). An evaluation method for stemming algorithms. *Proceedings of the 17th annual international ACM SIGIR conference on Research and development in information retrieval*, 42-50.

Fisher, D. (1996). Iterative Optimization and Simplification of Hierarchical Clustering. *Journal of Artificial Intelligence, 4*(1), 147–179. doi:10.1613/jair.276

Fung, B. C. M., Wang, K., & Ester, M. (2003). Hierarchical Document Clustering Using Frequent Itemsets. *Proceedings of Third SIAM International Conference on Data Mining*, *30*(5), 59-70.

Gowda, C. K., & Krishna, G. (1978). Agglomerative Clustering Using the Concept of Mutual Nearest Neighborhood. *Pattern Recognition*, *10*(2), 105–112. doi:10.1016/0031-3203(78)90018-3

Huang, A. (2008). Similarity Measures for Text Document Clustering. *Proceedings of New Zealand Computer Science Research Student Conference (NZCSRSC)*, 49-56.

Jing, L., Ng, M. K., & Huang, J. Z. (2010). Knowledge-based vector space model for text clustering. *Knowledge and Information Systems*, *25*(1), 35–55. doi:10.100710115-009-0256-5

Khairuddin, N. N., & Hashim, K. (2008). Application of Bloom's Taxonomy in Software Engineering Assessments. *Proceedings of the 8th WSEAS International Conference on Applied Computer Science*, 66-69.

Nguyen, D. T., & Chan, C. K. (2012). Clustering with Multiview point-Based Similarity Measure. *IEEE Transactions on Knowledge and Data Engineering*, *24*(6), 988–1001. doi:10.1109/TKDE.2011.86

Nivattanakul, S., Singthongchai, J. Naenudorn, E. & Wanapu, S. (2013). Using of Jaccard coefficient for keywords similarity. *Proceedings of International Multi-Conf. Engineers and Computer Scientists*, 380-384.

Soucy, P. (2005). Beyond TFIDF weighting for text categorization in the vector space model. *Proceedings of the 19th International Joint Conference on Artificial Intelligence (IJCAI)*, 1130-1135.

Srinivas, M., & Patnaik, M. (1994). Adaptive Probabilities of Crossover and Mutation in Genetic Algorithms. *IEEE Transactions on Systems. Man and Cybernetics*, *24*(4), 656–667. doi:10.1109/21.286385

Subhashini, R., & Kumar, V. J. S. (2010). Evaluating the Performance of Similarity Measures Used in Document Clustering and Information Retrieval. *Proceedings of first International Conference on Integrated Intelligent Computing (ICIIC)*, 27-31. 10.1109/ICIIC.2010.42

Turney, P. D., & Pantel, P. (2010). From Frequency to Meaning: Vector Space Models of Semantics. *Journal of Artificial Intelligence Research*, *37*(1), 141–188. doi:10.1613/jair.2934

Wang, Z. (2011). A new partitioning-based algorithm for document clustering, *Proceedings of 8th International Conference on Fuzzy Systems and Knowledge Discovery (FSKD)*, 26-28. 10.1109/FSKD.2011.6019857

Yeh, L. C., & Lin, S. P. (2003). The research of Bloom's taxonomy for educational objects. *The Journal of Educational Research, 105*, 94–106.

Chapter 3

Question Selection in Template–Based Test Paper Models

ABSTRACT

The success of any educational program depends on its evaluation system. Examinations are a part of learning process which acts as an element in evaluation. For the smooth conduct of examinations of various universities and academic institutions, the test paper generation process would be helpful. However, examination test paper composition is a multi-constraint concurrent optimization problem. Question selection plays a key role in test paper generation systems. Also, it is the most significant and time-consuming activity. The question selection is handled in traditional test paper generation systems by using a specified test paper format containing a listing of weightages to be allotted to each unit/module of the syllabus.

RELATED WORK

Automatic test paper/test paper generation is considered as the process of searching test items/questions from a Question Bank (QB) and composing it on the basis of the test paper specifications (Van der Linden, W. J. and J. J Adema. 1998; Lirong, X. and Jianwei, S. 2010). The process of test paper generation needs huge searching space, complex computing and multi-objective optimization. Intelligent algorithms employ the process of multi-

DOI: 10.4018/978-1-7998-3772-5.ch003

objective optimization to compose a test paper. The representative algorithms of intelligent optimization approach generally found suitable for question selection in adaptive testing are evolutionary computation based genetic algorithm and swarm algorithm type (Deb, K.,et.al. 2002; Laumanns, M., et.al.2000; Chen, M.R. and Lu, Z. 2008; Subhashini, R. and Kumar, V. J. S. 2010). In this chapter, three different multi-objective evolutionary optimization approaches namely evolutionary approach, elitist evolutionary approach and elitist differential evolution approach have been discussed. A Multi-Objective Question Selection Algorithm (MOQSA) supported by all the three approaches have been designed for solving the multi-objective optimization problem of question selection in template-based test paper model. The template generated in chapter 2 guaranteed the generation of a test paper with proportionate allocation of weightages to modules of a subject, proportionate allocation of weightages to cognitive processing levels, of taxonomy and maximum marks, but did not assure the quality of a test paper based on other criteria such as time duration, number of questions of each question type, total number of questions, difficulty level of questions on the basis of number of times the question was asked in the previous examination (exposure limit), etc. Hence, it was significant to accept the Test paper Template (QPT) generated in chapter 2 as one of the inputs, and to provide additional question selection constraints specified above and complete the process of question selection in the test paper model (Paul et al, 2014; Paul et al, 2013). Our question selection process includes the following five main steps-

1. Formulate a set of question selection vectors under each cell of the QPT satisfying the module level weightages of the cell.
2. Generate random initial population of question selection vectors using any of the evolutionary approach. Perform selection of Question Set (QS) on the basis of the generated question selection vector population.
3. Evaluate QS and apply Multi-Objective evolutionary approach-based operators such as selection, crossover and mutation to optimize the computing process of question selection.
4. Continue iterative population generation of selection vectors using Evolutionary Approach.
5. Terminate evolutionary approach after the user specified number of iterations or after completion of the optimal question selection process (whichever is earlier).

The terminology used in this chapter is already explained in chapter 1, Table 1 and Table 2 on section 1.1. Also, the structure of the QPT is presented in chapter 1 Table 3 on section 1.1. In this chapter, the terms unit and module are used interchangeably and are treated as synonyms. Also, the terms paper-setter and instructor are treated as synonyms. While considering Bloom's taxonomy levels, the terms Comprehension and Understanding are also used interchangeably and are treated as synonyms.

One of the problems of Multi-Objective Evolutionary Algorithm (MOEA) discussed in chapter 1 is that an evolutionary algorithm might lose the best solution during generations by performing recombination among the solutions. A remedy to this problem is the so called Elitist MOEAs. Elitism (or an elitist strategy) is a mechanism which is employed in some EAs which ensures that the individuals of the most highly t member(s) or fittest individuals of the population are passed on to the next generation without being altered by evolutionary operators. Using elitism, it is ensured that the minimum Fitness of the population can never reduce from one generation to the next. Also, Elitism usually brings about a more rapid convergence of the population (Deb, K., et.al.,2002; Laumanns, M.,et.al., 2000; Chen, M.R. and Lu, Z. 2008 & Subhashini, R. and Kumar, V. J. S. 2010). As already discussed in chapter 1, evolutionary optimization algorithm has many features such as population-based collective learning process, self-adaptation and robustness that allow optimization of fitness function of discrete variables. These kinds of techniques use iterative trial- and-error progress, similar to the development and evolution in living creatures to find better fitness at the given circumstances. Evolutionary computing techniques were initiated in 1950s, and work with the idea of using Darwinian principles for automated problem solving (Dennett, D. C. (1995). The search and optimization process follow the principle of the survival of the fittest to generate successively better results over generations to finally approximate the optimal solutions, if not the global optimum one. They have been used in numerous occasions as generic global optimization tools. On the other hand, a variety of levels of performance of different EAs on different specific optimization problem often lead to disagreement on their appropriateness as universal generic optimization tool. This is mainly because evolutionary algorithms selected need to be problem specific in order to have an optimal performance. The greatest drawback of EAs is that they occasionally create the problem of pre- mature convergence. This problem occurs due to poorly known fitness functions, random solutions and local convergence. Therefore, EAs as global optimization tools have to tackle challenges of peculiarities of a variety of objective functions to avoid degrading performances. This is generally not considered to be an easy task, and hence it was necessary to introduce other enhanced approaches such as Differential Evolution (DE) as an alternative to EAs.

Differential Evolution (DE) algorithm (Zamuda, A. and Brest, J. 2007; Storn, R. and Price, K. 1997), an alternate approach to evolutionary algorithm has been proposed as a simple and powerful population-based stochastic optimization, which is originally motivated by the mechanism of natural selection. This algorithm searches solutions using three basic operators: mutation, crossover and greedy selection. DE applies mutation as a search mechanism and selection to direct the search towards the potential regions in the feasible region. The purpose of mutation is to allow search diversity in the parameter space as well as to direct the existing object vectors with suitable amount of parameter variation in a way which will lead to better results at an appropriate time. It keeps the search robust and explores new areas in the search domain. Therefore, the principal difference between EAs and DEs is that EAs rely on crossover, a mechanism of probabilistic and useful exchange of information among solutions to locate better solutions, while DEs use mutation as the primary search mechanism. The procedure of working of DEs is as follows: Mutation is used to create a mutant vector by adding differential vectors obtained from the difference of several randomly chosen parameter vectors to the parent vector. Subsequently, crossover operator generates the trial vector by combining the parameters of the mutated vector with the parameters of a parent vector selected from the population. Lastly, according to the fitness value, selection determines which of the vectors should be chosen for the next generation by implementing one-to-one completion between the generated trial vectors and the corresponding parent vectors. In order to step up the convergence speed and avoid the local optima, several variations of DE have been proposed to enhance the performance of the standard DE. More- over, DE has been proved to be efficient for solving real life optimization problems (Qin, A, et.al.2009; Xue, F, et.al.,2004; Brest, J., et.al.,2006; Rahnamayan, S., et.al,.2008; Robic T. and Filipic, B. 2005 & Tusar, T. and Filipic B. 2007). Unlike the conventional evolutionary algorithms which depend on predefined probability distribution function for mutation process, differential evolution uses the differences of randomly sampled pairs of parent vectors for its mutation process. Another attribute of differential evolution is that the crossover rate and fitness do not require the same ne tuning which is necessary in many other EAs. Also, unlike EA, DE ensures that newly generated population is always better than the population in the preceding generation. According to Price (Price, K. 1999), DE incorporate numerous advantages such as fast and simple for application and modification, efficient global optimization capability, parallel processing nature, self-referential mutation operation, effective on integer and discrete parameter optimization, ability to provide multiple solutions in a single run, etc.

Evolutionary Approach, Elitist Evolutionary Approach and Elitist Differential Evolution Approach for Question Selection from Question Bank

The question selection is handled in traditional test paper generation systems by using a specified test paper format containing a listing of weightages to be allotted to each unit/module of the syllabus. They do not consider other constraints such as total time duration for completion of the paper, total number of questions, difficulty level of the questions in the test paper, etc. In this chapter, we have modeled question selection Problem as a multi-objective optimization problem and designed evolutionary computation-based approaches using evolutionary approach, elitist evolutionary approach and elitist differential evolution approach for the experimentation of the same. The iterative process of evolutionary computation-based algorithms does a simultaneous search of different regions in the search space. Starting with a population, a set of individuals or candidate solutions are generated at the initial iteration. The best candidates are selected based on their fitness value which measures the quality of each individual. Best candidates act as parents of a new group of individuals generated by modifying (recombining and mutating) the parents, which will compose a new population to be used in the next iteration of the algorithm. In the entire iterative process, both selection and evolutionary recombination operators play an important role. The selection decides which of the individuals will become parents of a new population. On the other hand, evolutionary operators determine how the genetic information is combined or modified, which in turn means, crossover and mutation allow passing information from parents to o spring, and jumping from a point to another of the search space, guaranteeing the genetic diversity, respectively.

As similar to other evolutionary computation-based approaches, the population based iterative process of initialization, evaluation (selection), recombination (crossover, mutation) and termination have been successfully adopted for completing the question selection process in our Evolutionary

Algorithm (EA) based multi-objective Question Selection Algorithm (MOQSA). The self-adaptation, collective learning process and robustness of population-based evolutionary approach have been experimented on a case study. The results obtained in the case study are interesting, but the evolutionary approach encountered significant run-time delay during the iterative QS generation. In order to improve the speed of convergence as well as to improve the global optimization capability of EA, a modified EA with elitism has been designed. Elitism means that the robust collection of individuals is guaranteed a position in the next generation, generally without undergoing mutation. The individuals selected under elitism to the next iteration are able to be selected as parents, in addition to being brought forward themselves. We adopted the elitist selection strategy in our EA, but the performance of MOQSA has not shown a major improvement. Hence, Differential Evolution (DE) Approach with Elitism has been experimented in the MOQSA. The principal difference between EAs and DEs is that EAs rely on crossover, a mechanism of probabilistic and useful exchange of information among solutions to locate better solutions, while DEs use mutation as the primary search mechanism. The predefined probability distribution function has been used for mutation process in EA. But DE uses the differences of randomly sampled pairs of parent vectors for its mutation process at each of the iteration. In this manner, the dependency on user-defined mutation probabilities has been sorted out to some extent, by using evolving/self-adapted mutation probabilities in DE.

METHODOLOGY USED

The methodology adopted for Evolutionary Approach consists of the following main steps-

Step 1-Formulate Selection Vectors (SV): K different selection vectors are generated for each cell of the QPT. The summation of the elements of a selection vector is equivalent to its x_{ij}, and is represented in the following manner. $x_{ij}=4$ is as same as $x_{ij}=4$ or $x_{ij}=2+2$ or $x_{ij}=2+1+1$ or $x_{ij}=2+1+1$ or $x_{ij}=1+1+1+1$.

Step 2-Generate Initial Population of SV using Evolutionary Approach: Use random initialization of population and generate an initial population P of SV. Each individual I of P is formed by randomly choosing an element from K different selection vectors corresponding to each x_{ij} such that I is an m x n combination of selection vector elements. paper-setter specifies the size of the population getting generated as q.

Step 3.1 Calculate Fitness of QS: Calculate fitness of each QS of P by applying Multi-Objective evolutionary fitness function.

Step 3.2 Apply Evolutionary Recombination Operators on QS: If paper-setter specified multi-constraint has not been satisfied by considering q different QS of P, then Evolutionary Approach continues iteratively by applying its selection, crossover and mutation to the selected QS of P. Selection operation selects the parent individuals for crossover as well as parent individuals for mutation based on the specified crossover probability and mutation probability respectively. The crossover operation applies single point (one-point) crossover on the parent individuals with a crossover probability of 0.5 (user specified). Mutation operator with its mutation probability 0.1, does random selection of 10% (user specified) of questions from parent individuals and replaces them with similar questions of QB.

Step 3.3 Termination: Repeat (step 3.1) and (step 3.2) for the paper-setter specified number of iterations or until the optimum solution has been found (whichever is earlier).

Step 4-Continue Iterative Population Generation of SV using Evolutionary Approach: Use Evolutionary Approach and generate next iterative population P from SV by applying the same method followed in step2. Repeat step3 on individuals of the iteratively generated population P.

Step 5-Terminate Iterative Population Generation of SV: Repeat step 4 for the paper-setter specified number of iterations or until the optimum solution has been found (whichever is earlier).

1. Modification for Evolutionary Approach with Elitism

In order to use Evolutionary Approach with Elitism, step 3 in the above Evolutionary Approach has been modified as follows:

During each of the iteration, the best 10% (user specified) of the individuals from the current population are copied to the next iteration without applying EA operators. Rest of the individuals continues to get applied with the EA operators and passes to the next iteration.

2. Modification for Differential Evolution Approach with Elitism

In order to use Differential Evolution Approach, step 3 in the first Evolutionary Approach has been modified as follows:

Step 3- Select Question Set (QS) corresponding to Initial Population of SV, Evaluate Question Set (QS), Apply Evolutionary Operators on QS: q different QS are randomly chosen from question bank, QB corresponding to each individual I of the generated population P at initialization.

Step 3.1 Calculate Fitness of QS: Calculate fitness of each QS of P by applying multi-constraint differential evolution fitness function.

Step 3.2 Apply Differential Evolutionary Recombination Operators on QS: If paper-setter specified multi-constraint has not been satisfied by considering q different QS of P, then Differential Approach continues iteratively by applying its mutation, crossover and selection to QS of P. The procedure for mutation is different in DE and is performed as follows.

1. Randomly select two individuals I_1, I_2 along with the individual with the best fitness value, I_{best} from the current population.
2. Create a Mutant Vector, $M = I_{best} + (I_1 - I_2)$, in such a way that the common questions of I_1 and I_2 are identified, and are substituted in I_{best}.
3. Perform binary crossover of M with every individual of current population. Select crossed individual if it improves fitness function or retain the original individual as a candidate for the next iteration. Here Elitism feature has also been automatically applied to generate population of next iteration.

Step 3.3 Termination: Repeat (step 3.1) and (step3.2) for the paper- setter specified number of iterations or until the optimum solution has been found (whichever is earlier).

PROBLEM DEFINITION

Given a QPT, same as the one presented in Table.2.3 on page number 16 of chapter 2, represented as m × n matrix with m number of modules and n number of levels, and a question bank QB for the same subject, the problem is to selectively choose questions from QB for each cell x_{ij} of QPT, such that the total set of selected questions satisfies all the constraints fixed by the paper-setter. The Fitness Function, (F) satisfied is represented as

$$F(X) = \sum_{i=1}^{m}\sum_{j=1}^{n} Fx_1 + \sum_{i=1}^{m}\sum_{j=1}^{n} Fx_2 + ... + \sum_{i=1}^{m}\sum_{j=1}^{n} Fx_n$$

where F_{x1}, $F_{x2,...}$, F_{xn} are the Paper Setter specified constraints.

Algorithm Details

MOQSA presented in Algorithm 4.1(a) and 4.1(b) consist of five main modules for question selection to accomplish the tasks listed below -

1. Generate Selection Vectors (SV)
2. Generate Initial Population from SV using one of the three Evolutionary based Approach
3. Select Question Set (QS) corresponding to Initial Population of SV
4. Evaluate Question Set (QS)
5. Apply Evolutionary Operators on QS based on the selected Evolutionary Approach

Algorithm 1 (a) Multi-Objective Question Selection Algorithm (MOQSA)

Procedure *Multi-Objective Question Selection (QPT, QB, sz)*

Input: QPT, QB

QPT : A template with m number of modules and n number of levels, represented as an m x n matrix with $U=<u_1, u_2,...,u_m>$, the vector of selected module weights where m_i is the weight assigned to the ith module, $L=<l_1, l_2,...,l_n>$, the vector of selected cognitive level weights of educational taxonomy where lj is the weight assigned to the jth cognitive level and $X=<x_{11}, x_{12}, x_{ij},..., x_{mn}>$, the vector of module-level-weights where x_{ij} is the weight assigned to the jth cognitive level of ith module.

QB: Question   Bank   with $Q=<q_1,   q_2,...,q_m>$,   the   vector   of   questions   having   attributes question_no(qno), module_no(mno), level_no(lno), total_marks(marks), difficulty_level(diff) and time_minutes (time).

sz=size of population

Output: SV, P, FQS

SV: Selection Vectors, $SV= <SV_{11}, SV_{12}, SVij,...,SV_{mn}>$, where $SVij=< svij1, svij2,..., svijk>$ for each x_{ij} of QPT, such that $x_{ij}= sv_{ij1}= sv_{ij2}= sv_{ij3}=...= sv_{ijk}$

P: Population of elements of selection vectors such that $P= \{I_0, I_1 I_2,..., I_{sz}\}$, where $I_0, I_1 I_2,..., I_{sz}$ are the set of individuals of the population, P and sz is the size of population.

FQS: Optimum set of questions, $FQS=<qs_1, qs_2,...,qs_m>$ from QB satisfying the Paper-setter specified fitness constraints.

//Apply Multi-Constraint Question selection
terminate-MOQSA=false
While terminate-MOQSA=false
{
Call Selection Vectors (QPT)
Call Initial Population (SV)
Call Select Question Set (P)
Call Calculate Fitness (QS)
terminate-MOQSA=true

}
// Generate Selection Vectors
procedure Selection Vectors (QPT)

  SV= {};
for i =1 to m do
  for j = 1 to n do
    extract x_{ij} of QPT;
    form $SV_{ij} = <sv_{ij1}, sv_{ij2}, sv_{ij3}, sv_{ij4}, sv_{ij5}..., sv_{ijk}>;
  end for
merge (SV, SV_{ij});
end for
return (SV);
end procedure

Algorithm 1(b) Multi-Objective Question Selection

```
procedure Initial Population (SV) //Generate Initial Population from SV
  sz = population size;
  P= {};
for s=1 to sz do
  for i=1 to m do
    for j=1 to n do
        r =randomly selected sv_ijk of SV_ij;
        merge (I_s , r) ;
    end for
  end for
merge (P, I_s);
end for
return (P)
end procedure
procedure Select Question Set (P) //Apply Question Set selection on P
QS← {};
for each I in P do
    search QB and form QS_I= <qs_1, qs_2,....,qst> ;
    merge (QS, QS_I)
next I
return (QS)
end procedure
 //Calculate Fitness of QS
Procedure Calculate Fitness (QS)
for each QS_I in QS do
    c = Paper-setter specified constraints
    if constraints (QS_I) == c then
        FQS = <qs_1, qs_2,....,qs_m>
        terminate (MOQSA) = true
        exit for
    end if
end for
if terminate (MOQSA) =false then
    if EA =Evolutionary Approach or EA=Elitist Evolutionary Approach then
        apply Evolutionary based Approach Selection (P)
        apply Evolutionary Approach Recombination (P)
        update P with new {I_0, I_1 I_2,..., I_sz}
    else
        apply Differential Evolution Recombination (P)
        apply Differential Evolution Selection (P)
        update P with new {I_0, I_1 I_2,.., I_sz}
    end if
end if
return (FQS)
end procedure
```

EXPERIMENTAL RESULTS

Implementation is done using PHP and MySQL on XAMPP Server with a 2GHz processor and 1GB RAM.

Evolutionary Approach with Elitism: The experimental case study has been carried out using Evolutionary Approach by considering the following data-

1. **Template (SEQPT) presented in Table 1 generated for Software Engineering:** (SE) subject of B.Sc Computer Science offered at the 6th semester of Goa University using Bloom's taxonomy. SE-QPT formulation is carried out with syllabus file of SE subject consisting of paper-setter specified first six modules (software requirement, re-engineering, legacy systems, requirement engineering, software prototyping and software architecture) of the syllabus file and first five levels (knowledge-know, understanding-under, application-appl, analysis-anal and synthesis-synth) of Bloom's taxonomy, for an examination test paper of Maximum Marks=100.

Table 1. SEQPT: An input for question selection case study

Module/ Level	know	under	appl	anal	synth	Module Weight
Software Requirement	7	6	6	6	5	30
Reengineering	7	4	4	4	1	20
Legacy Systems	5	3	3	3	1	15
Requirement Engineering	5	3	3	3	1	15
Software Prototyping	3	2	2	2	1	10
Software Architecture	3	2	2	2	1	10
Level Weight	30	20	20	20	10	100

2. **Question Bank (SEQB) shown in Table.2 and Table.3 for SE Subject:** Each question is stored with its respective module details, cognitive level details, difficulty level and completion time. Questions displayed in SEQB are few but are relevant for the experimental case study. Attributes used for storing each question in the question bank are: question_no(qno), module_no(mno), level_no(lno), total_marks(marks), difficulty_level(diff) and time_minutes (time). Module numbers p_1,

$p_2..., p_6$ correspond to the six selected modules of SE. Similarly, level numbers $q_1, q_2..., q_5$ correspond to the five selected levels of Bloom's taxonomy. We have currently fixed the difficulty level of a question by mapping to the Bloom's taxonomy level to which a question belongs to (Wiemer-Hastings, P., Wiemer-Hastings, K. & Graesser, A. C. 1999). Based on Bloom's taxonomy, paper setter assigns each question with a difficulty level ranging from 0.5-1.0. Questions belonging to knowledge level are assigned low (0.5) score, similarly, understanding level is low (0.6), application is medium (0.7), analysis is medium (0.8), synthesis is high (0.9) and evaluation is high (1.0).

Table 2. SEQB: sample format of SE question bank

SNo	qno	Mno	lno	marks	diff	time
1	Q1	p_1	l_1	3	0.5	4
2	Q2	p_1	l_1	2	0.5	3
3	Q3	p_1	l_1	2	0.5	2
50	Q50	p_1	l_2	6	0.6	8
69	Q69	p_1	l_3	6	0.7	8
90	Q90	p_1	l_4	6	0.8	8.
100	Q100	p_1	l_5	3	0.9	5
105	Q105	p_1	l_5	2	0.9	4
110	Q110	p_2	l_1	3	0.5	4
111	Q111	p_2	l_1	2	0.5	4
112	Q112	p_2	l_1	2	0.5	4
119	Q119	p_2	l_2	2	0.6	4

After accepting SEQPT and SEQB as input, the sequence of steps carried out in this case study for SE MCQSP is as follows-

Step1- Formulate Selection Vectors (SESV): Result obtained after formulation of all possible selection vectors of SEQPT is shown in Table.4.

Step2- Generate Initial Population of SESV using Evolutionary Approach: Table 5 below represents a sample of the initial population consisting of only 4 individuals out of 100.

Table 3. SEQB: Sample format of SE question bank

120	Q120	p_2	l_2	2	0.6	4
223	Q223	p_2	l_3	4	0.7	7
229	Q229	p_2	l_4	2	0.8	4
230	Q230	p_2	l_4	1	0.8	2
231	Q231	p_2	l_4	1	0.8	2
300	Q300	p_2	l_5	1	0.9	2
526	Q526	p_3	l_1	2	0.5	4
527	Q527	p_3	l_1	2	0.5	4
528	Q528	p_3	l_1	1	0.5	1
589	Q589	p_3	l_2	3	0.6	6
595	Q595	p_3	l_3	2	0.7	4
596	Q596	p_3	l_3	1	0.7	2
756	Q756	p_3	l_4	3	0.8	6
797	Q797	p_3	l_5	1	0.9	6
828	Q828	p_4	l_1	3	0.5	5
829	Q829	p_4	l_1	2	0.5	4
946	Q946	p_4	l_2	2	0.6	3
947	Q947	p_4	l_2	1	0.6	2
1000	Q1000	p_4	l_3	3	0.7	5
1050	Q1050	p_4	l_4	3	0.8	5
1100	Q1100	p_4	l_5	1	0.9	2
1120	Q1120	p_5	l_1	2	0.5	4
1121	Q1121	p_5	l_1	1	0.5	4
1125	Q1125	p_5	l_2	2	0.6	4
1297	Q1297	p_5	l_3	1	0.7	2
1298	Q1298	p_5	l_3	1	0.7	2
1320	Q1320	p_5	l_4	2	0.8	4
1329	Q1329	p_5	l_5	1	0.9	2
1400	Q1400	p_6	l_1	3	0.5	6
1427	Q1427	p_6	l_2	2	0.6	4
1460	Q1460	p_6	l_3	2	0.7	4
1478	Q1478	p_6	l_4	2	0.8	4
1500	Q1500	p_6	l_5	1	0.9	2

Table 4. Selection vectors for module-level-weights in SEQPT

Modules/Levels	know	under	appl	anal	synth	Module weight
Software Requirement	7 [(7)/(6,1)/(5,2)/(4,3)/ (4,2,1)/(3,3,1)/ (3,2,2)/(3,2,1,1)/ (3,1,1,1)/(2,2,2,1)/ (2,2,1,1,1)/(2,1,1,1,1,1)/ (1,1,1,1,1,1,1)]	6 [(6)/(5,1)/(4,2)/ (4,1,1)/(3,3)/ (3,2,1)/ (3,1,1,1)/ (2,2,2)/(2,1,1,1,1,1) /(1,1,1,1,1,1)]	6 [(6)/(5,1)/(4,2)/ (4,1,1)/(3,3)/ (3,2,1)/ (3,1,1,1)/ (2,2,2)/(2,1,1,1,1)/ (1,1,1,1,1,1)]	6 [(6)/(5,1)/(4,2)/ (4,1,1)/(3,3)/ (3,2,1)/(3,1,1,1)/ (2,2,2)/(2,1,1,1,1,1) /(1,1,1,1,1,1)]	5 [(5)/(4,1)/(3,2)/ (3,1,1)/(2,2,1)/ (2,1,1,1)/ (1,1,1,1,1)]	30
Reengineering	7 [(7)/(6,1)/(5,2)/(4,3)/ (4,2,1)/(3,3,1)/ (3,2,2)/(3,2,1,1)/ (3,1,1,1)/(2,2,2,1)/ (2,2,1,1,1)/(2,1,1,1,1,1)/ (1,1,1,1,1,1,1)]	4 [(4)/(3,1)/(2,2)/ (2,1,1)/(1,1,1,1)]	4 [(4)/(3,1)/(2,2)/ (2,1,1)/(1,1,1,1)]	4 [(4)/(3,1)/(2,2)/ (2,1,1)/(1,1,1,1)]	1 [(1)]	20
Legacy Systems	5 [(5)/(4,1)/(3,2)/(3,1,1)/ (2,2,1)/(2,1,1,1)/ (1,1,1,1,1)]	3 [(3)/(2,1)/(1,1,1)]	3 [(3)/(2,1)/(1,1,1)]	3 [(3)/(2,1)/(1,1,1)]	1 [(1)]	15
Requirement Engineering	5 [(5)/(4,1)/(3,2)/(3,1,1)/ (2,2,1)/(2,1,1,1)/ (1,1,1,1,1)]	3 [(3)/(2,1)/(1,1,1)]	3 [(3)/(2,1)/(1,1,1)]	3 [(3)/(2,1)/ (1,1,1)]	1 [(1)]	15
Software Prototyping	3 [(3)/(2,1)/(1,1,1)]	2 [(2)/(1,1)]	2 [(2)/(1,1)]	2 [(2)/(1,1)]	1 [(1)]	10
Software Architecture	3 [(3)/(2,1)/(1,1,1)]	2 [(2)/(1,1)]	2 [(2)/(1,1)]	2 [(2)/(1,1)]	1 [(1)]	10
Level weight	30	20	20	20	10	100

Step3- Evaluate SE Question Set (SEQS) and Apply Evolutionary Operators on SEQS: A sample of the selected individual of SESV from Table.5 for applying question selection is displayed in Table.6. Perform selection of SE Question Set (SEQS) on individual of Table 7. On SEQS, apply paper-setter specified three different constraints namely the total number of questions=45, total time for answering the paper=3 hours and overall difficulty level of test paper=medium. Verify whether SEQS of Table 4.7 satisfies all the above specified constraints and if satisfied, the problem terminates successfully. The identified question set of Table.4.7 is considered as an optimal solution to this case study and is displayed in Table.4.8. In all the other cases, individuals of initial population undergo the evolutionary recombination operation. If none of the question set of the initial population satisfies all the conditions specified by the paper-setter, then the problem continues iteratively for the paper-setter specified number of iterations or till the optimum solution is identified (whichever is earlier). Default value used for the number of iterations in SEMOQSA is 100.

Evolutionary approach-based operators such as selection and recombination were not applied on this case study as the optimal set of questions were extracted at the initial stage of SEMOQSA. The problem terminated after the first iteration. This case study has been designed to show the working of an evolutionary approach. In real experimental analysis, the optimal set of questions may not get extracted even after running the algorithm for the paper-setter specified number of iterations.

Differential Evolution Approach with Elitism

The set of stages for accepting the paper Setter specified constraints and SEQPT template generation is presented in Figure.1, Figure 2 and Figure.3 respectively. Figure.1 and Figure.2 shows the input screen for accepting the paper-setter specified constraints for the MOQSA of SE test paper generation. It include the following attributes - Total Number of Questions, Total Marks, Total Time for Answering the Test paper, Overall Difficulty Level of the Test paper, Exposure Limit of Question Set (number of times each question of the question set appeared in previous examination test paper), Type of Questions and the Type of Test paper Template (QPT) for SE test paper generation. Figure.3 shows the Pareto-optimal evolutionary approach based QPT generated using the syllabus le of SE subject consisting of the paper-setter

Table 5. Sample population of SE selection vectors using evolutionary approach

7	6	6	6	5	7	4	4	1	5	3	3	3	1	5	3	3	3	1	2	2	2	1
232	6	33	6	32	421	22	42	1	32	111	3	21	1	221	21	21	3	1	2	2	2	1
7	33	6	6	32	7	4	22	1	5	21	111	3	1	32	3	3	3	11	11	2	2	1
.	.	.	.	.	.	.	.	.	.	.	.	.	.	.	.	.	.	.	.	.	.	.
322	6	6	6	32	322	22	211	1	221	3	21	3	1	32	21	3	3	21	2	2	2	1

Table 6. Chosen individual of SE selection vector population of Table 5

322	6	6	32	322	22	211	221	21	3	21	21	1	21	32	3	3	3	1	11	2	2	1

Table 7. Optimal set of questions of SEQS selected from SEQB

Q1 Q2 Q3	Q50	Q69	Q90	Q100 Q105	Q100 Q111 Q112	Q119 Q120	Q223	Q229 Q230 Q231	Q300	Q526 Q527 Q528	Q589	Q595 Q596	Q756	Q797
Q828 Q829	Q946 Q947	Q1000	Q1050	Q1100	Q1120 Q1121	Q1125	Q1297 Q1298	Q1320	Q1329	Q1400	Q1427	Q1460	Q1478	Q1500

selected first six modules (Software Requirements, Re- engineering, Legacy Systems, Requirement Engineering, Software Prototyping and Software Architecture) and first four levels (knowledge, Understanding/Comprehension, Application and Analysis) of Bloom's taxonomy for an examination test paper of Maximum Marks=100. Template formulation is carried out using pareto-optimal Evolutionary Approach of Chapter 1, Section 1.4. Sample format of SEQB used in this experimental study is presented in Table.2 and Table.3 discussed in this chapter under the evolutionary approach-based case study.

After accepting SEQPT and SEQB as input, the sequence of steps carried out in this Differential Evolutionary Approach with Elitism for SEMO- QSA is as follows-

Step1- Formulate Selection Vectors: A snapshot of the result obtained after formulation of all possible selection vectors of SEQPT is shown in Figure.4 below.

Figure 1. Screenshot of Paper setter specified input for multi-constraint question selection problem for SE test paper generation

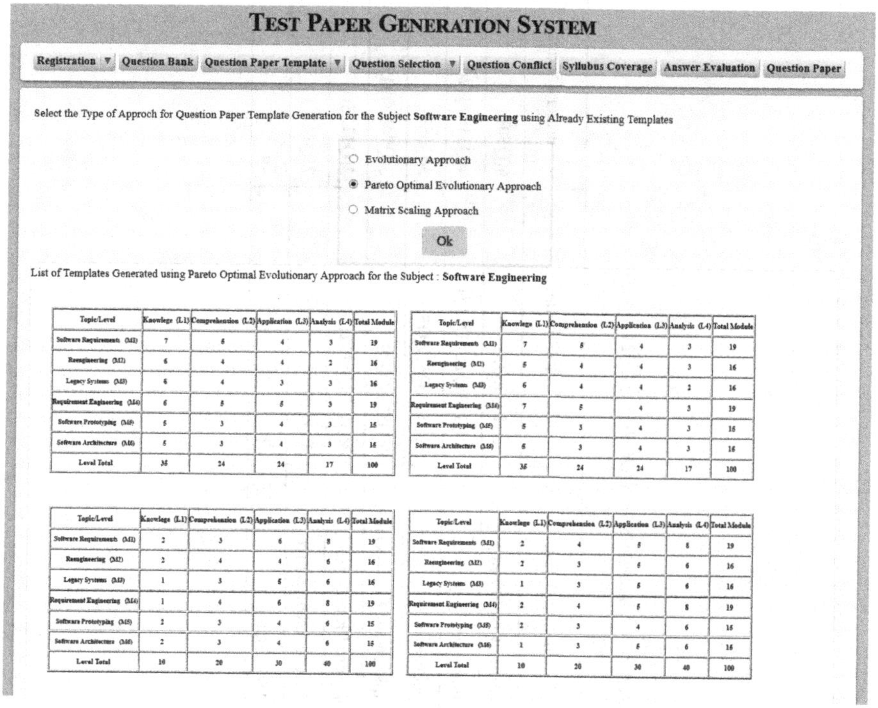

Topic/Level	Knowlege (L1)	Comprehension (L2)	Application (L3)	Analysis (L4)	Total Module
Software Requirements (M1)	7	5	4	3	19
Reengineering (M2)	6	4	4	2	16
Legacy Systems (M3)	6	4	3	3	16
Requirement Engineering (M4)	6	5	5	3	19
Software Prototyping (M5)	5	3	4	3	15
Software Architecture (M6)	5	3	4	3	15
Level Total	35	24	24	17	100

Topic/Level	Knowlege (L1)	Comprehension (L2)	Application (L3)	Analysis (L4)	Total Module
Software Requirements (M1)	7	5	4	3	19
Reengineering (M2)	5	4	4	3	16
Legacy Systems (M3)	6	4	4	2	16
Requirement Engineering (M4)	7	5	4	3	19
Software Prototyping (M5)	5	3	4	3	15
Software Architecture (M6)	5	3	4	3	15
Level Total	35	24	24	17	100

Topic/Level	Knowlege (L1)	Comprehension (L2)	Application (L3)	Analysis (L4)	Total Module
Software Requirements (M1)	2	3	6	8	19
Reengineering (M2)	2	4	4	6	16
Legacy Systems (M3)	1	3	6	6	16
Requirement Engineering (M4)	1	4	6	8	19
Software Prototyping (M5)	2	3	4	6	15
Software Architecture (M6)	2	3	4	6	15
Level Total	10	20	30	40	100

Topic/Level	Knowlege (L1)	Comprehension (L2)	Application (L3)	Analysis (L4)	Total Module
Software Requirements (M1)	2	4	5	8	19
Reengineering (M2)	2	3	5	6	16
Legacy Systems (M3)	1	3	6	6	16
Requirement Engineering (M4)	2	4	5	8	19
Software Prototyping (M5)	2	3	4	6	15
Software Architecture (M6)	1	3	5	6	15
Level Total	10	20	30	40	100

Table 8. Optimal solution for SEMOQSA

Modules/Levels	knowledge	understanding	Application	Analysis	synthesis	Module weight
Software Requirements	7(Q1,Q2,Q3)	6(Q50)	6(Q69)	6(Q90)	5(Q100,Q105)	30
Reengineering	7(Q110,Q111,Q112)	4(Q119,Q120)	4(Q223)	4(Q229,Q230,Q231)	1(Q300)	20
Legacy systems	5(Q526,Q527,Q528)	3(Q589)	3(Q595,Q596)	3(Q756)	1 (Q797)	15
Requirement Engineering	5(Q828,Q829)	3(Q946,Q947)	3(Q1000)	3(Q1050)	1(Q1100)	15
Software Prototyping	3(Q1120,Q1121)	2(Q1125)	2(Q1297,Q1298)	2(Q1320)	1(Q1329)	10
Software Architecture	3(Q1400)	2(Q1427)	2(Q1460)	2(Q1478)	1(Q1500)	10
Level weight	30	20	20	20	10	100

Figure 2. Screenshot of paper setter specified multi-constraints for multi- objective question selection problem for SE test paper generation

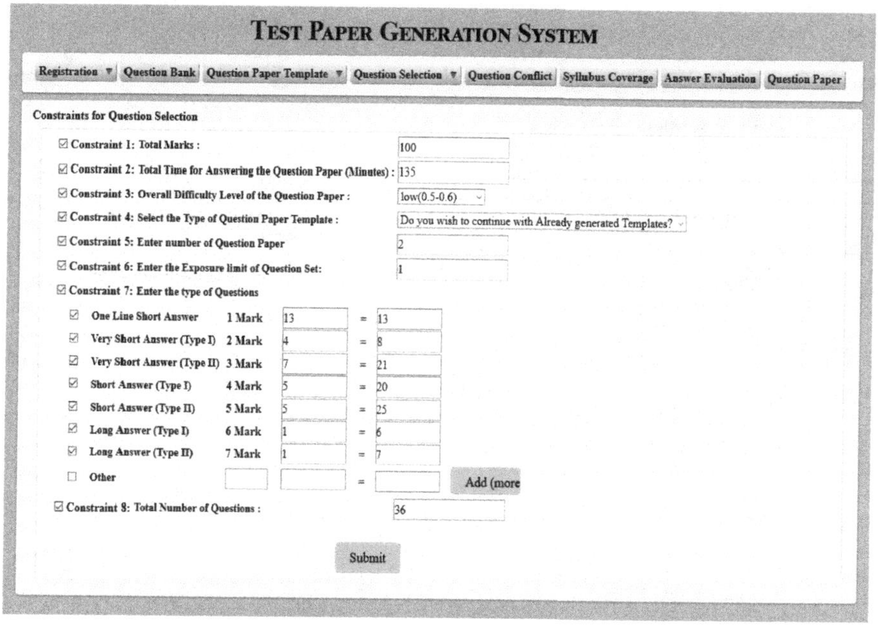

Figure 3. Display of paper setter specified (pareto-optimal evolutionary approach) based test paper template for SE test paper generation

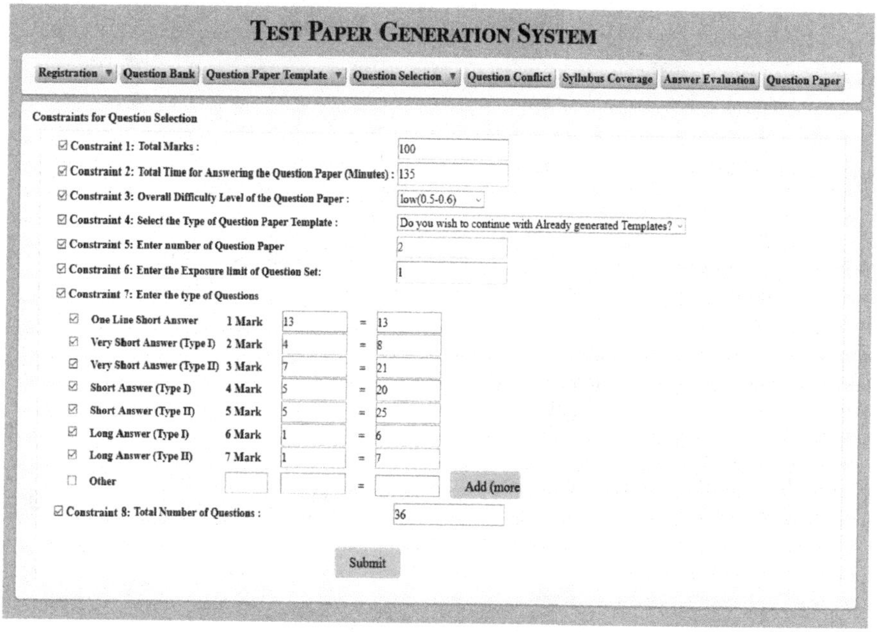

Figure 4. Display of selection vectors for module-level-weights in the Selected QPT of SE

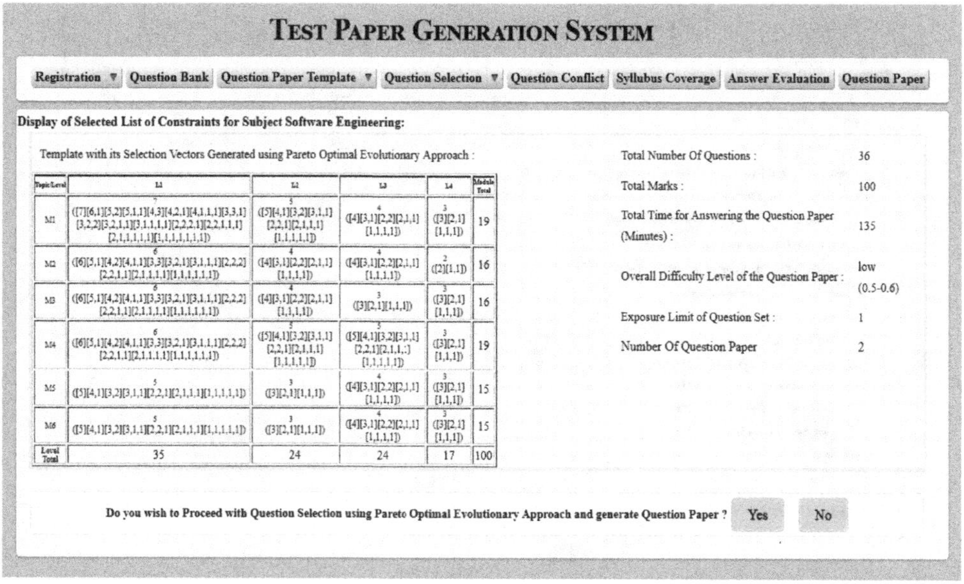

Figure 5. Calculated average deviation of paper setter specified four constraints (in addition to template types) for initiating SEMOQSA

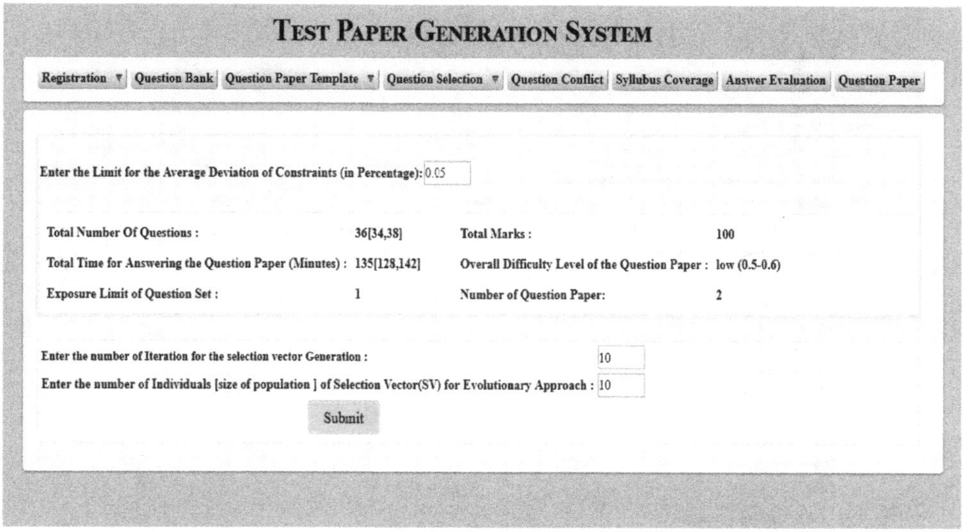

Figure 6. Sample initial population of selection vectors for SEQPT using MOQSA approach

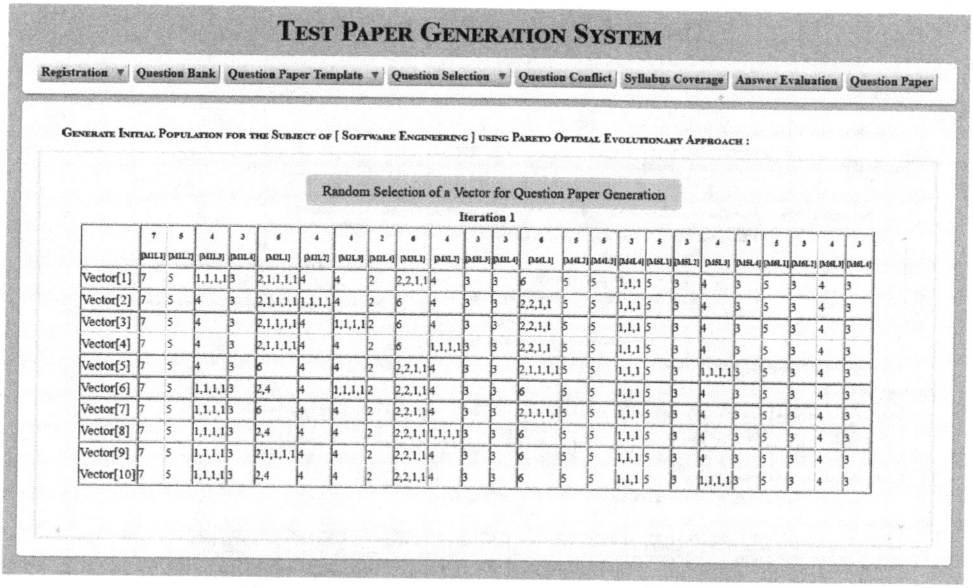

	7	5	4	3	6	4	4	2	6	4	3	3	6	5	5	3	5	3	4	3	5	3	4	3
	[M1L1]	[M1L2]	[M1L3]	[M1L4]	[M2L1]	[M2L2]	[M2L3]	[M2L4]	[M3L1]	[M3L2]	[M3L3]	[M3L4]	[M4L1]	[M4L2]	[M4L3]	[M4L4]	[M5L1]	[M5L2]	[M5L3]	[M5L4]	[M6L1]	[M6L2]	[M6L3]	[M6L4]
Vector[1]	7	5	1,1,1,1	3	2,1,1,1,1	4	4	2	2,2,1,1	4	3	3	6	5	5	1,1,1	5	3	4	3	5	3	4	3
Vector[2]	7	5	4	3	2,1,1,1,1	1,1,1,1	4	2	6	4	3	3	2,2,1,1	5	5	1,1,1	5	3	4	3	5	3	4	3
Vector[3]	7	5	4	3	2,1,1,1,1	4	1,1,1,1	2	6	4	3	3	2,2,1,1	5	5	1,1,1	5	3	4	3	5	3	4	3
Vector[4]	7	5	4	3	2,1,1,1,1	4	4	2	6	1,1,1,1	3	3	2,2,1,1	5	5	1,1,1	5	3	4	3	5	3	4	3
Vector[5]	7	5	4	3	6	4	4	2	2,2,1,1	4	3	3	2,1,1,1,1	5	5	1,1,1	5	3	1,1,1,1	3	5	3	4	3
Vector[6]	7	5	1,1,1,1	3	2,4	4	1,1,1,1	2	2,2,1,1	4	3	3	6	5	5	1,1,1	5	3	4	3	5	3	4	3
Vector[7]	7	5	1,1,1,1	3	6	4	4	2	2,2,1,1	4	3	3	2,1,1,1,1	5	5	1,1,1	5	3	4	3	5	3	4	3
Vector[8]	7	5	1,1,1,1	3	2,4	4	4	2	2,2,1,1	1,1,1,1	3	3	6	5	5	1,1,1	5	3	4	3	5	3	4	3
Vector[9]	7	5	1,1,1,1	3	2,1,1,1,1	4	4	2	2,2,1,1	4	3	3	6	5	5	1,1,1	5	3	4	3	5	3	4	3
Vector[10]	7	5	1,1,1,1	3	2,4	4	4	2	2,2,1,1	4	3	3	6	5	5	1,1,1	5	3	1,1,1,1	3	5	3	4	3

Step2- Generate Initial Population Differential Evolution Approach: Figure.4 displays the paper-setter specified four different constraints namely the total number of questions=36, total marks=100, total time for answering the paper=135 minutes and overall difficulty level of the test paper=low (0.5-0.6). The expected limit for average deviation of the value of the constraint namely total time for answering the paper has been computed and also is displayed in Figure.5. Figure.6 represents a sample of the initial population of selection vectors consisting of paper-setter specified input of 10 individuals (Population Size=10) shown as Vector [1]-Vector [10].

Step3-Apply Question Selection: Randomly chosen selection vector individual namely vector 3 out of the selection vector population of Figure.6 for question selection is shown in Figure.7. Figure.7 also displays the randomly selected five different question sets corresponding to Selection Vector 3 (Question Set Population Size=05) for applying the paper-setter specified constraints.

Figure 7. Randomly selected question Set (QS) corresponding to the selected individual of figure 6 for SEMOQSA

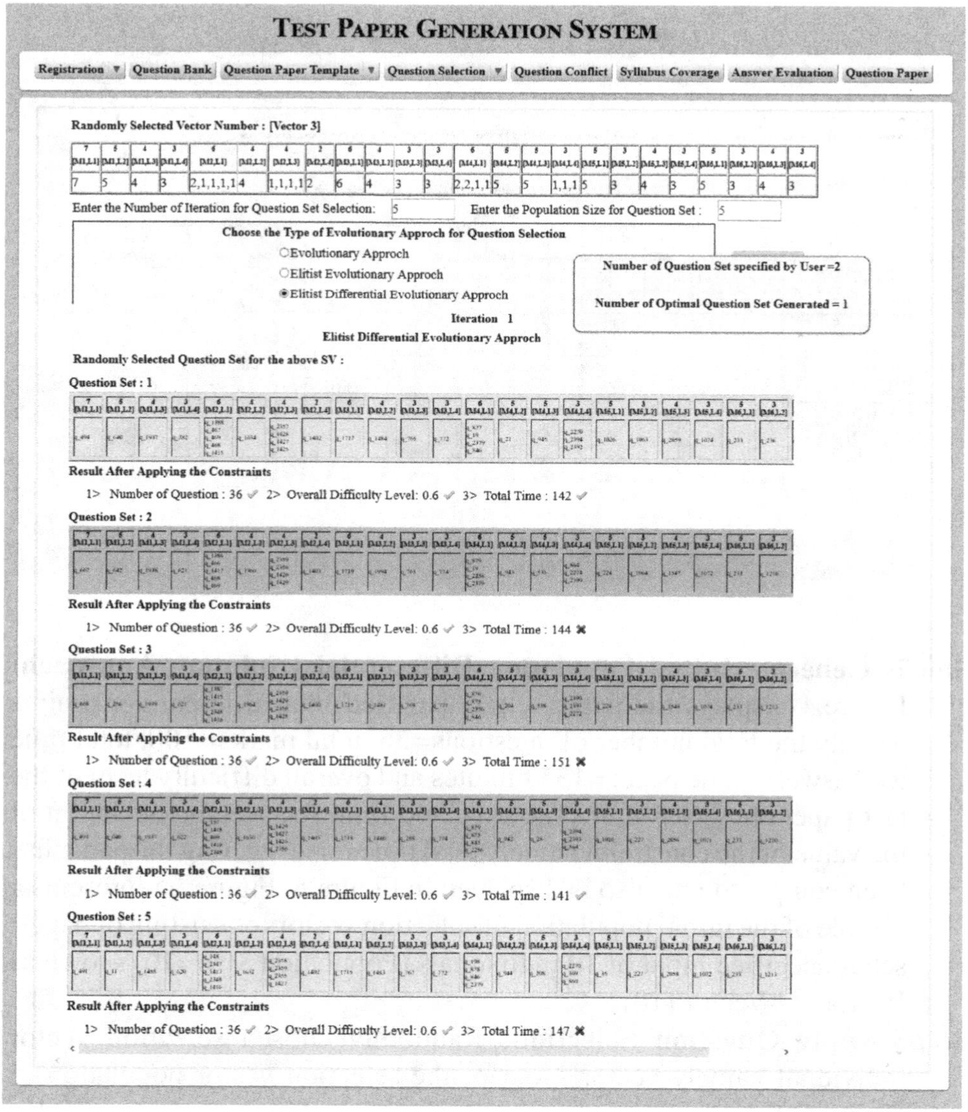

Figure 8. Randomly selected next question Set (QS) corresponding to the selected individual of figure 6 for SEMOQSA

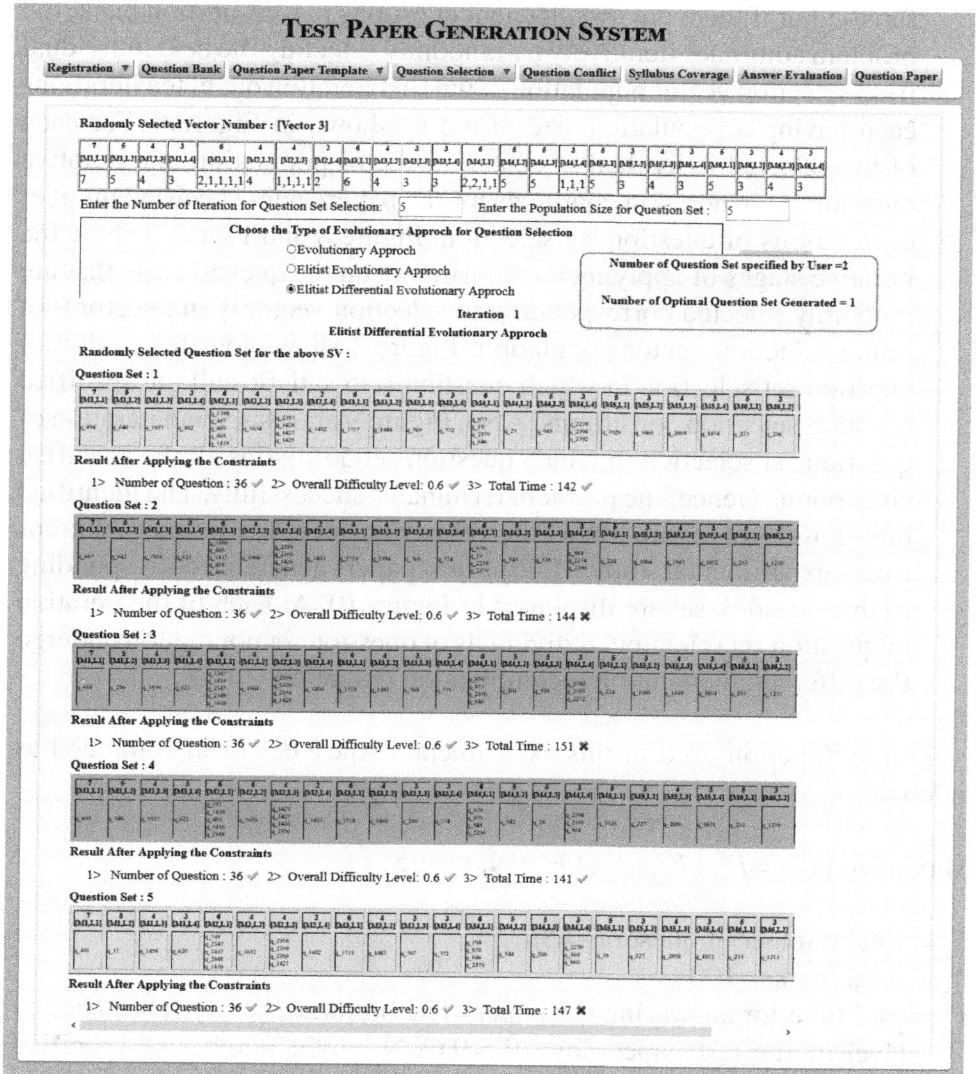

Step4-Apply Differential Evolution Operators: Paper-setter specified four different question set exclusive constraints namely Number of Questions, Overall Difficulty Level, Exposure Limit of Question Set and Total Time have been applied on the selected questions of Figure.7. Verify whether the selected questions of Figure.7 satisfy all the four different constraints or whether the questions in the question bank are insufficient to satisfy the constraints. If the constraints are not getting satisfied or if there are no sufficient questions in the question bank, the problem continues iteratively by randomly selecting the next individual from selection vector population of the first iteration out of ten iterations each having a population size of ten as shown in Figure.6. For each of the selected individual of selection vector population, the iterative question set generation continues for the paper-setter specified number of iterations of question set selection. Figure.8 and Figure.9 show the iterative stages of applying the constraints on the question sets that are randomly selected corresponding to selection vector 8 and vector 9 of initial selection vector population. Figure.8 shows fourth iteration of question set selection in which question set5 satisfies all the specified question selection constraints. Also, Figure.9 shows second iteration of question set selection in which question set 5 satisfies all the specified constraints. Hence, the problem terminates successfully. The identified question sets of Figure.8 and Figure 9 are considered as optimal solutions to this experimental study. Multiple test papers generated corresponding to this question set are displayed in Figure.10. At each of the iteration of question set selection, individuals of question set population undergo the differential evolution recombination operation.

Fitness function used in this experimental study has been computed as below:

Maximize F(x) = $F_{x1} + F_{x2} + F_{x3} + F_{x4})/N$, where

F_{x1} = total number of questions=36
F_{x2} = total marks=100
F_{x3} = total time for answering the paper=135 minutes F_{x4} = overall difficulty level of the test paper=low (0.5-0.6) N =total number of specified constraints=4

Second optimal question set selected in Figure.9 generate the values for variables F_{x1}, F_{x2}, F_{x3} and F_{x4} as follows. F_{x1} = (36/36), F_{x2} = (100/100), F_{x3} = (140/135) and F_{x4} = (0.6/0.6). The optimum value for the fitness function (F1) is achieved as below.

Maximize F(x) = ((1) + (1) + (1.037) + (1))/4
= (4.037/4)
=1.009 » 1.00

Figure 9. Randomly selected last question set (QS) corresponding to the selected individual of figure 6 for SE MOQSA

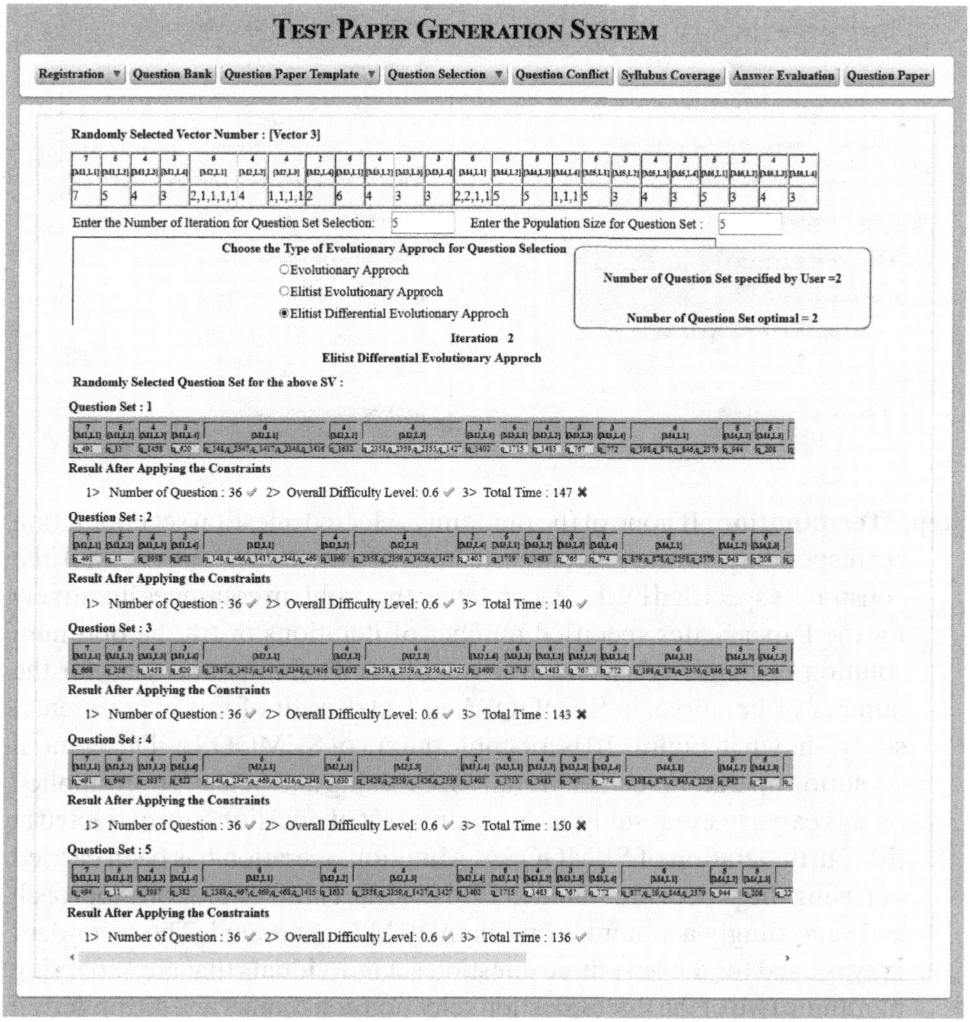

Figure 10. Optimal solution for SEMOQSA using elitist differential evolution approach

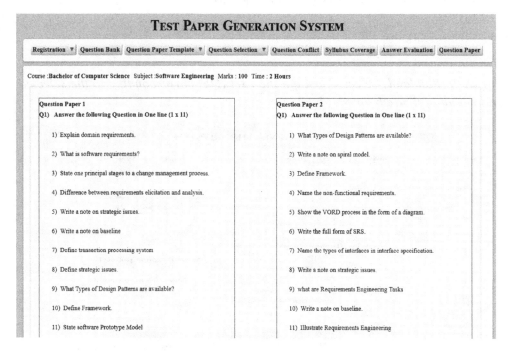

Step5-Termination: If none of the randomly selected question set population corresponding to the selection vectors of Iteration 1 satisfies all the constraints specified by the Paper Setter, the problem continues iteratively for the Paper Setter specified number of iterations or till the optimum solution is identified (whichever is earlier). Default value used for the number of iterations in SEMOQSA is 100. Result of this experimental study, shown in Figure.10 is a sample output of SEMOQSA. Differential evolution operators such as Mutation, Crossing and Selection are applied on this experimental study as the optimal set of questions are extracted at the fourth iteration of SEMOQSA. Mutation operation has been carried out using the procedure stated in Elitist Differential Evolution Approach and accordingly a mutant vector namely M is generated. The color dark grey is used for the first three question set individuals that are satisfying minimum two of the three question selection constraints and are preferred for forming the mutant vector in each of the initial iteration of question selection. Crossover has been carried out by performing a binary crossover operation of M with every parent individual shown in light grey color in each of the initial iteration in such a way that all individuals of the question set population gets crossed with M. The successfully crossed individuals are shown with a combination of dark grey and light grey colors in the successive iterations of question selection. In this manner, by incorporating an enhanced mutation operation with adaptive mutant vector and a modified crossover strategy with a binary crossover operation, MOQSA successfully completes the optimal question set generation. The problem terminates after the fourth iteration.

SUMMARY

Question Selection problem has been modeled as a multi-constraint optimization problem that aims at generating test papers satisfying multiple constraints proposed by the paper-setter. Due to the limitation of matching many constraints while generating a mathematical model for Question Selection, we have used three different Evolutionary Approaches for the multi-constraint question selection problem. Evolutionary Approach implements global parallel search and also applies its evolutionary operators such as mutation, crossing and selection to generate optimal solution during the search process. Experimental study shows that Differential Evolutionary Approach with Elitism (Elitist Differential Evolution Approach) can solve the issue of intelligent generation of test papers satisfying multiple constraints. We have used only Bloom's taxonomy cognitive processing levels to allot difficulty levels to the questions in the Question Bank in our case study. Other criteria that can also be incorporated for calculating the difficulty level are the frequency of occurrence of the question in previous examinations, the last time it appeared in some test paper, the way students attempted the question in previous examinations, etc. If additional criteria are used, then the weighted average of all these criteria can be used for assigning the difficulty level for each question in the Question Bank.

CONCLUSION

A question bank, also known as a repository of test questions is critical in storing and selecting examination content securely and accurately. Test paper developers always focus on designing test papers that accurately measure the knowledge, skills and abilities necessary for competence. A standard question selection module of a test paper generation system provides the test paper developers/paper- setters/instructors with a set of tools to facilitate the creation, review, editing and selection of test questions as well as the tools to complete the test paper composition process. An excellent question selection module also provides automation, standardization, and scalability essential for developing and maintaining effective test papers. In our multi-objective question selection problem, the Test paper Template (QPT) has been able to incorporate innovative formats while providing assurance that every candidate is assessed on a common set of knowledge, skills and abilities. During question selection, many versions (forms) of a test paper as well as multiple test papers for the same examination satisfying the specified constraints are able to get designed by using multi-objective evolutionary approaches. Among the three different multi-objective approaches namely evolutionary approach, elitist evolutionary approach and elitist differential evolution approach, elitist differential evolution approach has been found to be most efficient in completing the successful generation of multiple test papers.

REFERENCES

Brest, J., Greiner, S., Boskovic, B., Mernik, M., & Zumer, V. (2006). Self-adapting control parameters in differential evolution: A comparative study on numerical benchmark problems. *IEEE Transactions on Evolutionary Computation*, *10*(6), 647–657. doi:10.1109/TEVC.2006.872133

Chen, M. R., & Lu, Z. (2008). A novel elitist multi-objective optimization algorithm: Multi-objective extremal optimization. *European Journal of Operational Research*, *127*(3), 637–651. doi:10.1016/j.ejor.2007.05.008

Deb, K., Pratap, A., Agarwal, S., & Meyarivan, T. (2002). A fast and elitist multiobjective genetic algorithm: NSGA II. *Proceedings of the IEEE Transaction on Evolutionary Computation*, *6*(2), 182–197. doi:10.1109/4235.996017

Dennett, D. C. (1995). *Darwin's Dangerous Idea: Evolution and the Mean ings of Life*. Simon Schuster.

Dimple, Paul, & Pawar. (2013). Dynamic Test paper Tem- plate Generation using Bi-proportional Scaling Method. *Proceedings of 5th IEEE International Conference on Technology for Education (T4E)*, 80-83.

Dimple, V. (2014). Elitist-Multi-Objective Differential Evolution for Multiple Test paper Generation. *International Journal of Web Applications*, *6*(2), 43–56.

Dimple, V. (2014). Use of Common-Word Order Syntactic Similarity Metric for Evaluating Syllabus Coverage of a Test paper. *International Journal of Web Applications*, *6*(2), 68–81.

Hu, X. M., & Zhang, J. (2009). An Intelligent Testing System Embedded with an Ant Colony Optimization Based Test Composition Method. *Proceedings of IEEE Congress on Evolutionary Computation (CEC)*, 1414-1421.

Laumanns, M., Zitzler, E., & Thiele, L. (2000). A unified model for Multi-Objective evolutionary algorithms with elitism. *Proceedings of the IEEE 2000 Congress on Evolutionary Computation, 1*, 46-53. 10.1109/CEC.2000.870274

Lirong, X., & Jianwei, S. (2010). Notice of Retraction Automatic Generating Test Paper System Based on Genetic Algorithm. *Proceedings of Second IEEE International Workshop on Education Technology and Computer Science (ETCS)*, 272-275.

Mehmet, Y. (2010). A genetic algorithm for generating test from a question bank. *Computer Applications in Engineering Education*, *18*(2), 298–305.

Price, K. (1999). An introduction to differential evolution, New Ideas in Optimization. McGraw Hill.

Qin, A., Huang, V., & Suganthan, P. (2009). Differential evolution algorithm with strategy adaptation for global numerical optimization. *IEEE Transactions on Evolutionary Computation*, *13*(2), 398–417. doi:10.1109/TEVC.2008.927706

Rahnamayan, S., Tizhoosh, H., & Salama, M. (2008). Opposition-based differential evolution. *IEEE Transactions on Evolutionary Computation*, *12*(1), 64–79. doi:10.1109/TEVC.2007.894200

Robic, T., & Filipic, B. (2005). DEMO: Differential Evolution for Multi-Objective Optimization. *Proceedings of the Third International Conference on Evolutionary Multi-Criterion Optimization (EMO)*, 520-533.

Storn, R., & Price, K. (1997). Differential evolution-a simple and efficient heuristic for global optimization over continuous space. *Journal of Global Optimization*, *11*(1), 341–359. doi:10.1023/A:1008202821328

Subhashini, R., & Kumar, V. J. S. (2010). Evaluating the Performance of Similarity Measures Used in Document Clustering and Information Retrieval. *Proceedings of first International Conference on Integrated Intelligent Computing (ICIIC)*, 27-31. 10.1109/ICIIC.2010.42

Tusar, T., & Filipic, B. (2007). Differential Evolution versus Genetic Algorithms in Multi-Objective Optimization. *Proceedings of the Fourth International Conference on Evolutionary Multi-Criterion Optimization (EMO),* 257-271.

Van der Linden, W. J., & Adema, J. J. (1998). Simultaneous assembly of multiple test forms. *Journal of Educational Measurement, 35*(3), 185–198. doi:10.1111/j.1745-3984.1998.tb00533.x

Wiemer-Hastings, P., Wiemer-Hastings, K. & Graesser, A. C. (1999). Improving an intelligent tutor's comprehension of students with Latent Semantic Analysis. *Artificial Intelligence in Education,* 545-542.

Xinran, L. (2014). A Quantum-behaved Particle Swarm Algorithm on Auto-generating Test Paper. *Journal of Information and Computational Science, 11*(8), 2601–2610. doi:10.12733/jics20103585

Xue, F., Sanderson, A. C., & Graves, R. J. (2004). Pareto-based Multi-Objective differential evolution. *Proceedings of IEEE Congress on Evolutionary Computation (CEC), 2,* 862-869.

Zamuda, A., & Brest, J. (2007). Differential Evolution for Multi-objective Optimization with Self Adaptation. *Proceedings of the 2007 IEEE Congress on Evolutionary Computation (CEC),* 3617-3624. 10.1109/CEC.2007.4424941

Zhen-hua, J., Hun-e, Z., & Hao-shuai, F. (2011). The research and application of general item bank automatic test paper generation based on improved genetic algorithms. *Proceedings of 2nd International Conference on Computing, Control and Industrial Engineering (CCIE),* 14-18.

Chapter 4
Syllabus Coverage Evaluation in Test Paper Models

ABSTRACT

A syllabus is a detailed instructional plan of materials, resources, teaching methods, and evaluation plans primarily designed to inform the students about the standards, requirements, and learning outcomes expected out of them in the course. It also expresses an "informal agreement" between the instructor and the students in completing the delivery of the content of the syllabus throughout the course. A syllabus also informs the coverage of contents to other educational institutions so that they can determine if it is equivalent to a similar one offered at their institutions. A modularized syllabus contains weightages assigned to different units/modules of a subject. Different criteria like Bloom's taxonomy, learning outcomes, etc. have been used for evaluating the syllabus coverage of a test paper.

RELATED WORK

Bloom's taxonomy has been commonly accepted as a guideline in designing reasonable examination questions belonging to various cognitive levels. The hierarchical models of Bloom's taxonomy are widely used in education fields for constructing questions, for distributing questions across different cognitive levels of taxonomy and for achieving student cognitive mastery (Swart, A.J. 2010; Starr, C.W., Manaris, B. and Stalvey, R. H. 2008; Jones, K. O. and Harland, J. 2009; Yusof, N. and ChaiJ, H. 2010 & Scott, T. 2003).

DOI: 10.4018/978-1-7998-3772-5.ch004

Learning outcomes (O'Neill, A., Birol, G. and Pollock, C. 2010) illustrate what learners will be able to do on achievement of a particular learning experience. Providing with well- articulated learning outcome in a subject avoids students uncertainty and anxiety about what they are expected to know, assists students to prepare for assessment and allows instructor to design assessment questions that are in alignment with the intended learning of the subject. For course learning outcomes to be a useful tool for guiding student learning, these learning outcomes must list not only the modules that students will be responsible for learning in the course but also the cognitive level at which the students will be assessed for each of these modules. One benchmark currently used to rank the cognitive level of learning outcomes is the cognitive domain of Bloom's taxonomy. The implemented tools were able to compare the learning outcomes and the examination questions of the subject, investigating whether the cognitive skill level of each learning outcome as written matched the level at which it was assessed (Wen-Chih, C. and Ming-Shun, C. 2009; Thompson, E., et.al.2008). To the best of our knowledge, existing work in test paper evaluation has failed to assign priority to the unit-weightages/module weightages while computing syllabus coverage of a test paper. Hence, we have focused on the problem of evaluating syllabus coverage of an examination test paper by analyzing the questions on different criteria such as the unit-weightages, taxonomy, learning outcomes, etc. Partition-based grouping algorithm has been designed for handling multiple conditions in the grouping problem of syllabus coverage evaluation.

Syllabus coverage evaluation adopts a similarity coefficient-based comparison of questions of a test paper against the university prescribed syllabus file in order to verify the effectiveness of an examination test paper for theoretical courses such as software engineering, information technology, etc. Each unit/module in the syllabus file is given a weightage that corresponds to the number of lecture hours to be allotted to the instructor to teach that unit. The weightage also indicates the importance assigned to that unit which is used by the instructor to decide on the depth to which the topics in that unit should be covered, considered by the paper-setter to decide on the allocation of marks under each unit and used by the students to allocate time-schedule for each unit while preparing for an examination. Similarity measure is computed using a similarity matrix which is a two-dimensional matrix representing the pair-wise similarity of keywords of question content with keywords of unit/module content. Text pre-processing techniques are used for extracting the keywords from question content and unit content. In this chapter, two different approaches have been considered for syllabus coverage evaluation. The first approach focuses on cosine similarity measure where as the second one applies word order similarity measure. Cosine similarity was discussed in chapter 2. Word order similarity measure between two sentence vectors is calculated as a normalized difference of word order. Word order similarity measure remains as one of the best measures to find the similarity between sequential words in sentences and is increasing in popularity due to its simple interpretation and easy computation (Islam, A. and Inkpen, D. 2008 and Canhasi,E. 2013). Henceforth word-order similarity measure has been refereed as word-order coefficient or word-order similarity. During the process of generation of the similarity matrix, the partition-based grouping algorithm formulates unit-wise question groups, matches question group weightage against syllabus content and evaluates syllabus coverage of a test paper. The method used by the grouping algorithm is as follows: select n questions of a test paper and m units of syllabus file, compute n × m similarity matrix by performing n × m pair-wise question content and syllabus content comparisons and uses the matrix in evaluating the syllabus coverage. The result of syllabus coverage evaluation has been identified to be a good assessment standard for the instructor or test paper-setter or test paper moderator to revise the questions of examination test paper accordingly (Paul et al, 2014). The terms unit and module have been used interchangeably in this chapter and are considered as synonyms. Also, the terms fairness and coverage have been used interchangeably.

Table 1. Terminology used for syllabus coverage evaluation

Term	Meaning
Test paper (QP)	QP includes questions with its details such as question-no) question-content and question-marks
Syllabus File (SF)	SF includes unit-wise syllabus contents organized as a set of topics and is assigned with unit-wise weightage
N	N is the total number of questions in a QP
M	M is the total number of units in the SF
n_i	n_i refers to the number of questions in which term i appears
m_j	m_j refers to the number of units in which term j appears
Question-Term-Set (question qst_i)	t is a set of terms extracted from each question by performing its tokenization) stop word removal) taxonomy verb removal and stemming
Syllabus-Term-Set($unit$unt$_j$)	t is a set of terms extracted from each unit by performing its tokenization) stop word removal) taxonomy verb removal and stemming

TERMINOLOGY USED

The terminology used in this chapter is listed in Table.1 and Table.2 respectively.

Table 2. Terminology used for syllabus coverage evaluation

Term	Meaning
$q\,freq_{ij}$	$qfreq_{ij}$ is the frequency of question-term i in question j
$s\,freq_{ij}$	$sfreq_{ij}$ is the frequency of syllabus-term i in unit j
qmaximum frequency($qmax\,freq_{ij}$)	$qmaxfreq_{ij}$ is the maximum frequency of a question-term in question j
smaximum frequency($smax\,freq_{ij}$)	$smaxfreq_{ij}$ is the maximum frequency of a syllabus-term in unit j
qterm frequency(qtf_{ij})	qtf_{ij} refers to the importance of a question-term *i* in question *j*. It is calculated using the formula: (qtf_{ij})=qfreq/ $qmaxfreq_{ij}$ (1)
sterm frequency(stf_{ij})	(stf_{ij}) refers to importance of a syllabus-term i in unit j. It is calculated using the formula: (stf_{ij})=sfreq/ $smaxfreq_{ij}$ (2)
q Inverse Document Frequency($qidf_i$)	$qids_i$ refers to the discriminating power of question-term i and is calculated as: $qidf_i$=log$_2$(N/n$_i$) (3)
s Inverse Document Frequency($sidf_i$)	$sidf_i$ refers to the discriminating power of syllabus-term i and is calculated as: $sidf_i$=log$_2$(M/m$_i$) (4)
qtf-qidf weighting (QW_{ij})	t is a weighting scheme to determine weight of a term in a question. t is calculated using the formula: QW_{ij}=qtf_{ij}/$qidf_i$(5)
stf-qidf weighting(SW_{ij})	t is a weighting scheme to determine weight of a term in a unit. t is calculated using the formula: SW_{ij}=stf_{ij}/$sidf_i$ (6)
Theshold) δ	User input threshold value to find the similarity

COSINE SIMILARITY MEASURE AND WORD ORDER SIMILARITY MEASURE FOR SYLLABUS COVERAGE EVALUATION

The procedure for finding similarity between question content and syllabus content consists of the following two main steps-

Step 1-Pre-processing of Question Content and Syllabus Content
Step 2-Computing Question-Vs-Syllabus Similarity Matrix

A brief description of the above steps is given below-

Step 1- Pre-processing of Question Content and Syllabus Content

Pre-processing of Question Content and Syllabus Content follows the same method as the one used in chapter 3 for Question Bank pre-processing. Therefore, in this chapter the five sub-steps involved in pre-processing of question content and respective syllabus content are briefly discussed below-

1. **Tokenization:** The set of questions of a test paper as well as the unit-wise contents of syllabus file are treated as collection of strings (or bag of words), which are then partitioned into a list of terms.
2. **Filtering Stop Words:** Stop words within the question content and also in the syllabus content are eliminated.
3. **Filtering Taxonomy Verbs:** The taxonomy verbs within the question content are identified and eliminated.
4. **Stemming the Terms:** Porter stemmer is considered here.
5. **Normalization:** We have used the techniques: 1) lowercase the terms 2) remove special characters, for performing normalization.

Step2- Computing Question-Vs-Syllabus Similarity Matrix

Similarity matrix computation has been carried out by considering matrix representation of vectors as similar to the similarity matrix for question clusters in chapter 3 for Generating Question Clusters) such that question vectors act as row headers and unit vectors act as column headers of the matrix respectively. n the two-dimensional matrix of N questions and M units say N × M matrix) each pair of question-term vector and syllabus-term vector gets compared to determine how identical they are by using the following two similarity measure computation approaches:

1. Cosine Similarity Measure
2. Word Order Similarity Measure
3. Cosine Similarity Measure

Refer to chapter 3 for cosine similarity measure.

1. Word Order Similarity Measure

The word order similarity between question vector and syllabus vector say QV1 and SV1 is computed in a two-step process. In the first step, the common words in QV1 and SV1 are identified and are inserted in the same order in which they appear into two other common word vectors say QCWV1 and SCWV1. In the second step, a unique index number that represent the order in which the words appear in QCWV1, is identified for each word in QCWV1 and is inserted to the corresponding index vector say Q NV1. Based on these unique index numbers in QCWV1, we also assign respective unique index numbers to words in SCWV1 and insert it to the corresponding index vector say SNV1. The word order similarity of question-vector and syllabus-vector is calculated by using the following formula-

$$\textbf{Similarity (qv}_1\textbf{, sv}_1) = \cos\theta = \frac{(qv1, sv1)}{(|qv1|, |sv1|)}. \tag{7}$$

where '.' denotes the dot product between vectors qv_1 and sv_1. $|qv_1|$ and $|sv_1|$ are the Euclidean norm of qv_1 and sv_1 vectors. The above formula can be expanded in the following manner.

$$\cos\theta = \frac{\sum_{i=1}^{n} wi, qv1 \times wi, sv1}{qrt(\sum_{i=1}^{n} wi * wi, qv1) \times sqrt(\sum_{i=1}^{n} wi * wi, sv1)} \tag{8}$$

During the process of computation of the similarity matrix, the formulation of unit-wise question groups, calculation of unit-wise question groups weightage and comparison of the calculated weightage against the actual unit-weightage in the syllabus file has also been carried out in parallel. The syllabus coverage evaluation performed using the similarity matrix is a good aid for the subject expert or test paper-setter or test paper moderator to revise the questions of a test paper so as to satisfy the unit-weightages. Choosing suitable threshold value for similarity computation is a difficult task and it is problem/person dependent. Precision (P)) Recall (R) and F-measure (F) has been used as the metrics to evaluate the accuracy of predictions and the coverage of accurate pairs of comparisons while performing syllabus coverage evaluation. They are computed as-

(P) =

$$\frac{\text{number of relevant question-to-syllabus matches retrieved by the tool}}{\text{total number of question-to-syllabus matches reterieved by the tool}}$$

(9)

(R) =

$$\frac{\text{number of relevant question-to-syllabus matches retrieved by the tool}}{\text{total number of question-to-syllabus matches given by the instructor}}$$

(10)

$$(F) = \frac{(2 \times P \times R)}{P + R}$$

(11)

Table 3. Similarity matrix representation for question to syllabus match

QV/SV	SV_1	SV_2	SV_3	SV_4	SV_5	SV_6	SV_7	...	SV_m
QV_1	sm_{11}	sm_{12}	sm_{13}	sm_{14}	sm_{15}	sm_{16}	sm_{17}	...	sm_{1m}
QV_2	sm_{21}	sm_{22}	sm_{23}	sm_{24}	sm_{25}	sm_{26}	sm_{27}	...	sm_{2m}
QV_3	sm_{31}	sm_{32}	sm_{33}	sm_{34}	sm_{35}	sm_{36}	sm_{37}	...	sm_{3m}
QV_4	sm_{41}	sm_{42}	sm_{43}	sm_{44}	sm_{45}	sm_{46}	sm_{47}	...	sm_{4m}
QV_5	sm_{51}	sm_{52}	sm_{53}	sm_{54}	sm_{55}	sm_{56}	sm_{57}	...	sm_{5m}
QV_6	sm_{61}	sm_{62}	sm_{63}	sm_{64}	sm_{65}	sm_{66}	sm_{67}	...	sm_{6m}
QV_7	sm_{71}	sm_{72}	sm_{73}	sm_{74}	sm_{75}	sm_{76}	sm_{77}	...	sm_{7m}
...	...	...	...	...	...	...	...	...	...
QV_n	sm_{n1}	sm_{n2}	sm_{n3}	sm_{n4}	sm_{n5}	sm_{n6}	sm_{n7}	...	sm_{nm}

Problem Statement

Given a test paper of subject S consisting of N questions represented as QP(S)=$qst_1,qst_2,...,qst_N$ and a syllabus file of S consisting of M units represented as SF(S)=$unt_1,unt_2,...,unt_M$, the problem is to find unit-wise similar question groups UQG_1, UQG_2,..., UQG_k. A question qst_i can be said to belong to unt_j

if similarity $(qst_i)\ unt_j) >= \delta$ where δ is the user input threshold value to find the similarity.

The similarity $(qst_i)\ unt_j)$ function could use any of the similarity measures available. We have used cosine similarity and word order similarity to perform the experimental study.

The main modules of syllabus coverage evaluation are represented in Figure.1 below.

Figure 1. Main modules of syllabus-coverage evaluator

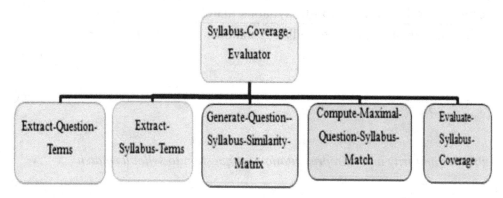

The brief details of modules of Syllabus-Coverage-Evaluator are presented below:

1. **Extract-Question-Terms:** Input qst_i (i=1 to N) and for each qst_i, it extracts terms qt_{ij} (j=1 to N_{ij}).
2. **Extract-Syllabus-Terms:** Input unt_j (j=1 to M) and for each unt_j in the syllabus file) it extracts terms st_{jk} (k=1 to M_j).
3. **Generate-Question-Syllabus-Similarity-Matrix:** Input question-terms qt_{ij} (j=1 to N_j) for all qst_i (i=1 to N) and also syllabus-terms st_{jk} (k=1 to M_j) for all unt_j (j=1 to M). For each pair of question-terms qst_i and syllabus-terms unt_j, compute similarity $(qst_p unt_j)$ for i=1 to N and j=1 to M using any standard similarity measuring scheme. Represent the result as a Question-Syllabus-Similarity- Matrix.
4. **Compute-Best-Question-Syllabus-Match:** For each question in the Question-Syllabus-Similarity-Matrix) it finds the highest value of similarity among the set of computed similarity $(qst_p unt_j) >= \delta)$ for i=1 to N and j=1 to M. If the highest value of similarity does not get

identified for a question) the question is considered to be in- directly associated with the syllabus and is represented as indirect question else the question is considered to be directly associated with the syllabus and is represented as direct question.

5. **Evaluate-Syllabus-Coverage:** Under each unit, it performs the summation of the marks of direct questions and represents the result of summation as unit-direct-question-marks. Also, it identifies whether the unit-direct-question-marks of each unit satisfies the-unit-weightage of the syllabus file. The term satisfies-the-unit-weightage means that the unit-direct-question-marks is less-than- or-equal-to ($<=$) the unit-weightage. If the unit-direct-question-marks is greater-than-or-equal-to ($>=$) the unit-weightage, then the value of unit-direct-question-marks gets replaced with the value of unit-weightage. This replacement process is carried out to limit the value of unit-direct-question-marks to the extent to which it matches with the unit-weightage. At the next stage, it adds up the unit-direct-question-marks of all the units and represents the result of addition as direct-question-weightage. Using the direct-question- weightage, it computes the Syllabus Coverage of the test paper. The computed syllabus coverage is represented as Poor or Average or Good or Excellent depending upon whether the percentage of direct-question-weightage falls in the range of 0-40 or 41-60 or 61-80 or 81-100 respectively.

Algorithm Details

Syllabus Coverage Evaluation has been carried out by performing the four main steps namely Extract-Question-Terms and Extract-Syllabus-Terms, Generate-Question-Syllabus-Similarity-Matrix, Evaluate-Maximal-Question-Syllabus-Match, Compute-Syllabus-Coverage using cosine similarity measure and word order similarity measure with Syllabus Coverage Evaluation Algorithm presented below -

Algorithm 1 (a) Syllabus Coverage Evaluation using Partition- based Grouping Algorithm

Procedure Question-Term-Extraction (QP(S) = {qst₁, qst₂,..., qstₙ})
 Input: $QP(S) = \{qst_1, qst_2, ..., qst_N\}$: *a question paper of subject S consisting of N questions*
Output: $QT = \{qt_1[\ ], qt_2[\ ], qt_3[\ ], ..., qt_N[\ ]\}$: *set of terms*
$QT = \{ \}$
for $i=1$ *to N do*
    extract terms from qst_i *and store it in array* $qt_i[\ ]$;
    remove stop words from $qt_i[\ ]$;
    remove taxonomy verbs from $qt_i[\ ]$;
    extract the stem of each term in $qt_i[\ ]$;
    $QT = QT \ U \ qt_i[\ ]$
end for
return $QT = \{qt_1[\ ], qt_2[\ ], qt_3[\ ], ..., qt_N[\ ]\}$
end procedure

Procedure Syllabus-Term-Extraction (SF(S)= {unt₁,unt₂,...,untₘ})
Input: $SF(S) = \{unt_1, unt_2, ..., unt_M\}$: *a syllabus file of S consisting of M units*
Output: $ST = \{st_1[\ ], st_2[\ ], st_3[\ ], ..., st_M[\ ]\}$: *set of terms in the syllabus file*
$ST = \{ \}$;
for $j=1$ *to M do*
    extract terms from unt_j *and store it in array* $st_j[\ ]$;
    remove stop words from $st_j[\ ]$;
    remove taxonomy verbs from $st_j[\ ]$;
    extract stem of each term in $st_j[\ ]$;
    $ST = ST \ U \ st_j[\ ]$;
end for
return $ST = \{st_1[\ ], st_2[\ ], st_3[\ ], ..., st_M[\ ]\}$
end procedure

Algorithm 1(b) Syllabus Coverage Evaluation using Partition-based Grouping Algorithm (Algorithm 1(a) Continued...)

```
Procedure Syllabus Coverage Evaluation (QT ST, δ)
// Syllabus Coverage Evaluation using Grouping Algorithm
Input: QT ST, δ
QT= {qt₁[ ], qt₂[ ], qt₃[ ], ..., qt₄[ ]} :set of question terms in the question paper
ST= {st₁[ ], st₂[ ], st₃[ ], ..., st₄[ ]} :set of unit terms in the syllabus file
where,
   qt₁ { qt₁, qt₂, qt₃,...,qtₚ} for p=1 to count(qti terms)  //set of terms in question i
   st₁ { st₁, st₂, st₃,...,stₐ} for q=1 to count(unit terms)  //set of terms in syllabus j
   N= {qst₁, qst₂,...,qstₙ} // number of questions in the question paper
   M= {unt₁, unt₂,...,untₘ} // number of selected units in the syllabus file
Threshold= δ: user input threshold value to find similarity
Output: k Unit_Question_Group UQG₁, UQG₂,... UQG_k where UQG consist of a set of   qst', questions of QP(S)
// Form unit-wise question groups and verify its syllabus coverage.
//Evaluate-Syllabus-Coverage by forming unit-wise question groups
//Initialization
cnt = 0; //counter for number of question-groups
direct_question_percentage=0; // counter for percentage of direct questions
unit_question_set = [ ];
//Unitwise-Question-Group-Formulation
   //Compare unit-wise marks of questions of QP(S) with unit-wise  weightages  in the syllabus
   for i=1 to M do
      cnt=cnt+1;
      //Formulate unit-wise new question groups
      UQG₁ New_Unit_Question_Group (unt,cnt)
      for j=1 to N do
         if qst not in unit_question_set then
            // Evaluate Best-Question-Syllabus-Match using the Similarity-Matrix
            if similarity (qst, unt) >=δ  then
               temp = similarity (qst, unt) ;
               for k=1 to M do
                  if similarity (qst, unt) >temp  then
                     exit for
                  end if
                  // Iterative stages of appending questions to each question-groups
                  Add qst to New_Unit_Question_Group p ;
               unit_question_set =  unit_question_set + qst
            end for
            end if
         end if
      end for
   end for
   // Evaluate Syllabus-Coverages using marks of unit-wise questions in question-groups
   for i=1 to cnt do
      Accept Unit_Question_Group (unt,i) ;
      marks_unt =sum (marks of all questions of Unit_Question_Group (unt,i))
      if marks_unt <=syllabus-weight(unt) then
         direct_question_percentage= direct_question_percentage+ marks_unt
      else
         direct_question_percentage= direct_question_percentage+ syllabus-weight (unt)
   end if
end for
end procedure
```

EXPERIMENTAL RESULTS

Implementation is done using Microsoft Visual Basic .NET as Front-End Tool and SQL Server as Back End Tool on a 2 GHz processor with 1GB RAM.

Input Dataset

The test paper of the third year of three year bachelor's degree course of computer science (B.Sc Computer Science) for Information Technology subject examination at Goa University contains 28 questions. 0ut of 28 questions, 21 of them are compulsory questions, and 7 are optional questions. The syllabus file for this subject includes five units. Details of experimental data used for similarity computation is as follows-

4.4.1.1 S= sub5= Information Technology (T)

4.4.1.2 QP(S)=qp7=$quest_1$, $quest_2$..., $quest_{10}$..., $quest_{28}$

4.4.1.3 SF(S)=$unit_1$, $unit_2$..., $unit_5$

4.4.1.4 δ=0.50

4.4.1.5 Sample Dataset of T Test paper and T syllabus File is displayed in Figure.2 and Figure.3 respectively.

Figure 2. Sample dataset of IT Test paper with 28 questions

Figure 3. Sample dataset of IT Syllabus File

subject_unit	subject_cd	unit_content	unit_weight
sub5unit1	sub5	authoring tool,definition,internet live stream,multimedia elements,multimedia applications and products,image types,audio types,video types, animation,viewing tool,creation and conversion,codecs,compression,transmission,bitrates,multicast,hi definition	16
sub5unit2	sub5	ecommerce technology,introduction of ecommerce,ecommerce today,ecommerce enablers,epayment systems,ecash, credit card payment, debit card payment,payment gateway, example, fake websites,digital certification spoof,eretail,ecarts,shopping cart,eshopping	16
sub5unit3	sub5	static website,dynamic website,web server, web security,web client,url,domain name,domain name definition,domain name,domain name format,http protocol ,https protocol,email,definition,email usage, email protocol,email clients,security,spam, phishing,information	20
sub5unit4	sub5	virus types,define virus,malware,malware, symptoms of attack,virus attack,virus attack prevention,antivirus and spyware detectors,define antivirus, choosing antivirus and spyware detection software, antivirus software installation, regular update virus definition,browser security,virus	18
sub5unit5	sub5	,piracy issues,user generated content,blogs,wikis,twitter,youtube, flickr, moodle,collaboration,social networks, multi user chat, application examples,google docs,file share,p2p, torrents, protocols, examples	10

1. Figure.4 presents the screenshot displaying paper-setter input for syllabus coverage evaluation. It provides the facility for entering general details for evaluation such as details of Syllabus, Test paper details, Stop Words and Bloom's Class details.

Figure 4. Screenshot with paper-setter input for syllabus coverage evaluation

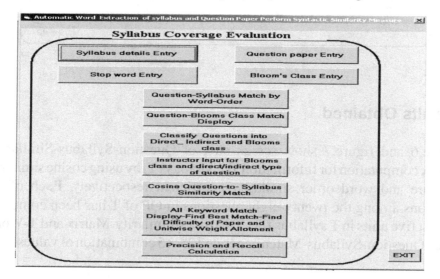

2.   A snapshot of the set of units $sub5unit_1, sub5unit_2,...,sub5unit_5$ with its extracted list of terms{anim,applic,audio,...},{shop,amazon,bank,card ,...},...,{attach, client,definit,distribut,...} etc.) and set of questions $qp7$ $quest_1, qp7quest_2,...,qp7quest_{10},..., quest_{28}$ with its extracted list of terms fake,website, what, browser,security, definition, need, regular, update, virus,file,issues, piracy,sharing etc., for qp7 is displayed in Figure.5. Extraction of terms from T subject's syllabus file and T subject's test paper has been carried out by performing four different pre-processing stages such as Tokenization, Stop Word Removal, Filtering Taxonomy Verbs and Normalization of Words.

Figure 5. Screenshot with paper-setter input for syllabus coverage evaluation

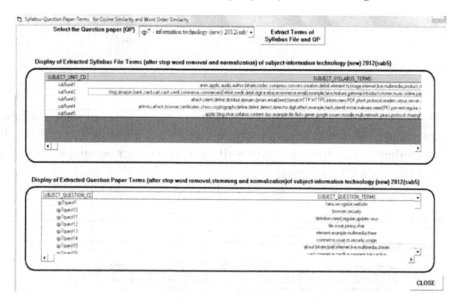

Results Obtained

Figure.6 and figure.7 show screen shot of Question-Syllabus-Similarity-Matrix computation for Information Technology (T) by using cosine similarity measure and word order similarity coefficient respectively. Each of the questions among the twenty-eight questions in QP of T has been compared against five units in T syllabus file. T-Cosine-Similarity-Matrix and T-Word-Order-Question-Syllabus-Match generated 28 × 5 combination of values. If no similarity exists between a pair of T question-terms and T unit-terms, cosine similarity and word order similarity return a value of zero and in every other case, it returns a value in the range of 0.0-1.0.

Figure 6. IT-cosine-similarity-matrix (question to syllabus match)

Cosine Similarity Matrix Computation

	sub5unit1	sub5unit2	sub5unit3	sub5unit4	sub5unit5
qp7quest1	0	1	0.16	0.02	0
qp7quest10	0	0.77	0.04	0.17	0
qp7quest11	0.05	1	0.06	0.27	0
qp7quest12	0	0.53	0	0	0.1
qp7quest13	0.2	1	0	0.02	0.16
qp7quest14	0	0.78	0.08	0.04	0
qp7quest15	0.39	1	0	0	0.08
qp7quest16	0	1	0	0	0
qp7quest17	0	1	0	0	0
qp7quest18	0.29	0.63	0	0.03	0
qp7quest19	0	0.75	0	0	0
qp7quest2	0.18	1	0	0	0.09
qp7quest20	0.2	0.79	0	0	0.1
qp7quest21	0	0.66	0.36	0.03	0
qp7quest22	0	1	0.04	0	0.02
qp7quest23	0	0.49	0.17	0	0
qp7quest24	0	1	0.37	0.01	0
qp7quest25	0	0.62	0.03	0.17	0
qp7quest26	0	0.56	0	0	0.43
qp7quest27	0.08	1	0.02	0.2	0
qp7quest28	0.08	1	0	0	0.46
qp7quest3	0.1	0.71	0.09	0	0
qp7quest4	0	0.66	0.38	0.02	0.03
qp7quest5	0	0.26	0.36	0	0
qp7quest6	0.1	0.53	0	0	0.2
qp7quest7	0	0.37	0.01	0.29	0
qp7quest8	0	0.92	0	0.44	0
qp7quest9	0.12	0.37	0	0.14	0

Figure 7. IT-word order-similarity-matrix (question to syllabus match)

Common Word Order Similarity Matrix

	sub5unit1	sub5unit2	sub5unit3	sub5unit4	sub5unit5
qp7quest1		0.667			
qp7quest10				1	
qp7quest11				1	
qp7quest12					0.4
qp7quest13	0.5				
qp7quest14		1			
qp7quest15	0.6				
qp7quest16		0.5			
qp7quest17		0.25			
qp7quest18	0.5				
qp7quest19		0.5			
qp7quest2	0.333				
qp7quest20	0.25				
qp7quest21			0.4		
qp7quest22					0.167
qp7quest23			0.75		
qp7quest24			0.75		
qp7quest25				0.5	
qp7quest26					0.75
qp7quest27				0.667	
qp7quest28					0.143
qp7quest3		1			
qp7quest4			0.6		
qp7quest5			0.25		
qp7quest6	0.5				
qp7quest7				0.25	
qp7quest9					1

Cosine similarity encountered a major disadvantage of term independence while comparing sequential terms in T question-content and T unit-content. n the tf-idf representation of cosine similarity, using the formula shown in Table.2, the term frequency of each term is normalized by the inverse document frequency (idf)) referred over here as $qid f_i$ for $sid f_i$. The idf normalization has been found to reduce the weight of terms which occur more frequently in the collection of T question-content as well as in T unit-content. This was not a major issue in the T question- content, as a single test paper normally doesn't include many similar questions or otherwise doesn't include similar question terms. Alternatively, in the syllabus wise unit content, most of the terms have been repeated across the unit sub-contents, as a specific unit describes mostly similar and associated concepts. This majorly deteriorated the entire tf-idf score of terms of T unit-content. Hence, the similarity matrix generated with cosine similarity does not display a good score for the true measure of similarity in most of the T question-content to T unit- content comparisons, even though it exists and on the other side displays a good score for the false measure of similarity in most of the T question- content to T unit-content comparisons, even though it doesn't exists. Also, the second limitation of cosine which represents terms as bag of words, and there by the underlying sequential information provided by the ordering of the words is typically getting lost is again identified as a major constraint in using the cosine similarity-based similarity matrix for syllabus coverage evaluation. Hence, the results of word order similarity matrix have been found more appropriate than cosine similarity matrix for syllabus coverage evaluation. Rest of our discussion continues only with experimental output of syllabus coverage evaluation using word order similarity coefficient. Figure.8 shows a screen shot of the process of generation of maximal common word pair vector match of each question with a specific unit. Among 28×5 combination of values of T-Word-Order-Question-Syllabus-Match, the maximal common word pair vector matches are identified and are displayed.

Figure.9 below represents the process of generation of T-unit-question-groups. For each question in the T-Common-Word Order-Similarity-Matrix, the highest value of similarity among a set of pair-wise similarity, (T- quest i, T- unit j)>=0.50) for i=1 to 28 and j=1 to 5 has been found. When highest value of similarity has been computed for a T-quest, the question is termed as direct, else the question is represented as indirect.

Figure.10 shows the evaluated measure of syllabus coverage. Under each T-unit, marks of direct questions were added up and were named as T-unit-direct-question-marks.

Figure 8. Computed maximal similarity measure for question to syllabus match

SL_NO	QUESTION_CD	QUESTION_KEYWORD_ORDER	UNIT_CD	UNIT_KEYWORD_MATCH_ORDER
1	qp7quest1	fake,websites,recognize	sub5unit2	fake websites
2	qp7quest10	browser,security	sub5unit4	browser security
3	qp7quest11	regular,update,virus,definition	sub5unit4	regular update virus definition
4	qp7quest12	meaning,file,share,peacy,issues	sub5unit5	file share
5	qp7quest13	multimedia,elements,with,example	sub5unit1	multimedia elements
6	qp7quest14	security,issues,mcommerce	sub5unit2	security issues mcommerce
7	qp7quest15	internet,live,stream,bitrate,multimedia	sub5unit1	internet live stream
8	qp7quest16	credit,card,payment,transactions,with,steps	sub5unit2	credit card payment
9	qp7quest17	meaning,ecommerce,technology,note	sub5unit2	ecommerce
10	qp7quest18	multimedia,applications	sub5unit1	multimedia
11	qp7quest19	shopping,cart,advanatge,etransactions	sub5unit2	shopping cart
12	qp7quest2	use,codec,multimedia	sub5unit1	multimedia
13	qp7quest20	lossy,lossless,compression,multimedia	sub5unit1	multimedia
14	qp7quest21	website,explain,static,dynamic,website	sub5unit3	static dynamic
15	qp7quest22	different,email,protocol,used,sending,receiving	sub5unit5	protocol
16	qp7quest23	url,relation,url,domain,names	sub5unit3	url domain
17	qp7quest24	usage,web,server,web,client	sub5unit3	web server
18	qp7quest25	pki,cryptography,web,security	sub5unit4	web security
19	qp7quest26	multiuser,chat,social,network	sub5unit5	social network multiuser
20	qp7quest27	three,virus,types	sub5unit4	virus types
21	qp7quest28	role,user,generated,content,known,moodle,blogs	sub5unit5	moodle
22	qp7quest3	ebanking,phishing	sub5unit2	ebanking phishing
23	qp7quest4	http,https,protocols,used,internet	sub5unit3	http protocols https
24	qp7quest5	information,distribution,using,pdf	sub5unit3	information
25	qp7quest6	multicast,multimedia	sub5unit1	multimedia
26	qp7quest7	virus,attack,prevention,methods	sub5unit4	virus
27	qp7quest9	hacking,types	sub5unit4	hacking types

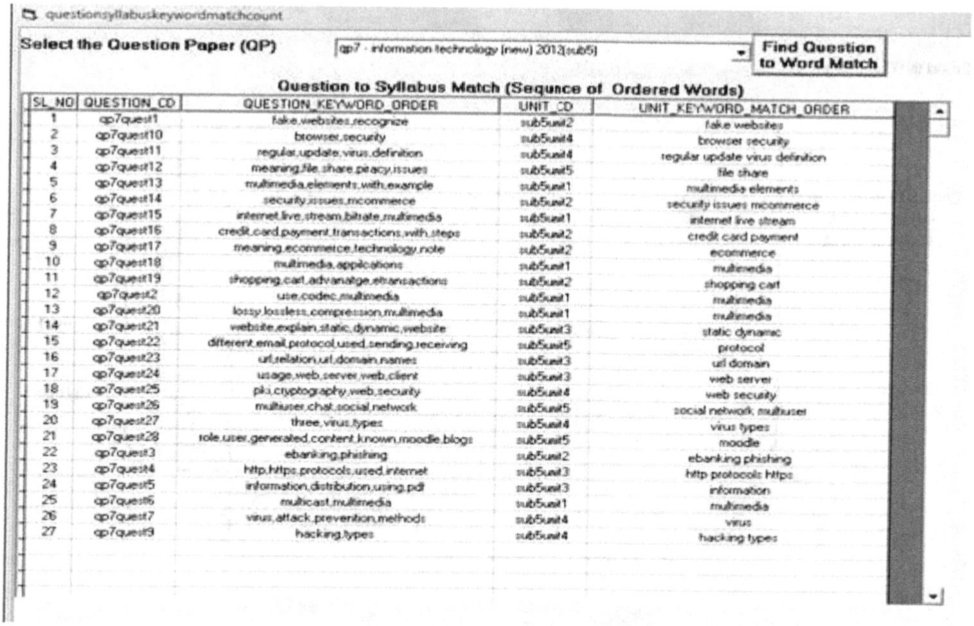

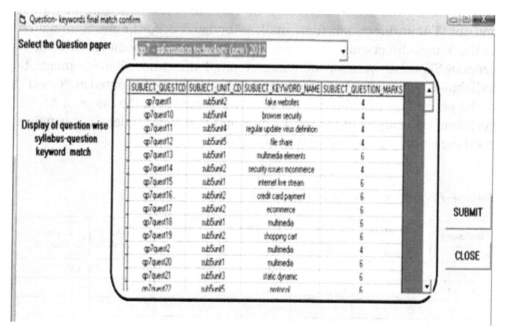

Figure 9. Iterative stages of unit-question-groups formulation

SUBJECT_QUESTCD	SUBJECT_UNIT_CD	SUBJECT_KEYWORD_NAME	SUBJECT_QUESTION_MARKS
qp7quest1	sub5unit2	fake websites	4
qp7quest10	sub5unit4	browser security	4
qp7quest11	sub5unit4	regular update virus definition	4
qp7quest12	sub5unit5	file share	4
qp7quest13	sub5unit1	multimedia elements	6
qp7quest14	sub5unit2	security issues mcommerce	4
qp7quest15	sub5unit1	internet live steam	6
qp7quest16	sub5unit2	credit card payment	6
qp7quest17	sub5unit2	ecommerce	6
qp7quest18	sub5unit1	multimedia	6
qp7quest19	sub5unit2	shopping cart	6
qp7quest2	sub5unit1	multimedia	4
qp7quest20	sub5unit1	multimedia	6
qp7quest21	sub5unit3	static dynamic	6
qp7quest22	sub5unit5	protocol	6

Figure 10. Computed syllabus-coverage measure using unit-question-groups

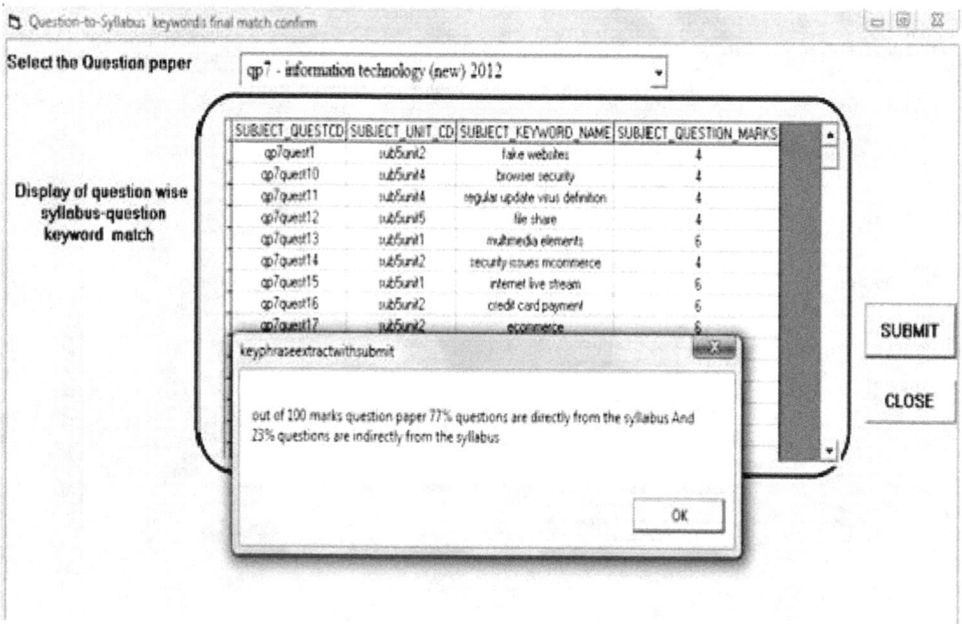

Whether or not the T-unit-direct- question-marks of each unit have been able to satisfy the T-unit-weightage of T-syllabus file is getting identified and the T-unit-direct-question- mark is updated accordingly. Summation of the T-unit-direct-question- mark of all the units has been carried out to generate SE-direct-question-weightage. Using T-direct-question-weightage, T-Syllabus-Coverage has been computed and is getting represented as "Good", as the percentage of SE-direct-question-weightage is in the range of 61-80. Performance analysis of the results indicates that Word Order similarity is a good measure in grouping similar questions.

Table 4. Performance evaluation of IT-syllabus-coverage

Test paper Code	Word Or- der Preci- sion	Word Order Recall	Word Order F- measure	Cosine Preci- sion	Cosine Recall	Cosine F- measure
T 2012	0.73	0.57	0.64	0.47	0.32	0.38
T 2010	0.78	0.57	0.66	0.46	0.32	0.37
T 2009	0.77	0.56	0.65	0.45	0.30	0.36
T 2008	0.75	0.56	0.64	0.49	0.39	0.43

Performance Evaluation

In order to carry out the performance evaluation of Word Order-similarity based T-syllabus-Coverage measure, we compute Precision, Recall and F-measure values for the T question-syllabus match. We have taken into consideration the T test papers of four different years. Each test paper consisted of roughly about 30 questions which are getting matched with the corresponding T syllabus content. The result of computation is shown in Table.4 below.

Summary

This chapter focused on a new approach for syllabus coverage evaluation of a test paper by performing (n × m) pair-wise question-vector and syllabus-vector comparisons. Similarity matrix computation has been successfully carried out using common word order similarity which is a commonly used similarity measure for short documents. Cosine similarity has been found to have a major disadvantage of tf-idf normalization and term independence and hence was substituted with word order similarity measure. Even though word order similarity also has a limitation of identifying the word order) this is not a major concern in our work as we deal with short text documents. Results obtained indicate that word order similarity is a good measure in formulating unit-wise question groups. The formulated question groups have been found successful in identifying the syllabus coverage of a test paper by comparing the unit-wise question groups weightages against the actual unit-weightage specified in the syllabus file. The question groups are useful in situations where novice instructors or the test paper-setter or test paper moderator needs to evaluate the syllabus coverage of a test paper and revise the questions of examination test paper accordingly. The primary objective of this study was to identify the effectiveness of statistical measures in formulating similar question groups and evaluating the coverage of a test paper. Our future work will focus on replacing the statistical approaches of similarity matrix generation by semantic approaches.

CONCLUSION

This chapter discussed the application of Partition-based Grouping Algorithm in the area of syllabus coverage evaluation of a test paper. Grouping algorithm is found suitable for syllabus coverage evaluation due to the following reasons: n the current educational scenario, criteria like Bloom's taxonomy, learning outcomes, etc. have been used for evaluating the syllabus coverage of a test paper. 13ut we had not come across any work that focuses on unit-weightages for computing the syllabus coverage. Hence, we focused on the problem of evaluating syllabus coverage of an examination test paper by analyzing the questions on different criteria such as unit-weightages) Bloom's taxonomy, etc. Cosine Similarity measure and word-order similarity measure have been used to compute the similarity between question content and syllabus content. Vector based Similarity measure computation is carried out by formulating the similarity matrix between question vectors and syllabus vectors. The similarity matrix is used as a guideline in grouping the module-wise questions, matching its weightage against syllabus file and evaluating the syllabus coverage of the test paper. 13ut due to the limitation of cosine which represent the terms as bags of words, the underlying sequential information provided by the ordering of the words was typically getting lost. In order to overcome this limitation, we extended the work by incorporating word-to-word syntactic similarity metric which computes the similarity between question content and syllabus content on the basis of word order similarity measure. Precision, Recall and F-measure computation of word- order based syllabus coverage evaluation has found it to be a good measure to be used by the subject expert or test paper- setter or test paper moderator to revise the questions of examination test paper accordingly.

REFERENCES

Canhasi, E. (2013). Measuring the sentence level similarity. *Proceedings of 2nd International Symposium on Computing in Informatics and Mathematics*, 35-42.

Dimple, Paul, & Pawar. (2014). A Syllabus-Fairness Measure for Evaluating Open-Ended Questions. In Advances in Signal Processing and Intelligent Recognition Systems. Springer International Publishing.

Dimple, V. (2014). Use of Common-Word Order Syntactic Similarity Metric for Evaluating Syllabus Coverage of a Test paper. *International Journal of Web Applications*, 6(2), 68–81.

Islam, A., & Inkpen, D. (2008). Semantic text similarity using corpus-based word similarity and string similarity. *ACM Transactions on Knowledge Discovery from Data, 2*(2).

Jones, K. O., & Harland, J. (2009). Relationship between Examination Questions and Bloom's Taxonomy. *39th ASEE/IEEE Frontiers in Education Conference*, 1-6.

O'Neill, A., Birol, G., & Pollock, C. (2010). A Report on the Implementation of the Blooming Biology Tool: Aligning Course Learning Outcomes with Assessments and Promoting Consistency in a Large Multi- Section First-Year Biology Course. *The Canadian Journal for the Scholarship of Teaching and Learning, 1*(1), 8. doi:10.5206/cjsotl-rcacea.2010.1.8

Scott, T. (2003). Bloom's Taxonomy Applied to Testing in Computer Science Classes. *Proceedings of Consortium for Computing Science in Colleges: Rocky Mountain Conference*, 267-274.

Starr, C. W., Manaris, B., & Stalvey, R. H. (2008). Bloom's Taxonomy Revisited: Specifying Assessable Learning Objectives in Computer Science. *Proceedings of ACM Special Interest Group on Computer Science Education (SIGCSE) Symposia*, 261-265.

Swart, A. J. (2010). Evaluation of Final Examination Papers in Engineering: A Case Study Using Bloom's Taxonomy. *IEEE Transactions on Education, 53*(2), 257–264. doi:10.1109/TE.2009.2014221

Thompson, E., Luxton-Reilly, A., Whalley, J., & Hu, L. (2008). Bloom's Taxonomy for CS Assessment. *Proceeding Tenth Australasian Computing Education Conference (ACE)*, 155-162.

Wen-Chih, C., & Ming-Shun, C. (2009). Automatic Applying Bloom's Taxonomy to Classify and Analysis the Cognition Level of English Question Items. *Proceedings of IEEE Joint Conferences on Pervasive Computing (JCPC)*, 727-733.

Yusof, N., & Chai, J. H. (2010). Determination of Bloom's Cognitive Level of Question Items using Artificial Neural Network. *Proceedings of 10th International Conference on Intelligent Systems Design and Applications*, 866-870. 10.1109/ISDA.2010.5687152

Chapter 5
Answer Evaluation of Short Descriptive Questions

ABSTRACT

Reforms in the educational system emphasize more on continuous assessment. The descriptive examination test paper when compared to objective test paper acts as a better aid in continuous assessment for testing the progress of a student under various cognitive levels at different stages of learning. Unfortunately, assessment of descriptive answers is found to be tedious and time-consuming by instructors due to the increase in number of examinations in continuous assessment system. In this chapter, an attempt has been made to address the problem of automatic evaluation of descriptive answer using vector-based similarity matrix with order-based word-to-word syntactic similarity measure. Word order similarity measure remains as one of the best measures to find the similarity between sequential words in sentences and is increasing its popularity due to its simple interpretation and easy computation.

RELATED WORK

The descriptive answers of short answer questions generally include four or five sentences and therefore similarity determination between descriptive answer content and its solution content has been identified as a demanding task. The descriptive answers of short answer questions can always be subjectively verified with the content of specified text book. The manual descriptive answer paper evaluation system commonly uses the master key

DOI: 10.4018/978-1-7998-3772-5.ch005

or the question solution key. Solution key for every question are prepared by the instructor or paper-setter who frames the examination test paper. The points in the solution key are collected from the specified text book and are used as a baseline in evaluating the student answer.

Assessment of objective answer by the computer is moderately easy and well supported in many automated systems. But, in case of descriptive answer, it is an open problem (Kaur, A., Sasikumar, M, Nema, S. & Pawar, S. 2013 & Chakraborty, P. 2012). The assessment of descriptive an- answers is found to be tedious and time consuming by instructors due to the increase in number of examinations in continuous assessment system. Latent Semantic Analysis (LSA) is a commonly used technique for automatic determination of document similarity. When measuring the similarity between text documents, LSA s accuracy improves with the size of the documents. Unfortunately, it does not take into account the word order and hence very short documents may not be able to receive the benefit of LSA (Kanejiya, D., Kumar, A. & Prasad, S. 2003 & Wiemer-Hastings, et.al 1999). Hence it is necessary to identify better approaches for automatic determination of similarity in short documents having its length ranging from one or two sentences to few sentences. Even though there are few attempts in automation or semi-automation of descriptive answer paper evaluation (Lin, C. and Och, F.J. 2004; Papineni, K., e.al.2002; Chodorow, M. 2003 & Wiemer-Hastings, P.2004), to the best of our knowledge none of them focuses on finding the co-occurrence match of multiple words in the student answer content as well as in the question solution key content. Hence, an attempt has been made to solve the problem of automatic evaluation of descriptive answer using vector-based similarity matrix with order-based word-to-word syntactic similarity measure.

TERMINOLOGY USED

The terminology used in this chapter for finding similarity between answer content and solution key content is represented in Table 1 below.

Table 1. Terminology used for question-answer evaluation

Term	Meaning
Subject	Paper in different semesters of a course.
Q	Test paper of a subject with T questions shown as Q= $\{q_1, q_2..., qT\}$
A	Answer paper of a subject with T answers represented as A= $\{a_1, a_2..., aT\}$
S	Question solution le of a subject with T solutions represented as S= $\{s_1, s_2..., sT\}$
a_i	An answer ai consist of a set of j answer vectors represented as $a_i = \{a_{i1}, a_{i2}..., ai_j\}$
s_i	A solution s_i consist of a set of k solution vectors, represented as $s_i = \{s_{i1}, s_{i2}..., sik\}$
$w_{i1}, wi_2..., wik$	Percentage of marks assigned to different solution vectors of solution, $s_i = \{s_{i1}, si_2..., sik\}$
SIM (a_i, si)	A two-dimensional matrix for each question, with a_i answer vectors and s_i solution vectors represented as $a_i \times s_i$ with computed pair-wise similarity, say $sima_{ij}, s_{ik}$ for every a_{ij} answer vector and s_{ik} solution vector.
similarity (a_{ij}, sik)	Pair-wise similarity, $sima_{ij}, s_{ik}$ for every a_{ij} answer vector & s_{ik} solution vector is represented as $similarity(a_{ij}, s_{ik})$.
Theshold,δ	User input threshold value to find the similarity
$n(a_i)$	Number of answer vectors in each a_i
$N(s_i)$	Number of solution vectors in each s_i
$wc(a_{ij}), wc(s_{ik})$	$wc(a_{ij})$ is the number of words in each answer vector, a_{ij} and $wc(s_{ik})$ is the number of words in each solution vector, s_{ik}
$ca_{ij}[w], cs_{ik}[w]$	$ca_{ij}[w]$ and $cs_{ik}[w]$ are the arrays of words common in answer vector a_{ij} and solution vector s_{ik}.
$va_{ij}[u], vs_{ik}[u]$	$va_{ij}[u]$ and $vs_{ik}[u]$ are the arrays of index numbers assigned to words in $ca_{ij}[w]$ and $cs_{ik}[w]$ for u=1 to $wc(ca_{ij}[w])$
instructor/ paper-setter	Carries out descriptive answer assessment.

WORD ORDER SIMILARITY MEASURE FOR EVALUATING DESCRIPTIVE ANSWER

Word-order similarity measure remains as one of the best measures to find the similarity between sequential words in sentences and is increasing its popularity due to its simple interpretation and easy computation (Lirong, X. and Jianwei, S. 2010; Hu, X. M. and Zhang, J. 2009). The metric acts as a guideline in computing the similarity measure of common word pair vectors of student answer content and question solution content, supports in representing the similarity measures of student answer to question solution in the form of a similarity matrix and provides input to the partition-based grouping algorithm for finding the marks obtained under each question in the subject examination. The grouping algorithm selects j answer contents and k solution contents for an answer, a_i, of question q_i, compute ij × ik similarity matrix by performing ij × ik pair-wise answer content and solution content comparisons, and uses the matrix in finding the marks for answer, ai, of question qi (Paul et al, 2014).

The word order similarity between answer vector a11 and solution vector s11 with its respective answer-words and solution-words is calculated by using the following formula:

$$\text{similarity } (a_{11}, s_{11}) = (1-(\text{norm } (a_{11}, s_{11}))) \tag{1}$$

where, norm (a_{11}, s_{11}) which normalizes the difference of common word order pairs in a_{11} and s_{11} can be expanded in the following manner-

$$\text{norm } (a_{11}, s_{11}) = \sum^{u}$$

$u\ i{=}1$

$|va_{11}[i]{-}vs_{11}[i]|$

$$|va_{11}[i]{+}vs_{11}[i]| \tag{2}$$

Sample of a similarity matrix with computed pair-wise similarity say sima_{ij}, s_{ik} for a1 answer vectors and s1 solution vectors corresponding to a question, q1 is represented in Table.2. The computation of similarity of j answers with k solutions of a question, q1 is carried out by calculating the similarity of a1 j × s1k pairs of answer vectors and solution vectors.

Table 2. Similarity matrix representation of answer content and solution content

s1/a1	$^s11$	$^s12$	$^s13$	...	^s1k
$^a11$	sima_{11}, s_{11}	sima_{11}, s_{12}	sima_{11}, s_{13}	...	sima_{11}, s_{1k}
$^a12$	sima_{12}, s_{11}	sima_{12}, s_{12}	sima_{12}, s_{13}	...	sima_{12}, s_{1k}
$^a13$	sima_{13}, s_{11}	sima_{13}, s_{12}	sima_{13}, s_{13}	...	sima_{13}, s_{1k}
$^a14$	sima_{14}, s_{11}	sima_{14}, s_{12}	sima_{14}, s_{13}	...	sima_{14}, s_{1k}
$^a15$	sima_{15}, s_{11}	sima_{15}, s_{12}	sima_{15}, s_{13}	...	sima_{15}, s_{1k}
...	...	...	...	...	...
^a1j	sima_{1j}, s_{11}	sima_{1j}, s_{12}	sima_{1j}, s_{13}	...	sima_{1j}, s_{1k}

PROBLEM STATEMENT

Given an answer a_i of answer paper A for question q_i of test paper Q for a subject S, consisting of j answer vectors represented as $a_i = \{a_{i1}, a_{i2}, ..., a_{ij}\}$ and its solution s_i consisting of k solution vectors, represented as $s_i = \{s_{i1}, s_{i2}, ..., s_{ik}\}$, the problem is to find the marks obtained for question q_i. An a_{ij} can be said to satisfy s_{ik} if similarity $(a_{ij}, sik) >= \delta$, where δ is the user input threshold value to find the similarity. The similarity (a_{ij}, sik) function could use any of the similarity measures available. We have used word order similarity to perform the experimental study.

The main modules of this problem are represented in Figure.1 below.

Figure 1. Main modules of question-marks-evaluator

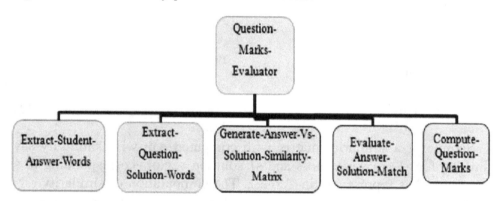

The brief details of modules are presented below:

1. **Extract-Student-Answer-Words:** Input a_i (i=1 to T) and for each ai in the answer le, it extracts answer vectors, $\{a_{i1}, a_{i2}..., aij\}$ for j=1 to $n(a_i)$. Under each a_{ij}, it extracts answer-words with their associated order, $a_{ijp}[p]$ for p=1 to $wc(a_{ij})$.
2. **Extract-Question-Solution-Words:** Input s_i (i=1 to T) and for each s_i in the solution le, it extracts solution vectors, $\{s_{i1}, s_{i2}..., sik\}$ for k=1 to $N(s_i)$. Under each s_{ik}, it extracts solution-words with their associated order, $s_{ikq}[q]$ for q=1 to $wc(s_{ik})$.
3. **Generate-Answer-Vs-Solution-Similarity-Matrix:** Input answer vectors a_{ij} (j=1 to $n(a_i)$) with answer-words $a_{ijp}[p]$ (p=1 to $wc(a_{ij})$) for each a_i (i=1 to T) as row headers and also input solution vectors s_{ik} (k=1

to N(s_i)) with solution-words $s_{ikq}[q]$ (q=1 to wc(s_{ik})) for each s_i (i=1 to T) as column headers in the Answer-Vs-Solution- Similarity-Matrix of a question q_i (i=1 to T). For each pair of answer vector a_{ij} and solution vector s_{ik} of

Answer-Vs-Solution-Similarity-Matrix, compute similarity (a_{ij}, s_{ik}) for j=1 to n(ai)and for k=1 to N(si) using any standard similarity measuring scheme. Represent the result of computation as Answer-Vs-Solution-Similarity-Matrix.

4. **Evaluate-Answer-Solution-Match:** For each answer vector in the Answer-Vs-Solution-Similarity-Matrix of a question, it finds the highest value of similarity among the set of computed similarity(a_{ij}, s_{ik}) >=δ, for i=1 to T, for j=1 to n (ai) and for k=1 to N (s_k).

If the highest value of similarity does not get identified for an answer vector, then the answer vector is considered to be incorrect and is represented as incorrect, else the answer vector is represented as correct.

5. **Compute-Question-Marks:** Using Answer-Vs-Solution-Similarity-Matrix of a question qi having its answer a_i with its answer vector a_{i1}, ai_2..., aij, the percentage of marks, w_{i1}, wi_2..., wik that corresponds to s_{i1}, si_2,...,s_{ik} of correct answer vectors is identified. The summation of all identified percentage of marks is computed and is represented as Question-Marks. Under each question qi, Grouping Algorithm does the selection of the highest pair-wise similarity among the successful answer vector, a_{i1}, ai_2..., ai_j to solution vector, s_{i1}, si_2,...,s_{ik} comparisons and carries out grouping of correct answer vectors along with their percentage of marks. The summation of percentage of marks of correct answer vectors of a group is represented as its Question-Marks.

Algorithm Details

Question-Marks-Evaluation has been carried out by processing five different modules namely-

1. Extract-Student-Answer-Words
2. Extract-Question-Solution-Words
3. Generate-Answer-Vs-Solution-Similarity-Matrix
4. Evaluate-Answer-Solution-Match

5.   Compute-Question-Marks with Question-Mark-Evaluation

Algorithm Presented Below

Algorithm 1 (a) Question-Marks-Evaluation using Partition-based Grouping Algorithm (QMEPBGA)

```
terminate-MEPBGA=true
While not terminate-MEPBGA=flase
{
    Call Answer-Word-Extraction (a_i = {a_{i1}, a_{i2}, ..., a_{ij}} for j=1 to n(a_i))
    Call Solution-Word-Extraction (s_i = {s_{i1}, s_{i2}, ..., s_{ik}} for k=1 to n(s_i))
    Call Question-Marks-Evalaution (AW SW, e)
    terminate-MEPBGA=flase

}
Procedure Answer-Word-Extraction (a_i = {a_{i1}, a_{i2}, ..., a_{ij}} for j=1 to n(a_i))
Input: a_i = {a_{i1}, a_{i2}, ..., a_{ij}} for j=1 to n(a_i)): answer a_i of answer paper A for question paper Q
Output: AW= {aw_{i1} [ ], aw_{i2} [ ], aw_{i3} [ ], ..., aw_{ij} [ ]}: set of answer words in answer vector of a_i
// Extract Answer-Words and its associated order by stop-word removal, taxonomy verb removal and stemming
    AW= { }
    for j=1 to n(a_i) do
        extract words from a_{ij} and store it in array aw_{ij}[ ];
        remove stop-words from aw_{ij} [ ];
        extract stem of each word in aw_{ij} [ ];
        AW= AW U aw_{ij}[ ];
    end for
    return(AW= {aw_{i1} [ ], aw_{i2} [ ], aw_{i3} [ ], ..., aw_{ij} [ ]})
end procedure

Procedure Solution-Word-Extraction (s_i = {s_{i1}, s_{i2}, ..., s_{ik}} for k=1 to n(s_i))
Input: s_i = {s_{i1}, s_{i2}, ..., s_{ik}} for k=1 to n(s_i)): solution s_i corresponding to a_i of answer paper
 A for question paper Q
Output: SW = {sw_{i1} [ ], sw_{i2} [ ], sw_{i3} [ ], ..., sw_{ik} [ ]: set of solution words in solution vector of s_i
// Extract Solution-Words and its associated order by stop-word removal, taxonomy verb removal and stemming
    SW= { }
    for k=1 to N(s_i) do
        extract words from s_i and store it in array sw_{ik}[ ]
        remove stop-words from sw_{ik} [ ]
        extract stem of each term in sw_{ik} [ ]
        SW= SW U sw_{ik}[ ]
    end for
    return (SW = {sw_{i1} [ ], sw_{i2} [ ], sw_{i3} [ ], ..., sw_{ik} [ ]})
end procedure
```

Algorithm 1 (b)Question-Marks-Evaluation using Partition-based Grouping Algorithm (QMEPBGA) (Algorithm 1(a)continued ...)

```
Procedure Question-Marks-Evalaution (AW, SW, ∂)
//Evaluate-Question-Mark
Input: AW, SW, ∂
AW= {aw_i1 [ ], awi_2 [ ], awi_3 [ ], ..., aw_ij [ ]}: set of answer words in the answer vector of a_i
SW= {sw_i1 [ ], swi_2 [ ], swi_3 [ ], ..., sw_ik[ ]}: set of solution words in the solution vector of s_i
where,
aw_ij[ ] = {aw_ij1, aw_ij2, ..., aw_ijp} for j=1 to n(a_i), p=1 to wc(a_ij) //set of answer vectors in a_i
sw_ik[ ] = { sw_ik1, sw_ik2, ..., sw_ikq } for k=1 to N(s_i),  q=1 to wc(s_ik) //set of solution vectors in s_i
Threshold =∂: user input threshold value to similarity computation
Output: Marks for q_i, where q_i is the i^th question in Q
//Evaluate- Marks for q_i, where q_i is the i^th question in Q
 ans_sol_match_set={} //Initialization
 answer_marks=0//counter for marks
//Compute Question-Marks
//Compare a_i of A with the corresponding s_i in S
 for  j=1 to 1 to n(a_i) do
       flag =true // flag for finding the best answer-to-solution match
      // Answer-Solution-Match using Similarity-Matrix
       for  k=1 to 1 to N (s_i) do
          if s_ik not in ans_sol_match_set  then
            if similarity(a_ij, s_ik) >=∂  and flag=true then
              ans_sol_similarity= similarity (a_ij,s_ik)
                ans_sol_match =  s_ik
                answer_marks= answer_marks+ w_ik
               flag =false
              else if similarity(a_ij, s_ik) > ans_sol_similarity then
                ans_sol_match =  s_ik
                ans_sol_similarity=similarity (a_ij, s_ik)
          end if
         end if
        end for
         ans_sol_match_set= ans_sol_match_set+ ans_sol_match
       ans_sol_match=null
      end for
     // Compute marks of a question
     Mark of q_i = answer_marks
     end procedure
```

EXPERIMENTAL RESULTS

Implementation is done using PHP and MySQL on XAMPP Server with a 2GHz processor and 1GB RAM.

Datasets Used

The descriptive examination test paper of Information Technology (IT), a subject offered in the first year of three year bachelor's degree course of computer science (B.Sc Computer Science) at Goa University includes thirteen very short answer questions of four marks and eight short answer questions of six marks. The answer paper of IT contains answers for twenty-one questions. For each of the question, the solutions given by the paper-setter/instructor has been used. The solution to each question is in the form of sentences/points. In this experimental study, same weightage is given to all points. Details of experimental data used for computing the marks of each question are as follows:

(1) $Q= \{q_1, q_2..., q_{10}..., q_{21}\}$
(2) $A= \{a_1, a_2..., a_{10}..., a_{21}\}$
(3) $S= \{s_1, s_2..., s_{10}..., s_{21}\}$
(4) $\delta=0.60$

1.   Sample Datasets S and A are displayed in Figure.2 and Figure.3 respectively. We are considering only 21 questions out of 28 questions in Q. The questions qp7quest22 till qp7quest28 are optional questions of Q.

Figure 2. Dataset S of IT having solutions for 21 questions

subject_quest_cd	ques	subject_quest_descr	sub	subject_answer_desc
qp7quest1	qp7	explain fake websites.how do we rec	4	the illegal practice of attempting to steal the identity by setting up
qp7quest2	qp7	What is use of codec in multimedia	4	codec is a small piece of software or hardware which allow us to wa
qp7quest3	qp7	Discuss meaning of ebanking	4	ebanking is a simple and convenient method to manage our money
qp7quest4	qp7	http and https protocols used in inter	4	http send plain text messages whereas https send encryped messag
qp7quest5	qp7	information distribution using pdf	4	pdf is a global standard for capturing and retrieving rich information
qp7quest6	qp7	Explain multicast in multimedia	4	multicast require one to one,one to many and many to many comm
qp7quest7	qp7	virus attack prevention methods	4	never open an email attachment from an unknown sender;update a
qp7quest8	qp7	antivirus software installation	4	good spyware detection tool provide the user with an easy to use s
qp7quest9	qp7	Discuss hacking types	4	network hacking are designed to block the computer network and c
qp7quest10	qp7	explain browser security	4	always use the most current version of the browser;check for the lo
qp7quest11	qp7	regular update virus definition	4	Virus definition is a unique set of binary pattern of virus,virus defin
qp7quest12	qp7	meaning of file share and piracy issue	4	file sharing is the practice of distributing or providing access to digit
qp7quest13	qp7	what are multimedia elements and a	6	multimedia include image types which are the graphical images hav
qp7quest14	qp7	security issues in mcommerce	4	risk of malware attacks;less memory on the mobile device;transacti
qp7quest15	qp7	internet live stream and bitrate in m	6	internet live streaming is the live delivery of live audio and video c
qp7quest16	qp7	credit card payment transactions with	6	credit card is a piece of plastic card containing information about a
qp7quest17	qp7	meaning of ecommerce technology a	6	ecommerce technology enable a business to easily reach across geo
qp7quest18	qp7	Write a note on multimedia applicati	6	multimedia is used in education and training;multimedia is used in
qp7quest19	qp7	shopping cart and its advanatge in et	6	eshopping cart allows to purchase multiple items from the same sel
qp7quest20	qp7	lossy and lossless compression in mu	6	lossy compression reduces the size of a file by eliminating the bits
qp7quest21	qp7	meaning of website.explain static an	6	websites are normally represented by different web pages containi

Figure 3. Sample dataset A of student1 for IT corresponding to questions in Figure.2

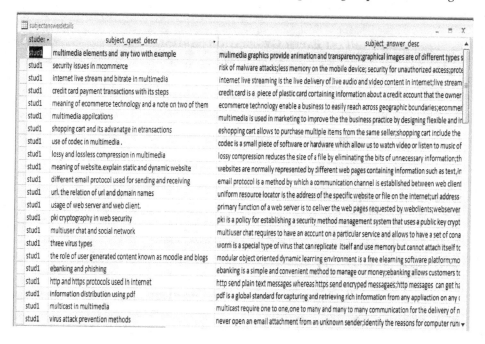

2. Figure.4 presents an extensive screenshot having two parts. First part of it shows Paper Setter input for computing question- wise marks. Paper Setter input includes general details such as Course Details, Subject Details, Test paper Details and Student Answer Details. Second part displays extracted terms of question-solution-content, extracted terms of student1-answer- content and extracted terms of student2-answer-content respectively. Second part of the input has been described in detail as follows. A snapshot of the set of question solutions, {qp7sol1k1, qp7sol1k2, qp7sol1k3,...,} with its extracted list of solution words {illegal, attempting, steal,...}, {fake, website, incorrect, url,...},..., {ebanking, simple, convenient, method,...}, etc., and the set of student answers of student1,{qp7ans1k1, qp7ans1k2, qp7ans1k3,....,} with its extracted list of answer words {illegal, attempt, steal},...,{codec, small, piece, software,} ,...,{ebank, simple, convenient, method, money,...}, etc., for IT is displayed in Figure 4. Extraction of words from IT answer paper and IT solution le has been carried out by performing four dif- ferent pre-processing stages such as Tokenization, Stop Word Removal, Stemming and Normalization of Words.

Figure 4. Screenshot -part1 paper setter's input for IT-question-marks computation, part2.

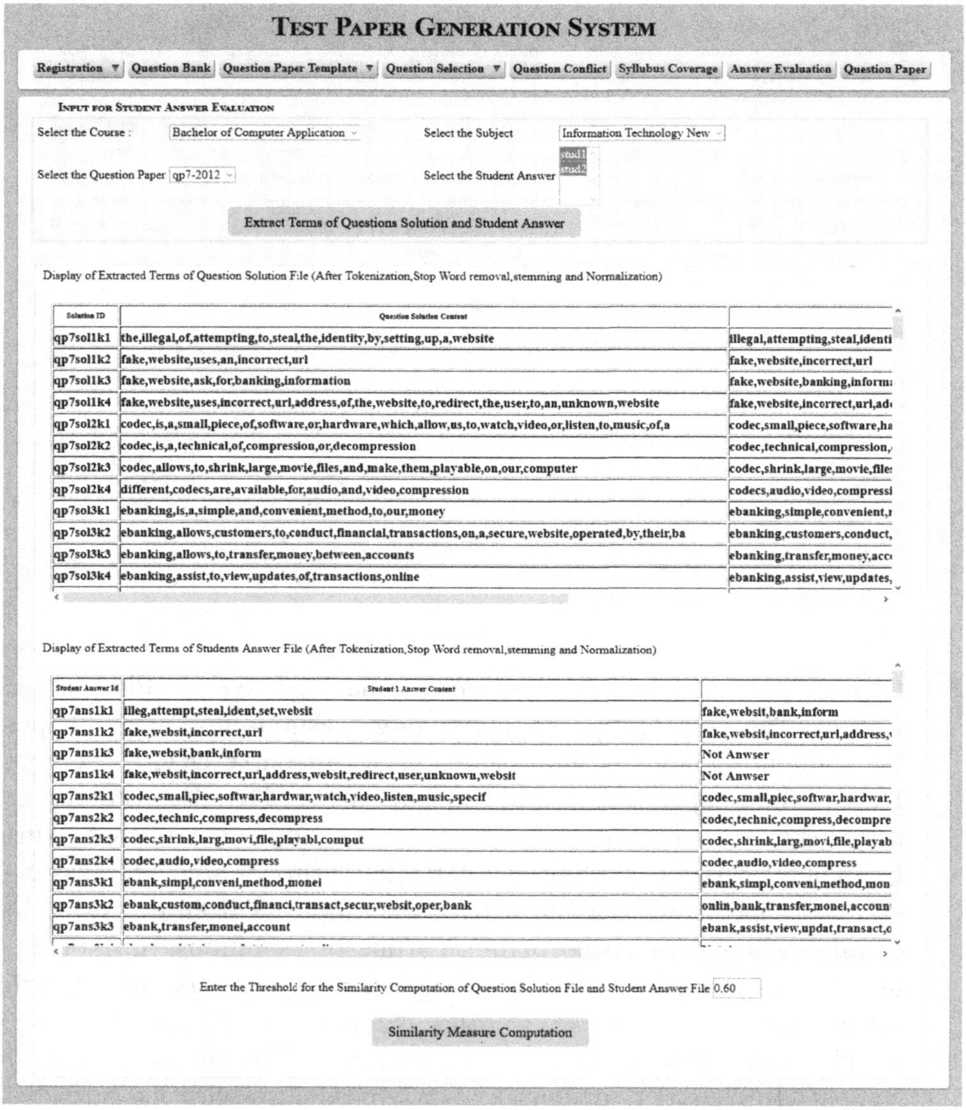

Extracted list of Words of Question Solution File S of IT, Student Answer File A of Student1 and Student2 respectively

RESULTS OBTAINED

Figure 5 shows a sample screen shot of similarity matrix computation carried out using word order syntactic similarity measure for each answer of IT answer paper. Each of the answer among the twenty-one answers in A has been compared against the twenty-one solutions in S. IT-Answer-Vs-Solution-Similarity-Matrix generation is carried out by formulating separate IT-Answer-Vs-Solution-Similarity-Sub-Matrix for each of the twenty-one answers using word order similarity. If no similarity exists between a pair of IT- answer vector to IT-solution vector comparison in an IT-Answer- Vs-Solution-Similarity-Sub-Matrix, word order similarity returns a value of zero and in every other case; it returns a value in the range of 0.0-1.0.

Figure 5. Screenshot of word order based answer-solution-similarity- matrix for computing IT-question-marks

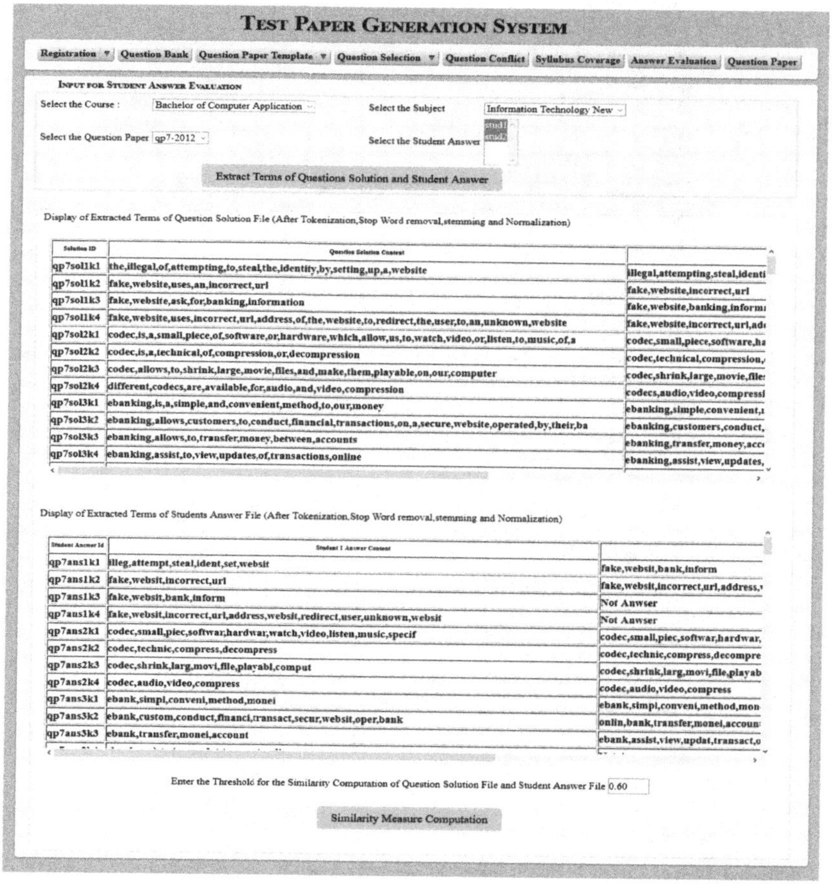

Figure.6 represents the process of generation of IT-Question-Marks for all questions. For each answer in the IT-Answer-Vs-Solution-Similarity-Matrix of $a_i \times s_j$ for q_i, the highest similarity among the pair-wise similarity, similarity $(a_{ij}, s_{ik}) >= 0.60$, for i=1 to 21, j=1 to n (a_i) and k=1 to N(s_i) has been found. The percentage of marks for each correct answer vector, a_{ij} of a_i is extracted from s_j. The summation of percentage of marks for all correct answer vectors of q_i is computed and the result of computation is represented as marks of q_i.

Figure 6. Screenshot of IT-question-wise-marks for it-question-marks computation

TEST PAPER GENERATION SYSTEM

| Registration ▼ | Question Bank | Question Paper Template ▼ | Question Selection ▼ | Question Conflict | Syllubus Coverage | Answer Evaluation | Question Paper |

QUESTION MARKS COMPUTATION

Display of Question wise Marks of Student1 and Student2 for the Subject Infomation Technology

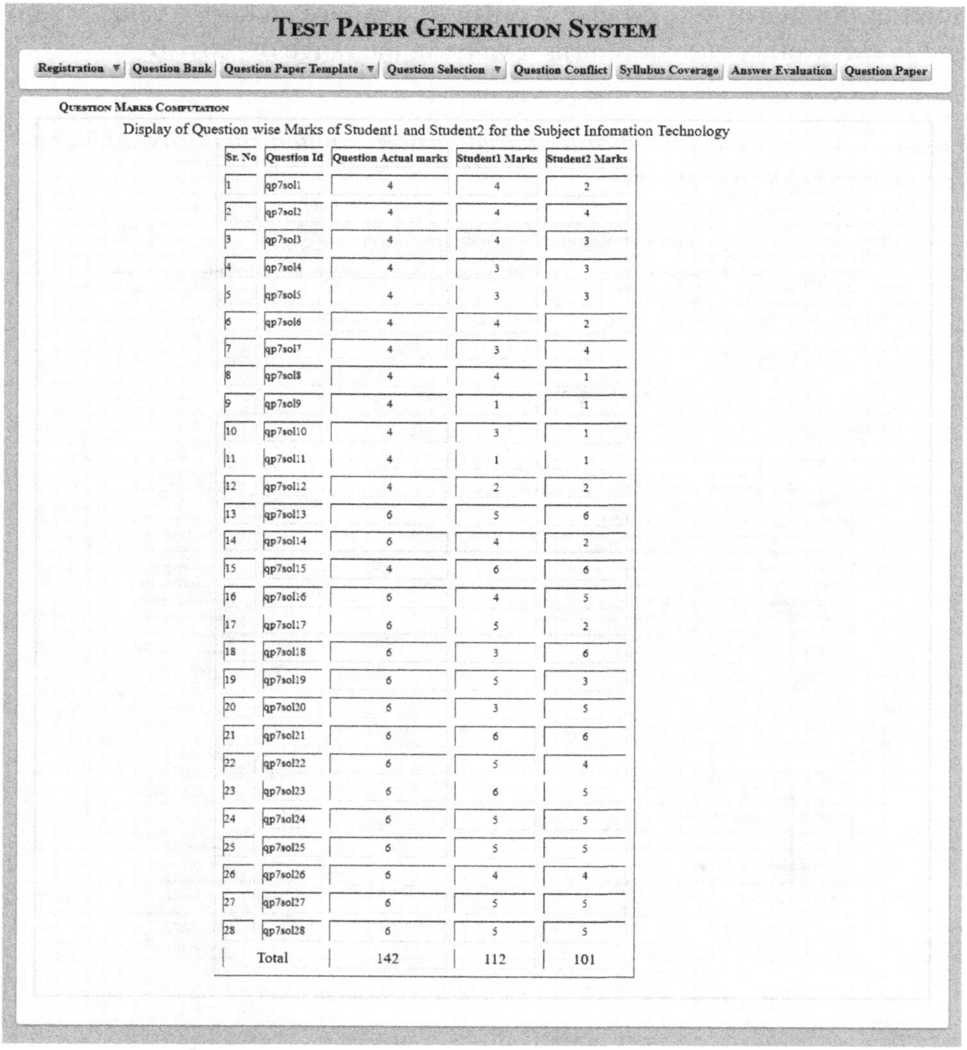

Sr. No	Question Id	Question Actual marks	Student1 Marks	Student2 Marks
1	qp7sol1	4	4	2
2	qp7sol2	4	4	4
3	qp7sol3	4	4	3
4	qp7sol4	4	3	3
5	qp7sol5	4	3	3
6	qp7sol6	4	4	2
7	qp7sol7	4	3	4
8	qp7sol8	4	4	1
9	qp7sol9	4	1	1
10	qp7sol10	4	3	1
11	qp7sol11	4	1	1
12	qp7sol12	4	2	2
13	qp7sol13	6	5	6
14	qp7sol14	6	4	2
15	qp7sol15	4	6	6
16	qp7sol16	6	4	5
17	qp7sol17	6	5	2
18	qp7sol18	6	3	6
19	qp7sol19	6	5	3
20	qp7sol20	6	3	5
21	qp7sol21	6	6	6
22	qp7sol22	6	5	4
23	qp7sol23	6	6	5
24	qp7sol24	6	5	5
25	qp7sol25	6	5	5
26	qp7sol26	6	4	4
27	qp7sol27	6	5	5
28	qp7sol28	6	5	5
	Total	142	112	101

Summary

This work focuses on a new approach for descriptive answer evaluation. Each of the answer ai in an answer paper has been matched with solution si in the solution le by performing $(a_{ij} \times s_{ik})$ pair-wise answer-vector and solution-vector comparisons. The matrix computation was carried out using common word order syntactic similarity which is a commonly used similarity measure for short documents. Results obtained indicate that word order similarity is a good measure in identifying the marks of descriptive answer.

CONCLUSION

This chapter focused on application of partition-based grouping algorithm in descriptive answer evaluation. The process of generation of similarity matrix for a question q_i, corresponding to its answer content Vs solution content, $a_i \times s_i$, has been carried out by performing $(a_{ij} \times s_{ik})$ pair-wise answer-vector and solution-vector comparisons. Grouping algorithm has been found efficient in performing the operations such as formulating groups of question-wise correct answer vectors, identifying percentage of marks assigned to each of the correct answer vectors and computing question-wise-marks in parallel with generation of similarity matrix of every question, q_i. Hence grouping algorithm acted as an aid in successful computation of marks of the entire answer paper. Primary objective of this study was to use partition-based grouping algorithm to identify effectiveness of statistical measures in evaluating descriptive answer. A domain-based WordNet is proposed to get incorporated in the future work to handle the synonyms in the answer content as well as in the question content.

REFERENCES

Chakraborty, P. (2012). Developing an Intelligent Tutoring System for Assessing Students' Cognition and Evaluating Descriptive Type Answer. *International Journal of Modern Engineering Research,* 985-990.

Chodorow, M. (2003). C-rater: Automated Scoring of Short-Answer Questions. *Computers and the Humanities, 37*(4), 389–405. doi:10.1023/A:1025779619903

Dimple, Paul, & Pawar. (2014). Use of Syntactic Similarity based Similarity Matrix for Evaluating Descriptive Answer. *Proceedings of 6th IEEE International Conference on Technology for Education (T4E), 253-256.*

Hu, X. M., & Zhang, J. (2009). An Intelligent Testing System Embedded with an Ant Colony Optimization Based Test Composition Method. *Proceedings of IEEE Congress on Evolutionary Computation (CEC), 1414-1421.*

Kanejiya, D., Kumar, A., & Prasad, S. (2003). Automatic evaluation of students' answers using syntactically enhanced LSA. *Proceedings of the HLT-NAACL workshop on Building educational applications using natural language processing, 2,* 53-60. 10.3115/1118894.1118902

Kaur, A., Sasikumar, M., Nema, S., & Pawar, S. (2013). Algorithm for Automatic Evaluation of Single Sentence Descriptive Answer. *International Journal of Inventive Engineering and Sciences, 1*(19), 6–9.

Lin, C., & Och, F. J. (2004). ORANGE: A Method for Evaluating Automatic Evaluation Metrics for Machine Translation. *Proceedings of the 20th International Conference on Computational Linguistics (COL- ING),* Article No.501. 10.3115/1220355.1220427

Lirong, X., & Jianwei, S. (2010). Notice of Retraction Automatic Generating Test Paper System Based on Genetic Algorithm. *Proceedings of Second IEEE International Workshop on Education Technology and Computer Science (ETCS),* 272-275.

Papineni, K., Roukos, S., Ward, T., & Zhu, W. (2002). BLEU: a method for automatic evaluation of machine translation. *Proceedings of the 40th Annual Meeting of the Association for Computational Linguistics (ACL),* 311-318.

Wiemer-Hastings, P., Allbritton, D., & Arnott, E. (2004). RMT: A dialog-based research methods tutor with or without a head. In *Proceedings of the 7th International Conference on Intelligent Tutoring Systems (ITS).* Springer-Verlag. 10.1007/978-3-540-30139-4_58

Wiemer-Hastings, P., Wiemer-Hastings, K. & Graesser, A. C. (1999). Improving an intelligent tutor's comprehension of students with Latent Semantic Analysis. *Artificial Intelligence in Education,* 545-542.

Chapter 6
Keyword Extraction

ABSTRACT

Keywords are defined as phrases that capture the main topics discussed in a document. As they offer a brief yet precise summary of document content, they can be utilized for various applications. In an IR (information retrieval) environment, they serve as an indication of document relevance for users, as the list of keywords can quickly help to determine whether a given document is relevant to their interest. As keywords reflect a document's main topics, they can be utilized to classify documents into groups by measuring the overlap between the keywords assigned to them. Keywords are also used proactively in information retrieval (i.e., in indexing).

TERMINOLOGY AND NOTATIONS USED

The general terminology used in this chapter is brie y discussed in Table 1.

RELEVANCE OF KEYWORDS IN PLAIN TEXT

As Keywords reflect a document's main topics, they can be utilized to classify documents into groups by measuring the overlap between the Keywords assigned to them. Keywords are also used proactively in information retrieval i.e., in indexing. Good Keywords mostly supplement full-text indexing by assisting users in finding relevant documents (Christos, B. 2006).

DOI: 10.4018/978-1-7998-3772-5.ch006

Table 1. Terminology used for keyword extraction

Notation	Term	Meaning
D	Document	A text document consisting of a set of words
W	Word	A sequence of non-blank characters
WL	Word List	A list of meaningful words
SW	Stop Words	A collection of stop words
S	Stemmed Word	The stem of the word
FC	Frequency count of a word	The number of times the word is found in the document
T	Frequency threshold	User Input criteria to find dense words
N	Document size	Total number of words found in the document
M	Extracted words size	Total number of words from document after removing stop words from the N words.
MS	Min Support	T * (N/ M)
DW	Dense Word	A word whose frequency count (FC) in the document is greater than or equal to the Min Support (MS)
CWx	Candidate Word phrase of length x in document, D	Sequence of x Dense Words which could be the Frequent Word phrase for the document, D
FWx	Frequent Word phrase of length x in document, D	Candidate Word phrase of length x whose FC is greater or equal to Min Support and can be considered as a keyword phrase of length x for Document, D
KW [i][j]	Keyword Set	A table (2 dim array) of frequent word phrases FWi,.i.e. ith row consists of all frequent word phrases of length i. KW[i] [j] represents the jth FWi, frequent word phrase of length i

Keywords are Meant to Serve Multiple Goals

1. When they are printed on the first page of a journal article, the goal is summarization (Christos, B. and Vassilis, T.2008). They enable the reader to quickly determine whether the given article is in the reader's fields of interest.
2. When they are printed in the cumulative index for a journal, the goal is indexing. They enable the reader to quickly find a relevant article when the reader has a specific need.
3. When a search engine form has a field labeled *keyword*s, (Fan, W., Wallace, L., Rich, S. & Zhang, Z. 2006). the goal is to enable the reader to make the search more precise. A search for documents that match a given query term in the *keyword* field will yield a smaller, higher quality list of hits than a search for the same term in the full text of the document.

Despite of these known advantages of Keywords (Yang, Y., and Pedersen, J.O.1997 & WitteI.H, Don, K. J., Dewsnip, M. and Tablan, V. 2004), only a minority of documents has Keywords assigned to them. This is because authors provide Keywords only when they are instructed to do, as manual assignment of Keywords is expensive and time-consuming. This need motivates research in finding automated approaches to Keyword generation. Most of the existing automatic Keyword generation programs view this task as a supervised machine learning classification task, where labeled Keywords are used to learn a model of how true Keywords differentiate themselves from other possible candidate phrases. The model is constructed using a set of features that capture the saliency of a phrase as a Keyword (Bouras, C. et.al 2006; Chengzhi, Z., Huilin, W., Yao, L. and Dan,W. 2008).

There are already some commercial software products that use Keyword extraction algorithms (An, J. & Chen, Y. 2005). For example, Microsoft uses automatic Keyword extraction in Word 97, to fill the *Keywords* field in the document metadata template (metadata is meta-information for document management). These Keywords mentioned above is based on the short list of fixed predefined phrases that captures the main topics of the document.

BACKGROUND

The value of **Text Mining** is well regarded by both academics and industry practitioners because of the existence of huge collections of untapped text documents. On the application side, well-known software vendors such as SAS, SPSS, and IBM (Zhang, Q & Segall, R. 2010; Dekhtyar, A., Hayes, J. Huffman, and Menzies, T. 2004). have devoted considerable resources to developing and customizing text-mining software for industry uses. Currently there is tremendous research work going on in the field of Document Classification (Uysal, A. K. & Gunal, S. 2014; Silverstein, C., Sergey B., and Rajeev M.1998). Keywords are particularly useful because they can be interpreted individually and independently of each other. They can be used in information retrieval systems as descriptions of the documents returned by a query, as the basis for search indexes, as a way of browsing a collection, and as a document classification technique (Arvinder, K., Deepti, C. 2016; Yves, K.1999; Witten, I.H. 2004 & Hayes, J., Dekhtyar, A. & Sundaram, S. 2005). Fundamentally there are two different approaches:

1. Keyword Assignment

2.   Keyword Extraction.

Both use machine learning methods, and require for training purposes a set of documents with keywords (Agrawal, R., Imielinski, T. and Swami, A. 1993; Mohammed, a. and Bassam, A. 2014; Sarkar, A. 2013 & Balázs, R, Ferenc, B., Lars, S.T. 2005) already identified. In **Keyword Assignment**, there is a predefined set from which all keywords are chosen (a controlled vocabulary). Then the training data provides, for each document, a specific predefined class that is associated with it. A classifier (predefined class) is created from all training documents using the ones associated with it as positive examples and the remainder as negative examples. A new document is processed by each classifier, and is assigned the keywords associated with those that classify it positively (Dell, Z. and Wee, S.L. 2006). Here, the only keywords that can be assigned are ones that is in the controlled vocabulary.

METHODOLOGY

Tokenizing the Document

Documents are considered as sequence of strings. Tokenize is a process of splitting the sentence into word tokens. It is considered as a sub task of parsing input. It is an important first step that seems easy but is fraught with small decisions: how to deal with numbers, alphanumeric strings, apostrophes and hyphens, capitalization, punctuation etc., whether to impose a maximum length on tokens, what to do with non-printing characters, and so on.

Stop Words Removal

Stop words, which are language-specific functional words, neither characterize document contents nor discriminate the documents (Jaideepsinh, K & Saini, J. 2016; Schofeld, A., Magnusson, M. & Mimno, D. 2017). They must be removed. Removal of stop word can expand words and enhance the discrimination degree between documents and can improve the system performance.

Applying Stemming Algorithm

Stemming converts words to their stems, which incorporates a great deal of language-dependent linguistic knowledge (Atharva, J., Nidhin, T. and Megha, D. 2016; Lovins, J.B., 1968 & Moral, C., de Antonio, A., Imbert, R., Ramírez, J. 2014). Behind stemming, the hypothesis is that words with the same stem or word root mostly describe the same or relatively close concepts in text and so words can be conflated by using stems. Word stemming can reduce the number of document terms and expand terms. Hence, it increases the system recall while the precision is decreased to some extent.

Keyword – Based Association Analysis

This analysis collects set of words or terms that occur frequently together and then finds the association or correlation relationships among them. Association analysis first preprocesses the text data by parsing, stemming, removing stop words and so on, and then evokes association-mining algorithms. In a document database, each document can be identified as a transaction, while a set of keywords in the document can be considered as a set of items in the transaction, that is, the database is in the format

{document_id, a_set_of_keywords}

A set of frequently occurring consecutive or closely located words may form a term or a keyword. The association mining process can help to detect compound associations, that is, domain dependent terms or keywords such as [Maximal Frequent Itemset], [Keyword Extraction] etc., within a document (Mladenic, D., Grobelnik, M. 1998).

Statistical Analysis for Keyword Extraction

A keyword is a single word or multiple words present in the documents that can characterize and summarize the topics covered by documents. Keyword extraction is a procedure of selecting important, topical phrases from documents (Christos, B. 2006). It is distinct from information extraction. The later involves extracting specific types of task dependent information while the former is not specific and aims to produce topical phrases for any type of factual document (Atika, M., Ali, A., and Ahmer, S. 2009). The approach used for automatic extraction of keyword from text is **Statistical Analysis.** It uses statistics to add a numerical dimension to unstructured text.

Statistical Analysis

By this method, keyword extraction may be viewed as a classification problem, where a document can be seen as a bag of words, where each word is counted for its number of occurrences. Later, techniques such as frequency counts are used to find word pairs, sequence of words and so on. One observation is that keywords often correspond to frequent noun phrase in the text. The following figure display the significance of Statistical Analysis.

Figure 1. Statistical analysis of documents

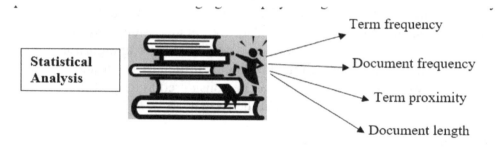

Predefined Class Creation for Document Classification

Assignment of keywords to predefined class is a supervised learning task and allows adding the knowledge acquired by a domain expert. A class is a generalized entity and all its keywords are the special attributes to characterize it (Dumais, S. T., et.al. 1998; Gregory, P.S., Chabane, D., Lise, G. and Robert, G. 2006 & Dell, Z. and Wee, S.L. 2006).

Stemming Algorithms

The Porter (1980) and Lovins (1968) stemming algorithm are two commonly used algorithms. They both use language-dependent heuristic rules to transform word suffixes. An alternative to heuristic rules is to use a dictionary that explicitly lists the stem for every word. In the practice, stemming is facultative. The following Table. 2 lists the behavior of three different stemming algorithms.

Table 2. Samples of the behavior of three different stemming algorithms

Word	Porter Stem	Lovins Stem	Iterated Lovins Stem
believes	believ	belief	belief
belief	belief	belief	belief
believable	believ	belief	belief
jealousness	jealous	jeal	jeal
jealousy	jealousi	jealous	Jeal
Police	polic	polic	pol
policy	polici	polic	Pol
assemblies	assembli	assembl	assembl
assembly	assembli	assemb	Assemb
probable	probabl	prob	prob
probabilities	probabl	prob	prob
probability	probabl	probabil	probabil

Example
user, users, used, using → stemmed output is, use
engineering, engineered, engineer → stemmed output is, engineer

Selection of **Porter Stemming Algorithm** (Wahiba Ben Abdessalem, K. 2013) for our work is due to the following characteristics.

- Improving effectiveness of IR and Text Mining
- Matching similar words
- Combining words with same roots will reduce indexing size by 40-50%

PROBLEM STATEMENT

Problem: Given a user document D, and user input frequency threshold T, find the keyword set, KW consisting of all keywords, K= {k_1, k_2, k_3, ..., k_n} of the document D.

Algorithm for Keyword Extraction

Pseudo Code for Keyword Extractor

Purpose: Generate a list of Keywords

Input: D - A text document, n- number of Keywords to be extracted, T-threshold for extracting documents

Pre Condition: The input document is a text document

Output: A set of keywords

Post Condition: If n is input by user, then n keyword phrases from the Keyword_Set starting from the longest width will be output as keywords, else all keywords from Keyword_Set will be output.

```
begin
1)          Call   Remove_ Stop_ Words (val document D,
var Stopwords SW,var WL)
2)          Call  Get_Stemmed_Words (val WordList WL, var
Stemwords S)
3)          Call  Gen_CW₁(val Stemwords S, var CW₁)
4)          Call  Find_FW₁ (val CW1,var FW₁)
5)          Keyword_Set[1] = FW₁;
6)          Call  Gen_CW₂(val FWI,          var CW₂)
7)       Call  Find_FW₂ (val CW₂,var FW₂)
8)          Keyword_Set[2]=FW₂;
9)        x = 2;
10)       while  (FWₓ != empty set)
11)       {
12)             Call   Gen_CWₓ (val FWₓ,var CWₓ)
13)           Call   Find_FWₓ (val CWₓ,var FWₓ)
14)           x = x+1
15)             Keyword_Set[x] = FWₓ;
16)       }
17)       maxlen = x-1 ; // maximum length of keyword
18)       //output keywords
19)       if  n  < > 0
20)       {
21)          x = maxlen; count = 0;
22)          while (count < n)
23)           {
24)             Cur_Keyword=first Keyword of Keyword_
Set[x];
25)               while (not end of (Keword_Set[x]))
26)               output  Cur_Keyword  of Keyword_
Set[x];
27)                ++ count;
28)               Cur_Keyword = next Keyword of Keyword_
Set[x];
29)                }
30)             if count < n
31)             - -x ;
32)         }
33)       else
34)         {
```

```
35)                 for (i= maxlen ; i > 0 ; i - -)
36)                   {
37)                      Output " Keywords of length i are -"
38)                      Output all Keywords of set Keyword_
Set[i];
39)                   }
40)               }
end
```

Procedures Used Above

1)   Remove_ Stop_Words (val document D, var Stopwords SW, var WL)
Function: This procedure checks the status of a word as a stop word or not. If it is a stop word, it is not added to the WordList.
Input: D - A text document, SW- Stop Word Collection
Output: WL- A list of meaningful words which are not stop words

2)   Get_Stemmed_Words (val WordList WL, var Stemwords S)
Function: This procedure accepts a word from the WordList and retrieves the stem of the accepted word. All stemmed words can be used to generate candidate word phrases.
Input: WL - A list of meaningful words
Output: S- A list of stemmed words
3)   Gen_CW1 (val Stemwords S, var CW1)
Function: This procedure accepts all the stemmed words and retrieves the candidate word phrase of length 1
Input: S - A list of stemmed words
Output: CW1- A list of candidate word phrase of length 1.
4)   Find_FW1 (val CW1, var FW1)

Function: This procedure accepts all the candidate word phrases of length 1 and finds the frequent word phrases of length 1 depending on the Min Support.
Input: CW1- A list of candidate word phrase of length 1.
Output: FW1- A list of frequent word phrase of length 1.

CHARACTERISTICS OF OUR KEYWORD EXTRACTOR

1. It yields an overall judgment on the document as a whole, and does not discard information by pre-selecting features. (i.e., No Generation of keywords from pre-defined vocabulary)
2. It avoids the messy problem of defining word boundaries. (No fixed width specified for the length of keywords)
3. It deals uniformly with morphological variants of words. (By Applying Stemming Algorithm to all words)

REFERENCES

Agrawal, R., Imielinski, T., & Swami, A. (1993). Mining association rules between sets of items in large database. *Proceedings of ACM SIGMOD Conference*, 207-216.

An, J., & Chen, Y. (2005). Keyword extraction for text categorization. *Proceedings of the 2005 International Conference on Active Media Technology*, 556 - 561.

Arvinder, K., & Deepti, C. (2016). Comparison of Text Mining Tools. *5th International Conference on Reliability, Infocom Technologies and Optimization (ICRITO) (Trends and Future Directions)*, 186-192.

Atharva, J., Nidhin, T., & Megha, D. (2016). Modified Porter Stemming Algorithm. *International Journal of Computer Science and Information Technologies*, 7(1), 266–269.

Atika, M., Ali, A., & Ahmer, S. (2009). Knowledge Discovery using Text Mining: A Programmable Implementation on Information Extraction and Categorization. *International Journal of Multimedia and Ubiquitous Engineering*, 4(2), 183–188.

Balázs, R., Ferenc, B., & Lars, S. T. (2005). On Benchmarking Frequent Itemset Mining Algorithms from measurement to practice. *Proceedings of the 1st international workshop on open source data mining: frequent pattern mining implementations*, 36–45.

Bouras, C., Dimitriou, C., Poulopoulos, V., & Tsogkas, V. (2006). The Importance of the Difference in Text Types to Keyword Extraction: Evaluating a Mechanism. *Proceedings of the 2006 International Conference on Internet Computing & Conference on Computer Games Development*, 43-49.

Chengzhi, Z., Huilin, W., Yao, L., & Dan, W. (2008). Automatic Keyword Extraction from Documents Using Conditional Random Fields. *Journal of Computer Information Systems*, *4*(3), 1169–1180.

Christos, B. (2006). The importance of the difference in text types to keyword extraction: Evaluating a mechanism. *Proceedings of the International Conference on Internet Computing & Conference on Computer Games Development*, 43-49.

Christos, B., & Vassilis, T. (2008). Improving Text Summarization Using Noun Retrieval Techniques. *International Conference on Knowledge-Based and Intelligent Information and Engineering Systems*, 593-600.

Dekhtyar, A., & Hayes, J. (2004). Text is Software Too. *Proceedings of the International Workshop on Mining of Software Repositories (MSR) 2004*, 22-27.

Dell, Z., & Wee, S. L. (2006). Extracting key-substring-group features for text classification. *Proceedings of the twelfth ACM SIGKDD international conference on Knowledge discovery and data mining*, 474–483.

Dumais, S. T., Platt, J., Heckerman, D., & Sahami, M. (1998). Inductive learning algorithms and representations for text categorization. *Proceedings of the 7th International Conference on Information and Knowledge Management*, 148-155. 10.1145/288627.288651

Fan, W., Wallace, L., Rich, S., & Zhang, Z. (2006). Tapping the Power of Text Mining. *Communications of the ACM*, *49*(9), 76–82. doi:10.1145/1151030.1151032

Gregory, P.S., Chabane, D., Lise, G., & Robert, G. (2006). What Are the Grand Challenges for Data Mining? KDD-2006 Panel Report. *ACM SIGKDD Explorations Newsletter*.

Hayes, J., Dekhtyar, A., & Sundaram, S. (2005). Text Mining for Software Engineering: How Analyst Feedback Impacts Final Results. *Software Engineering Notes*, *30*(4), 1–5. doi:10.1145/1082983.1083153

Jaideepsinh, K., & Saini, J. (2016). Stop-Word Removal Algorithm and its Implementation for Sanskrit Language. *International Journal of Computers and Applications*, 15–17.

Lovins, J. B. (1968). Development of a Stemming Algorithm. *Mechanical Translation and Computational Linguistics*, *11*(1/2), 22–31.

Mladenic, D., & Grobelnik, M. (1998). Word Sequences as Features in Text Learning. *Proceedings of Seventh IEEE Electrotechnical and Computer Science Conference*, 145 – 148.

Mohammed, A., & Bassam, A. (2014). An improved Apriori algorithm for association rules. *International Journal on Natural Language Computing, 3*(1), 21-29.

Moral, C., de Antonio, A., Imbert, R., & Ramírez, J. (2014). A Survey of Stemming Algorithms in Information Retrieval. *Information Research*, *19*(1), 605–627.

Sarkar, A. (2013). Modified Apriori Algorithm to find out Association Rules using Tree based Approach. *International Journal of Computer Applications*, 25-28.

Schofeld, A., Magnusson, M., & Mimno, D. (2017). Pulling out the stops: rethinking stopword removal for topic models. *Proceedings of the fifteenth Conference of the European Chapter of the Association for Computational Linguistics*, *2*(1), 432–436. 10.18653/v1/E17-2069

Silverstein, C., Sergey, B., & Rajeev, M. (1998). Beyond Market Baskets: Generalizing Association Rules to Dependence Rules. *Data Mining and Knowledge Discovery*, *2*(1), 39–68. doi:10.1023/A:1009713703947

Uysal, A. K., & Gunal, S. (2014). The impact of preprocessing on text classification. *Information Processing & Management*, *50*(1), 104–112. doi:10.1016/j.ipm.2013.08.006

Wahiba Ben Abdessalem, K. (2013). A New Stemmer to Improve Information Retrieval. *International Journal of Network Security & Its Applications*, *5*(4), 143–154. doi:10.5121/ijnsa.2013.5411

Witten, I. H. (2004). Adaptive text mining: Inferring structure from sequences. *Journal of Discrete Algorithms*, 2(2), 137–159. doi:10.1016/S1570-8667(03)00084-4

Witten, I. H., Don, K. J., Dewsnip, M., & Tablan, V. (2004). Text mining in a digital library. *International Journal on Digital Libraries*, *4*(1), 56–59. doi:10.100700799-003-0066-4

Yang, Y., & Pedersen, J. O. (1997). A comparative study on feature selection in text categorization. *Proceedings of the fourteenth International Conference on Machine Learning*, 412-420.

Yves, K. (1999). Knowledge discovery in texts: A definition, and applications. *International Symposium on Methodologies for Intelligent Systems, ISMIS 1999: Foundations of Intelligent Systems*, 16-29.

Zhang, Q., & Segall, R. (2010). Commercial Data Mining Software. *The Data Mining and Knowledge Discovery Handbook*, 1245-1268.

Chapter 7
Document Classification

ABSTRACT

Keywords can be used as attributes for mining rules or as a basis for measuring the similarity of new (unclassified) documents with existing (classified) ones. The focus is on the problem of extracting keywords from document collection in order to use them as attributes for document classification. Document classification is a hot topic in machine learning. Typical approaches extract "features," generally words, from document, and use the feature vectors as input to a machine learning scheme that learns how to classify documents. This "bag of keywords" model neglects keyword order and contextual effects.

DOCUMENT CLASSIFICATION: ROLE OF KEYWORDS

Survey shows that text classification is a typical scholarly activity in literary study, and automatic text classification methods can be used in three scenarios.

1. The first is **Information Organization** - A classifier can learn the target category concepts (e.g. news article about trade, acquisition, etc.) from the training documents, and then assign new documents into these predefined categories.
2. The second purpose is **Knowledge Discovery** - A successful classifier can provide insights to understand a target concept by revealing the correlations between the features and the concept.

DOI: 10.4018/978-1-7998-3772-5.ch007

3.   The third purpose is **Example-based Retrieval** - A classifier might be able to learn a concept from a small number of training documents with the help of semi-supervised learning or active learning methods, and then retrieve more documents similar to the training examples from a large collection.

Automatic document classification methods are tremendously used in research domain of textual documents due to,

- The numerous and important domains of application
- The indispensability in many applications
- The implausibility of manual alternative
- The productivity of machine learning
- Large amount of digital form of documents

NEED FOR DOCUMENT CLASSIFICATION

The goal of text classification is to (semi) automate the categorization process. It is also useful for reducing cost and improving performance (including accuracy and consistency) of text processing.

Scope of Text Classification

Text Classification could be considered as the application of (semi) automatic methods in order to choose, from a set of predefined classification codes, the appropriate one (category / class) for a given new document. Various studies have focused on the construction of a model (Rule or Tree) related to the existence of keywords in order to assign the class of the unclassified document. The text collection is divided into documents and each document is characterized by a number of keywords (Yang, Y., and Pedersen, J.O, 1997). In automatic document classification, for example, for classifying newspaper articles into predefined categories such as politics and sports, the crucial step is how to select appropriate keywords. With traditional classification methods based on the vector space model, frequent words are emphasized and therefore low- frequency words tend to be disregarded. However, there often exist low-frequency words that are effective for classification. For instance, technical phrases can appear in specific categories whose frequencies are generally low, even though they are effective keywords. The two main trends for automation are (Dumais, S. T., et.al 1998),

- **Knowledge Based Approach**
- **Learning Based Approach**

Knowledge Based Approach

Knowledge about classification is obtained from experts and codified in the form of classification rules.

Learning Based Approach

- Experts are requested not to explain but to classify examples
- Information Retrieval (IR) and Machine Learning (ML) techniques are used to induce an automatic classifier
- The knowledge acquisition problem is reduced

METHODOLOGY

The construction of the keyword list is considered as an important and useful research subject in the domain of document classification. We have proposed an algorithm that is based on the idea that the appropriate text classification method is the one that is based on automatic keyword generation. These keywords are frequent within the documents of only one or few classes in the training set. This algorithm reduces the search space by matching the extracted keyword list to the predefined classes with well-defined set of keywords. The knowledge-based approach of text classification is selected to create the predefined vocabulary of classes.

PROBLEM STATEMENT

Problem: Let, $C = \{c_1, c_2, ... c_m\}$ be a set of classes and $CKi = \{\{k_{ij}, w_{ij}\}, j=1$ to $m\}$ represent the m number of (keyword, weight) pairs assigned to each class i by the class/domain/category experts. These value pairs could also be generated during the training phase. But we have considered them as being assigned by experts in that class/category.

The task of text classification consists of assigning to an input document D, consisting of keywords say Key1, Key2, ..., KeyN, a class C_k such that the CWK(D, C_k) *Cumulative Weight of Keywords* of document D in class C_k, is maximum compared to that in any other class. The *Cumulative Weight of Keywords* of a document in a class is defined as sum of the corresponding weights of keywords of document in that class. That is CWK (D, C_k) = Summation of (w_{kj} of all keywords k_{kj} in class C_k which are keywords of document D).

Algorithm for Document Classifier

Pseudo Code for Document Classifier

```
 Purpose:              Identification of the class depending on
the extracted Keyword_Set of document D
 Input:                A set of some predefined classes - C =
{c1, c2, c3, ..., cn} and  Keyword_Set - one dimensional array
of extracted Keywords  of document D
 Pre-Condition: CK_i = { {k_ij,w_ij} } j=1 to m} representing the  m
number of (keyword, weight) pairs that  are assigned to each
class i (i = 1 to n) by the class/domain experts.
 Output:              Selected class C of the document,D
 begin
1.         for each class C_i
2.         find the CWK (D, C_i);
3.         Sort the classes C_i in descending order of CWK (D,
C_i) found in step 2 above.
4.         Selected class C of document D = the first class in
the sorted list.
5.         If there is restriction on number of documents that
can be assigned to a class and if
     first class is full, then the next class in sorted list
is selected and so on...
 end
```

CHARACTERISTICS OF OUR DOCUMENT CLASSIFIER

- Knowledge based approach to classification
- Automatically group related documents based on their contents

- No predetermined training sets or taxonomies
- Predefined Weights to keywords of each class

REFERENCES

Dumais, S. T., Platt, J., Heckerman, D., & Sahami, M. (1998). Inductive learning algorithms and representations for text categorization. *Proceedings of the seventh international Conference on Information and Knowledge Management.* 10.1145/288627.288651

Yang, Y., & Pedersen, J. O. (1997). A comparative study on feature selection in text categorization. *Proceedings of the 14th International Conference on Machine Learning*, 412-420.

Chapter 8
System Analysis and Design for Document Classification

ABSTRACT

The text-mining process starts with a keyword search in text collections. Current text processing technology allows a search technique beyond simple Boolean searches by using natural language queries. Since search engines can recognize any of thousands of keywords and phrases but not the concepts behind the text, it is necessary for researchers to construct an automatic keyword extractor to generate the "Keyword List" for each document. Later, this list can act as the knowledge base to associate unorganized documents to meaningful classes. Failures in identifying the keywords for a certain concept will result in missing values or data for that specific concept.

FACT FINDING

Technology is nearly at a point that Text Classification can apply automated **Text Mining** approaches to develop strategic information. Much of the relevant information is contained on Textual documents and is freely available if one can gain access to it. **Text Mining** applications are expensive and relatively crude, but as interest grows in this, prices will diminish and functionality will improve. Domain intelligence plays an important role when **Text Mining** tools make strategic and operational decisions.

One particular focus for IT has been on using Data Mining techniques to extract meaningful patterns and build predictive customer relationship

DOI: 10.4018/978-1-7998-3772-5.ch008

models from textual data. Although widely used, data mining is currently widely available only to structured, numeric databases. However, a majority of business information exists in the form of unstructured or semi structured text documents or in Web based data sources. The traditional way of processing text information involves human actions in information gathering, analysis, and dissemination. This requires substantial investment of money, time, and human resources.

Moreover, it is difficult to combine qualitative text data with quantitative numeric data in business analyses. Therefore, there is a pressing need to develop a method that can accurately extract business intelligence from large text collections and integrate the fragmented information into business intelligence databases.

The text-mining process starts with a keyword search in text collections. Current text processing technology allows a search technique beyond simple Boolean searches by using natural language queries. Since search engines can recognize any of thousands of keywords and phrases but not the concepts behind the text, it is necessary for researchers to construct an automatic keyword extractor to generate the "Keyword List" for each Document. Later, this list can act as the knowledge base to associate unorganized Documents to meaningful Classes. Failures in identifying the keywords for a certain concept will result in missing values or data for that specific concept.

DATA FLOW DIAGRAM FOR DOCUMENT CLASSIFIER

Figure 1. Context level (Level 0) of data flow diagram

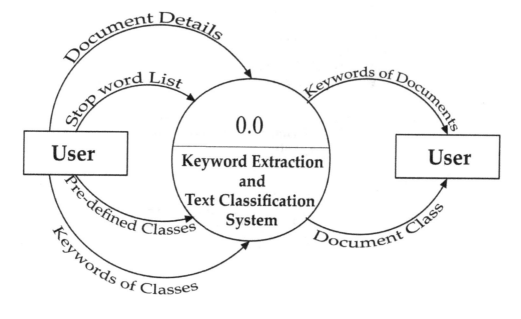

Figure 2. Level 1 of data flow diagram

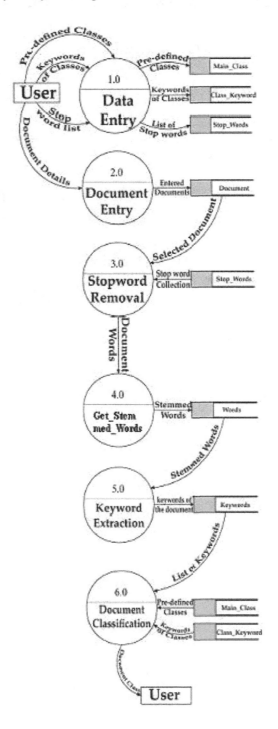

ENTITY RELATIONSHIP DIAGRAM
OF DOCUMENT CLASSIFIER

Figure 3. Entity, relationship and cardinality of document classifier

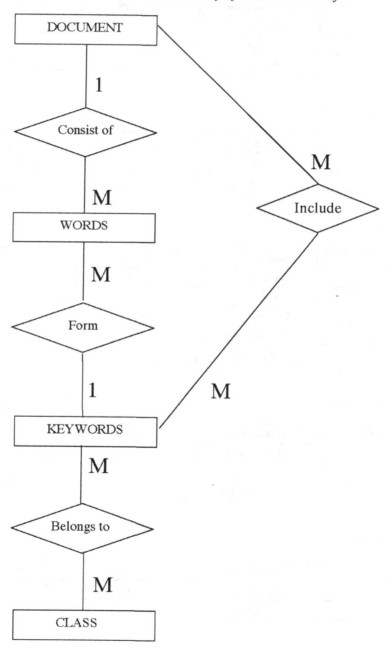

DATABASE DESIGN OF DOCUMENT CLASSIFIER

Table 1. Document

Sr.No	Attribute Name	Data Type	Size
	doc_id (p)	Text	10
	doc_content	Memo	
	doc_path	Text	100

Table 2. Stop_Words

Sr.No	Attribute Name	Data Type	Size
	sw_id (p)	Text	10
	sw_name	Text	50

Table 3. Words

Sr.No	Attribute Name	Data Type	Size
	freq_word_id (p)	Text	10
	doc_id (f)	Text	10
	freq_word_stem	Text	100
	freq_word_full	Text	100
	freq_word_loc	Number	

Table 4. Keywords

Sr.No	Attribute Name	Data Type	Size
	keyword_id (p)	Text	10
	doc_id (f)	Text	10
	keyword_name	Text	100

Table 5. Class

Sr.No	Attribute Name	Data Type	Size
	main_class_id (p)	Text	10
	class_name	Text	50

Table 6. Class_Keyword

Sr.No	Attribute Name	Data Type	Size
	sub_class_id (p)	Text	10
	main_class_id (f)	Text	
	sub_keyphrase	Text	100

Data Dictionary

Table 7. Document

Sr.No	Attribute Name	Description
	Doc_id (p)	Unique identification number for each document
	Doc_content	Document Description
	Doc_path	Document's directory path of attachment

Table 8. Stop_Words

Sr.No	Attribute Name	Description
	sw_id (p)	Unique identification number for each stop word
	sw_name	Stop word

Table 9. Words

Sr.No	Attribute Name	Description
	Freq_word_id (p)	Unique identification for each word of a document
	Doc_id (f)	Unique identification number for each document
	Freq_word_full	Full word before stemming
	Freq_word_stem	Stemmed root of each word
	Freq_word_loc	Position of each word within each document

Table 10. Keywords

Sr.No	Attribute Name	Description
	Keyword_id (p)	Unique identification number for each keyword
	Doc_id (f)	Unique identification number for each document
	Keyword_name	Full keyword

Table 11. Class

Sr.No	Attribute Name	Description
	Main_Class_id (p)	Unique identification number for each classification
	Class_name	Category name of each class

Table 12. Class_Keyword

Sr.No	Attribute Name	Description
	Sub_Class_id (p)	Unique identification number for each category under one class
	Main_Class_id (f)	Unique identification number for each classification
	Sub_keyphrase	Predefined keyword name

PLATFORM FOR DOCUMENT CLASSIFIER

1. Hardware Requirements
   a. Intel Pentium 4 Processor or Above
   b. 4GB RAM or above
2. Software Requirements
   a. Operating System
      Microsoft Windows 2000/XP or above
   b. Application Tools
      i. SQL Server Manager Studio
      ii. Visual Studio.net or above

Chapter 9
Input Output for Document Classifier

ABSTRACT

The report generated displays a list of automatically generated keywords in each document. A document is allowed to have any number of keywords. As the keywords are getting generated at any pass of the loop, there is no restriction on the width of keywords. Another report is also generated to display the list of the document class. If a document finds its match with more than one class (overlapping classes), the selection of the final class for a document is done on the basis of the maximum weight of the keywords in each class.

DOI: 10.4018/978-1-7998-3772-5.ch009

MENU DESIGN

Figure 1. The hierarchy chart of the menu interface of the document classifier

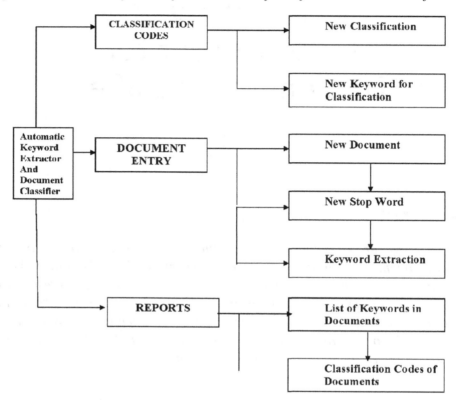

INPUT DESIGN

Welcome Screen

Figure 2.

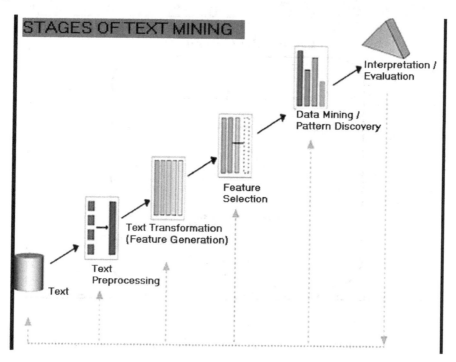

This form displays the sequence of processes carried out in Text Mining such as

1. Text Preprocessing (Syntactic/Semantic Text Analysis)
2. Features Generation (Bag of Words)
3. Feature Selection (Simple Counting, Statistics)
4. Text/Data Mining (Classification- Supervised Learning)
5. Classification (Unsupervised Learning)
6. Analyzing Results

Automatic Keyword Extraction and Text Classification (Main Form)

Figure 3.

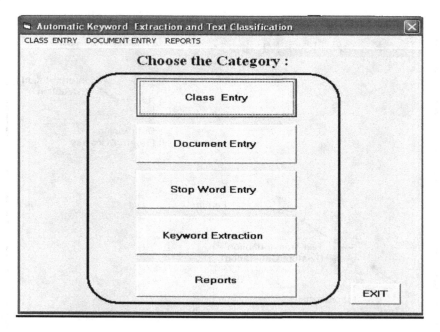

This is the main form for the system. It gives access to individual form designs such as

1. Class Entry
2. Document Entry
3. Stop Word Entry
4. Keyword Extraction
5. Reports

Buttons Used

Figure 4.

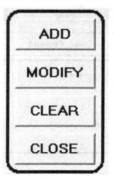

Add: This button allows adding records to tables.

Modify: This button is used to perform modifications to the existing records of the specified table. As the records are getting populated in the "Display Matrix" of each form, it is possible to fetch the needed record from the matrix, update the record and save it to table.

Clear: If the operation is not valid, this button clear the entries made on the form.

Close: This button allows closing the currently active form and reverting to main form.

Exit: This button is used to Exit the project.

Predefined Class Entry Form

Figure 5.

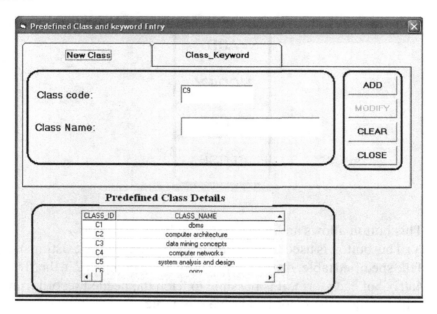

Here it is possible to add details of new class. Each new class is identified with its code and corresponding keyword details are entered. The examples of classes in computer science could be,

1. Data base management system
2. Data mining concepts
3. Computer architecture
4. Computer networks etc.,

Predefined Keyword Entry Form

Figure 6.

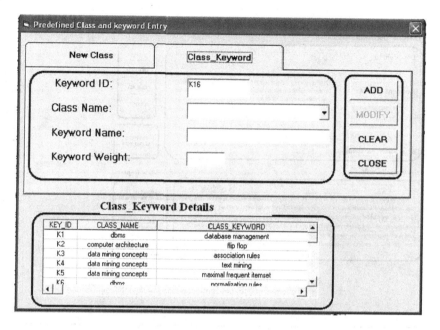

This form allows adding keywords for all the predefined classes. It is possible to include any number of keywords for each class. This predefined keyword list of each class is getting verified by every new document to identify the class to which they belong to. If a new document finds it's match with two or more classes (Overlapping classes), then it is put to a class where the cumulative weights of the keywords are more.

Document Entry Form

Figure 7.

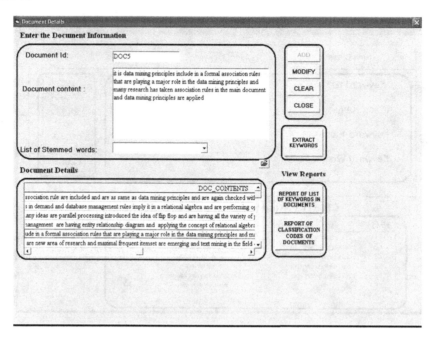

This form enables the entry of new documents. An entered document is spitted to words after stop word removal and stemming. The list of stemmed words of each document is displayed. Each word of the document is passed through two procedures, namely, Remove_Stop_Words and Get_Stemmed_Word. This allows removing all the Stop words from the document as well as generating the stem or root of all meaningful words.

It also includes provision to view the reports of the all the automatically extracted keywords of documents and the document class. There is also a link to the form, which extracts keywords of the given document.

A new document content could get typed in the content entry space or could get attached as follows:

Document Entry Form with File Attachment

Figure 8.

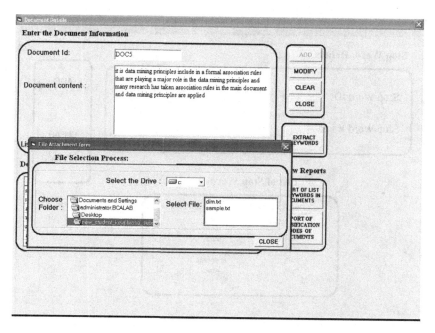

File attachment process allows contents of any file from any folder in any drive of the machine to be copied as the content of the current document. This content is editable as it is automatically copied to the Document Content entry space.

Stop Word Entry Form

Figure 9.

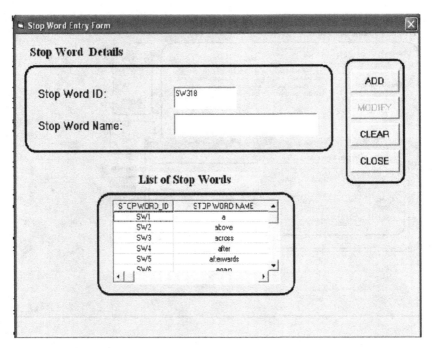

This form is specially included to add the list of stop words. Depending on the context, users are allowed to add any new stop words of their choice. Each of them is uniquely identified by their stop_word_id.

Keyword Extraction: Threshold Entry Form

Figure 10.

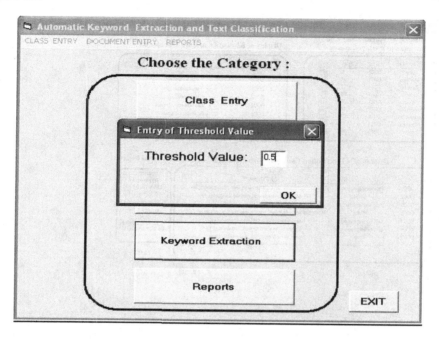

In order to generate keywords, the threshold limit is accepted from the user. This value used to generate the minimum support limit (Min Support) .A phrase is identified as a keyword depending on the calculated Min Support.

Keyword Extraction Form

Figure 11.

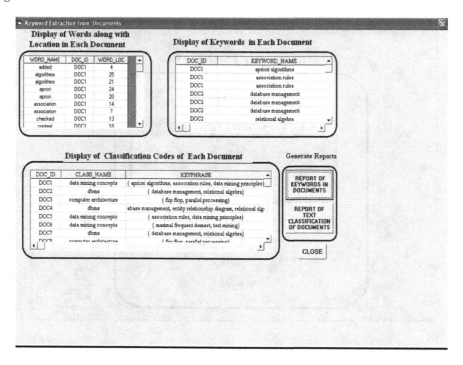

Our first problem is to automatically extract keywords. Keyword Extraction procedure is getting invoked in this form. The keywords are getting generated automatically. This form comprises of three different display matrices. They are

1. **Display of Words Along With Location in each Document**: populate the full list of all words and their corresponding locations in each document.
2. **Display of Keywords in Each Document:** Shows the automatically generated list of keywords of each document.
3. **Display of Document Class:** identifies the class of each document.

OUTPUT DESIGN

Reports Selection Form

Figure 12.

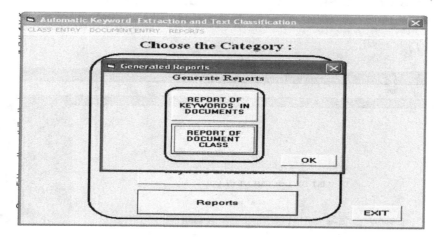

Report of list of Keywords in Documents

Figure 13.

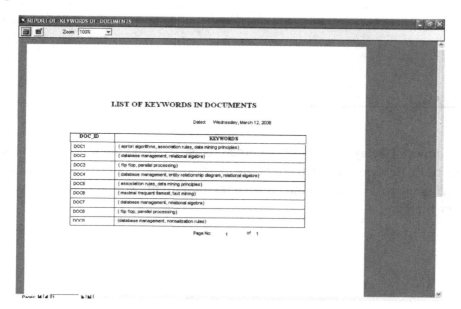

This report displays the list of automatically generated keywords in each document. A document is allowed to have any number of keywords. As the keywords are getting generated at any pass of the loop, there is no restriction to the width of keywords.

Reports of Classification Codes of Documents

Figure 14.

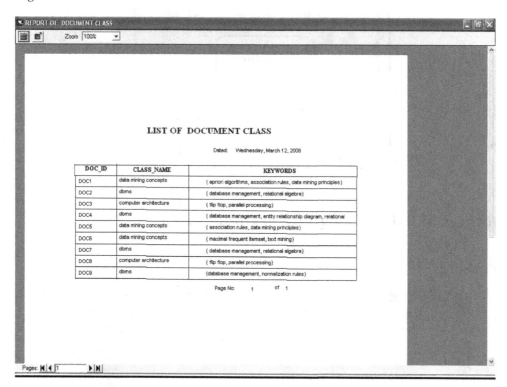

This report displays the list of document class .If a document find it's match with more than one class (overlapping classes), the selection of the final class for a document is done on the basis of the maximum weight of the keywords in each class.

Chapter 10
Implementation and Testing Details of Document Classification

ABSTRACT

It is trivial to achieve a recall of 100% by returning all documents in response to any query. Therefore, recall alone is not enough, but one needs to measure the number of non-relevant, for example by computing the precision. The analysis was performed for 30 documents to ensure the stability of precision and recall values. It is observed that the precision of large documents is less than a moderate length document, in the sense that some unimportant keywords get extracted. The reason for this may be attributed to the frequent occurrence and its unimportant role in the sentence.

SYSTEM TESTING

Reuters Data Set

Researchers have used benchmark data, such as the Reuters- 21578 corpus of newswire test collection (Sholom M. W., Indurkhya, N., Zhang, T. and Damerau, F. 2010), to measure advances in automated text classification. We performed testing of our system using a sample of the same.

DOI: 10.4018/978-1-7998-3772-5.ch010

Modules of Execution

1. Document Entry
2. Stop Word removal
3. Stemming
4. Keyword generation
5. Document Classification

Document Entry

Doc_id : DOC1

Doc_content :

Table 1. Words after tokenization

hard
problem
text
classification
aspects
potential
solution
keyword
extraction
maximal
frequent
item
set
used
attributes
mining
association
rules
basis
measuring
similarity
new
documents
existing
association rules
issue
keyword
extraction
text
collection
emerging
research
filed
promotes
maximal
frequent
item
set
generation

"The hard problem of the Text Classification usually has various aspects and Potential solutions. Keyword extraction and maximal frequent item set can be used as attributes for mining association rules or as a basis for measuring the similarity of new documents with existing association rules. The issue of keyword extraction from text collection is an emerging research field. It also promotes maximal frequent item set generation."

Stop Word Removal (Tokenize and Remove Stop Words)

We are using white space as delimiter to tokenize a document string. A tokenized document contains only language-specific alphabets in lower case and all unnecessary characters such as "," will be removed from the list. Table 1 shows that the tokenization process is not only splitting the words but also changing entire tokenized words into a lowercase format. All tokenized words will then undergo the process of removing stop words.

There are many stop words exist in the above document. To purge them out, a list of predefined stop words must be developed first. The program will then identify and finally remove all the stop words in the document based on the predefined list. Table 2 displays the list of stop words.

Table 2. Removed set of stop words

the
of
usually
has
various
and
can
be
a
used
as
or
for
with
is
an
from
it
also

Stemming

We have used Porter Stemmer algorithm for implementation, for which the source code is available online (Priya, G., Ravichandran, K. S. 2017). The Porter Stemmer cannot stem irregular nouns and verbs. It can recognize past tense and present tense verbs applying the "-ed/-ing" stemming rules. But this stemmer cannot separate plural nouns from third-person singular verbs because it uses the same rule "-s" on both of them. For example, the stemmer chops "sets" to "set" no matter if the context is a verb phrase "sets up" or a noun phrase "feature sets". Consequently the stemming rules by themselves cannot separate nouns and verbs. Examples of terms that have gone through the stemming processes are shown in Table 3.

Keyword Generation

Accept Threshold value, T, from user $= 0.75$
Minimum Support $= T*$ (number of words in the document) / (No. of words extracted)
$= 0.75* (66/25)$
$= 0.75* 2.64$
$=$ Round (1.98)
$= 2$

Process

Rather than attempting an NLP approach, we decided to use an approach that captures the association between words appearing in each document depending upon their location. This is based on automatically identifying frequently co-occurring localized word patterns. By expanding the search for these word patterns to the whole content of a document, our approach models the associations between sequence of words and considers it as a keyword if that specific word pattern repeats to the extent of the user generated Min Support.

Each pass of the loop generates words of corresponding length. (Eg:- First pass can generate words of length one, Second pass generate words of length 2 etc.,).At the end of each pass, a phrase is identified as a sequence of words for the next pass if the frequency count of the same match with the calculated minimum support.

Table 3. Stemmed words

Original Word		Stemmed Word
hard		hard
problem		problem
text		text
classification		classification
aspects		aspect
potential		potential
solution		solution
keyword		keyword
extraction		extraction
maximal		maxim
frequent		frequent
item		item
set		set
use		use
attribute		attribute
mine		mine
associ		associ
rule		rule
basis		basis
measuring		measur
similarity		similarity
new		new
documents		document
existing		exist
association rule		associ
issue		rule
keyword		issue
extraction		keyword
text		extract
collection		text
emerging		collect
research		emerg
filed		research
promotes		filed
maximal		promote
frequent		maxim
item		frequent
set		item
generation		set
		generation

Accordingly, after first pass of the loop, we extract all the phrases of length 1, whose frequency count is more than or equal to the calculated minimum support, i.e., 2. After second pass of the loop, we extract all phrases of length 2, whose frequency count is more than or equal to the calculated minimum support, i.e., 2. The loop terminates when no more sequence of words (x width) matching to the minimum support can be generated.

Result After the First Iteration of the Algorithm

Table 4. Contents of keyword table after first iteration

keyword_name	keyword_loc
associ	27
associ	19
extract	32
extract	11
frequent	40
frequent	13
item	41
item	14
keyword	31
keyword	10
maxim	39
maxim	12
rule	28
rule	20
set	42
set	15
text	33
text	3

The field, **keyword _loc** in the above table signifies the position of the corresponding word in the document. This position is allotted to a word after removing all stop words from the given document.

Result After the Second Iteration of the Algorithm

Table 5. Contents of keyword table after second iteration

keyword_name	keyword_loc
associ rule	28
associ rule	20
frequent item	41
frequent item	14
item set	42
item set	15
keyword extract	32
keyword extract	11
maxim frequent	40
maxim frequent	13

Result After the Third Iteration of the Algorithm

Table 6. Contents of keyword table after third iteration

keyword_name	keyword_loc
frequent item set	42
frequent item set	15
maxim frequent item	41
maxim frequent item	14

Result After the Fourth Iteration of the Algorithm

Table 7. Contents of keyword table after fourth iteration

keyword_name	keyword_loc
maxim frequent item set	42
maxim frequent item set	15

The loop terminates after fourth pass as no more sequence of words can be generated. At the end of fourth pass, the list of identified keywords is-

Extracted Keyword List

Table 8. Contents of keyword table after keyword extraction

keyword_name
associ rule
maxim frequent item set
keyword extract

DOCUMENT CLASSIFICATION

Process

The knowledge-base approach of text classification helps to create the predefined classes by a domain expert. The expert stores the list of keywords of all classes. There is no restriction to the number of keywords per class. It is also possible to add a new class at any time with its own set of keywords.

This is the last module of the system. It checks two predefined tables namely, **Class** and **Keyword_Class**. The generated list of keywords is getting compared with the predefined list of keywords to generalize the class of the given document.

Class

Table 9. Contents of class table

class_id	class_name
C1	Software engineering
C2	computer architecture
C3	data mining
C4	computer networks

Keyword_Class

Table 10. Part of the Content of Keyword_Class Table

class_id	subclass_keyphrase
C3	association rules
C3	text mining
C3	maximal frequent item set
C3	keyword extraction
C3	apriori algorithms
C3	classification rule

Output

Table 11. Final Content of Keyword_Class Table

Doc_id	Keyword_name	Keyword_full	class
DOC1	associ rule	association rule	data mining
DOC1	maxim frequent item set	maximal frequent item set	data mining
DOC1	keyword extract	Keyword extraction	data mining

Finally, the given document is generalized to be of the class - "**Data Mining**". But if this document was getting matched to more than one class, selection of the class to which it should be put would have been done on the basis of the maximum cumulative weight.

PERFORMANCE MEASURES IN TEXT MINING – PRECISION AND RECALL

Precision (P) and Recall **(R)** are the standard metrics for retrieval effectiveness in information retrieval. Many samples of the above data were used to compute the standard information retrieval metrics of precision and recall, using the calculation as follows:

$P = NC / NW$
$R = NC / NM$

Where,

NC = Total number keywords common to both manual and computationally derived list.

NW = Total number of keywords found in the computationally derived list and not found in the manually derived list.

NM = Total number of keywords found in the manually derived list and not found in the computationally derived list.

Recall and precision are often inversely related, meaning that, in an actual text mining system, the precision often goes down when the recall goes up and vice versa. Measuring recall is difficult because it is often difficult to know how many relevant records exist in a database. In binary classification, recall is called sensitivity. So it can be looked at as the probability that a relevant document is retrieved by the query. It is trivial to achieve recall of 100% by returning all documents in response to any query. Therefore, recall alone is not enough but one needs to measure the number of non-relevant documents also, for example by computing the precision. Analysis was performed for 30 documents to ensure stability of precision and recall values. Sample of precision and recall measure for a set of 10 documents is as follows:

It is observed that precision of large documents is less than moderate length document, in the sense that some unimportant keywords get extracted. The reason for this may be attributed to frequent occurrence and its unimportant role in the sentence.

Table 12. Sample data for precision and recall

Docs	NM	NW	NC	Precision	Recall
Doc1	4	4	3	0.75	0.75
Doc2	4	5	3	0.60	0.75
Doc3	5	5	4	0.80	0.80
Doc 4	5	5	3	0.60	0.60
Doc 5	3	3	2	0.67	0.67
Doc6	5	5	3	0.60	0.60
Doc7	4	4	3	0.75	0.75
Doc8	4	4	3	0.75	0.75
Doc9	4	5	3	0.60	0.75
Doc10	5	5	4	0.80	0.80
Average				0.69	0.72

REFERENCES

Priya, G., & Ravichandran, K. S. (2017). Modified stemmer for a medical system — evaluated using predefined metrics. *International Conference on Energy, Communication, Data Analytics and Soft Computing (ICECDS)*, 746-750.

Sholom, M. W., Indurkhya, N., Zhang, T., & Damerau, F. (2010). *Text Mining: Predictive Methods for Analyzing Unstructured Information.* Springer-Verlag Inc.

Chapter 11
Software Tool for Test Paper Generation

ABSTRACT

In this chapter, the authors discuss the features of the tool which is developed using the algorithms designed and implemented as part of the research work carried out. They have named it a test paper generation system (TPGS). At some places, they have used question paper generation system (QPGS) instead of its alias TPGS. The main modules of this tool are (1) test paper template generation, (2) question conflict detection, (3) test paper template-based question selection, (4) syllabus coverage evaluator for test paper, (5) and answer paper evaluator.

INTRODUCTION

In this chapter we discuss the features of the tool which is developed using the multi-objective algorithms designed and implemented as a part of the research work carried out. We have named it as Test paper Generation system (TPGS). Main modules of the tool are-

1. Test paper Template Generation
2. Question Conflict Detection
3. Test paper Template based Question Selection
4. Syllabus Coverage Evaluator for Test paper
5. Answer Paper Evaluator

DOI: 10.4018/978-1-7998-3772-5.ch011

TPGS has been implemented using PHP as front-end and MySQL as back-end on XAMPP server with 2GHz processor and 1GB RAM. It is a web-based tool designed to facilitate automatic generation of qualitative test paper satisfying subject's module constraint, taxonomy's cognitive level constraint, time constraint, type of question constraint, exposure limit of question constraint, question conflict constraint, syllabus coverage constraint, solution key constraint, etc. and there by provide a benchmark for test paper generation system.

THE TPGS TOOL

The functionalities supported by the first module namely Test paper Template Generation is as follows-

Test Paper Template Generation: The two-dimensional test paper template generation is considered as a multi-objective optimization problem. The best approach to generate dynamic examination test paper is by selecting an efficient algorithm to generate a two-dimensional dynamic template. By using the evolutionary computational search technique of evolutionary approaches and the cognitive level assignments of educational taxonomies, this module experimentally proves that the generated test paper templates are most appropriate for dynamic examination test paper generation. The evolutionary approach-based algorithms such as the evolutionary algorithm and the pareto-optimal evolutionary algorithm along with the incremental bi-proportional matrix scaling algorithm outperformed traditional algorithms in terms of coverage of units/modules of a subject, cognitive learning domains of educational taxonomies and marks distribution in the generated test paper. The dynamic template provided the flexibility to select all/few modules of a subject; all/few levels of the cognitive learning domain as well as assign varying total marks and thereby design various types of user specified templates for generating different types of test papers for examinations such as in-semester (20 marks), end- semester (80 marks) and practical (50 marks).

The Figure.1 displays the screenshot for accepting the input of test paper template generation using evolutionary approaches. Flexible options are provided to select module(s) of a subject, select taxonomy level(s), specify the percentage of importance assigned to module coverage as well as percentage of importance assigned to cognitive level coverage. Also, the user is permitted

Figure 1. Input screen for test paper template generation

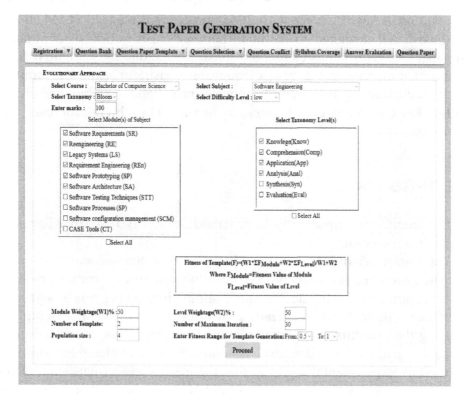

to mention the number of templates required, size of the population for the evolutionary approach, number of iterations for evolutionary approach as well as the range of fitness values to be considered for initial population and successive iterative population generation.

Figure. 2 displays the evolutionary approach based iterative stages of test paper template generation. The population size specified by the user is 4, and therefore, four different templates are getting generated at the initial iteration as well as at the successive iterations. Mutation rate assigned within the source code is 0.5 and therefore one among the two templates undergoes its mutation operation by identifying the module- level-weight(s) of the cells which highly vary its value as compared to other cell values. The identified module-level-weight(s) are progressively applied with (+1) or (-1) operation and accordingly are adjusted to the nearest value as close to the rest of cell values. Also, during the entire mutation operation, many other cell values automatically get adjusted so as to draw out the template satisfying the module

Figure 2. Iterative stages of evolutionary test paper template generation

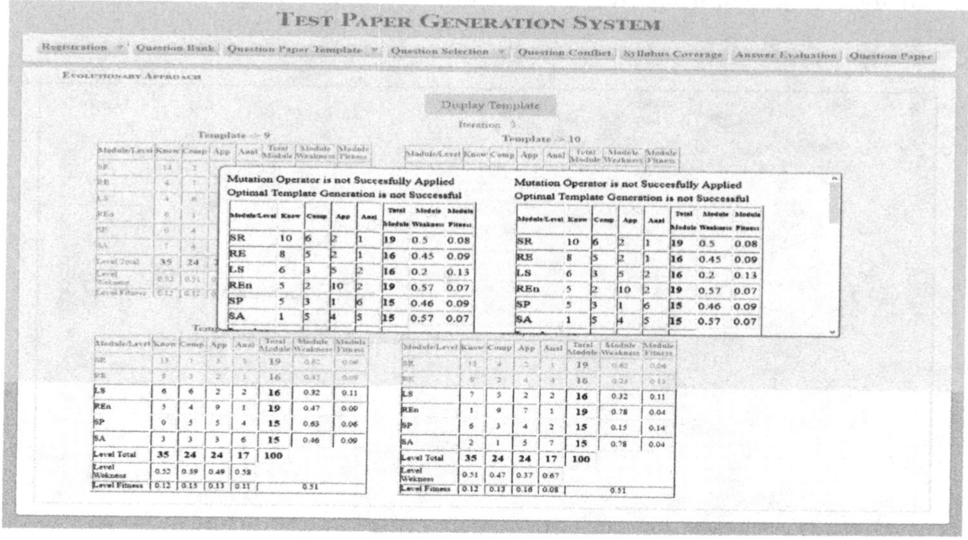

weightages and level weightages. The white window overlapping the actual screen on Figure. 2 does the mutation operation.

Figure.3 displays the successful generation of user specified number of near optimal template(s) at the end of the 28th iteration having template number 112 as the last generated template. The white window overlapping the actual screen on Figure. 3 shows the status of near optimal template(s) generation.

Figure 4 displays the evolutionary approach based final output screen for near optimal template generation with its left-hand side showing the near optimal templates generated before mutation and right-hand side showing the near optimal templates with improved fitness values after mutation. The generated templates are identified to be near optimal as their fitness values are in the range of 0.6-1.0 which is the user specified fitness range. In order to consider a template to be an optimal one, its fitness value is expected to be equivalent to 1.

The evolutionary approach-based test paper templates generated in Figure.2, Figure.3 and in Figure.4 had a major disadvantage that they used randomized approach for assigning module-level weights. Even though it generated population of test paper templates iteratively, several of them were not satisfactory in terms of its fitness. During the iterative population

173

Figure 3. Iterative stages of evolutionary test paper template generation showing the number of optimal template generated at the end of each of the iteration

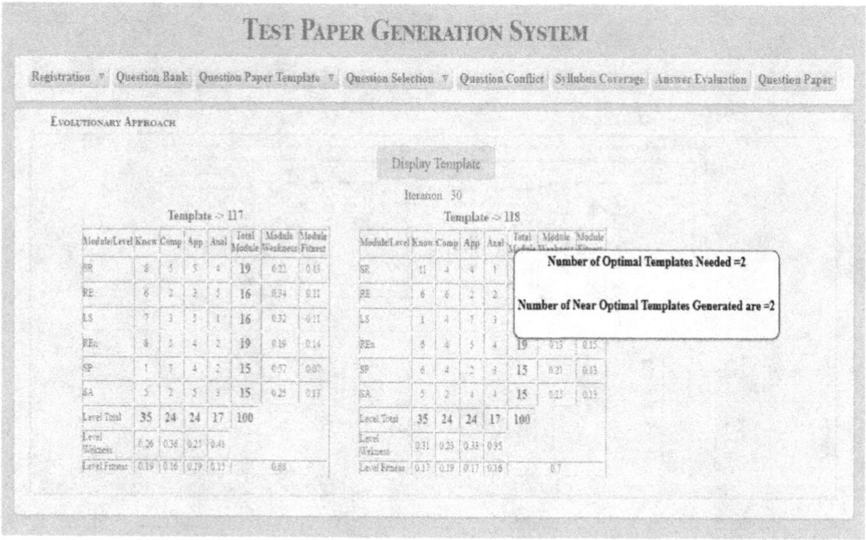

generation, significant runtime delay was encountered. This is mainly because of the wastage of time in identifying a set of random module-level-weights that satisfied both module weights and level weights. Also, this evolutionary programming approach never guaranteed the generation of user specified number of optimal templates even after running it for the user specified number of iterations. In order to overcome these limitations of evolutionary programming, we have implemented an incremental evolutionary approach namely pareto-optimal based evolutionary algorithm that aims to find a set of optimal trade-off solutions or non-dominating solutions known as the pareto-optimal set. Figure.5 represents the initial stage of pareto-optimal test paper template generation for the subject of Software Engineering using the same set of input of evolutionary approach. The template of Figure.5 includes two different module-level-weights in each cell, calculated by using the formula: $x_{mn} = (u_m \times l_n) / TM$, where u_m is the module-weightage, $l_n)$ is the level weightage and TM is the total marks, such that the module-level-weightages finally get adjusted to its nearest integer values.

The iterative stage of pareto-optimal test paper template generation is shown in Figure.6. The significance of using pareto-optimal evolutionary approach for template generation has been highlighted in Figure.6 by showing

Figure 4. Final stages of evolutionary test paper template generation showing two mutated near optimal templates generated at the end of evolutionary approach

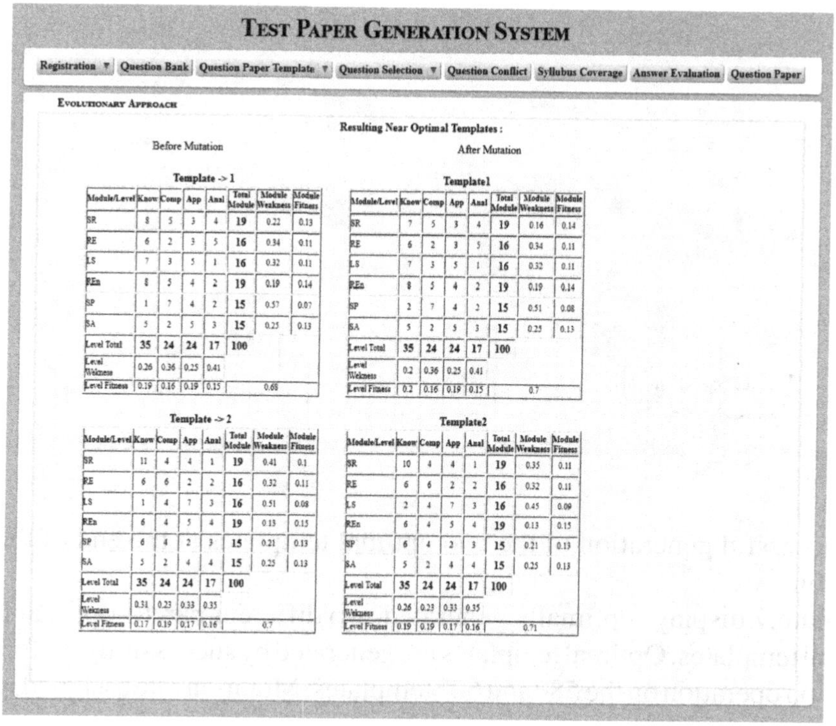

Before Mutation — Template -> 1

Module/Level	Know	Comp	App	Anal	Total Module	Module Weakness	Module Fitness
SR	8	5	3	4	19	0.22	0.13
RE	6	2	3	5	16	0.34	0.11
LS	7	3	5	1	16	0.32	0.11
REn	8	5	4	2	19	0.19	0.14
SP	1	7	4	2	15	0.57	0.07
SA	5	2	5	3	15	0.25	0.13
Level Total	35	24	24	17	100		
Level Weakness	0.26	0.36	0.25	0.41			
Level Fitness	0.19	0.16	0.19	0.15	0.68		

After Mutation — Template1

Module/Level	Know	Comp	App	Anal	Total Module	Module Weakness	Module Fitness
SR	7	5	3	4	19	0.16	0.14
RE	6	2	3	5	16	0.34	0.11
LS	7	3	5	1	16	0.32	0.11
REn	8	5	4	2	19	0.19	0.14
SP	2	7	4	2	15	0.51	0.08
SA	5	2	5	3	15	0.25	0.13
Level Total	35	24	24	17	100		
Level Wekness	0.2	0.36	0.25	0.41			
Level Fitness	0.2	0.16	0.19	0.15	0.7		

Before Mutation — Template -> 2

Module/Level	Know	Comp	App	Anal	Total Module	Module Weakness	Module Fitness
SR	11	4	4	1	19	0.41	0.1
RE	6	6	2	2	16	0.32	0.11
LS	1	4	7	3	16	0.51	0.08
REn	6	4	5	4	19	0.13	0.15
SP	6	4	2	3	15	0.21	0.13
SA	5	2	4	4	15	0.25	0.13
Level Total	35	24	24	17	100		
Level Weakness	0.31	0.23	0.33	0.35			
Level Fitness	0.17	0.19	0.17	0.16	0.7		

After Mutation — Template2

Module/Level	Know	Comp	App	Anal	Total Module	Module Weakness	Module Fitness
SR	10	4	4	1	19	0.35	0.11
RE	6	6	2	2	16	0.32	0.11
LS	2	4	7	3	16	0.45	0.09
REn	6	4	5	4	19	0.13	0.15
SP	6	4	2	3	15	0.21	0.13
SA	5	2	4	4	15	0.25	0.13
Level Total	35	24	24	17	100		
Level Wekness	0.26	0.23	0.33	0.35			
Level Fitness	0.19	0.19	0.17	0.16	0.71		

Figure 5. Initial stage of pareto-optimal test paper template generation

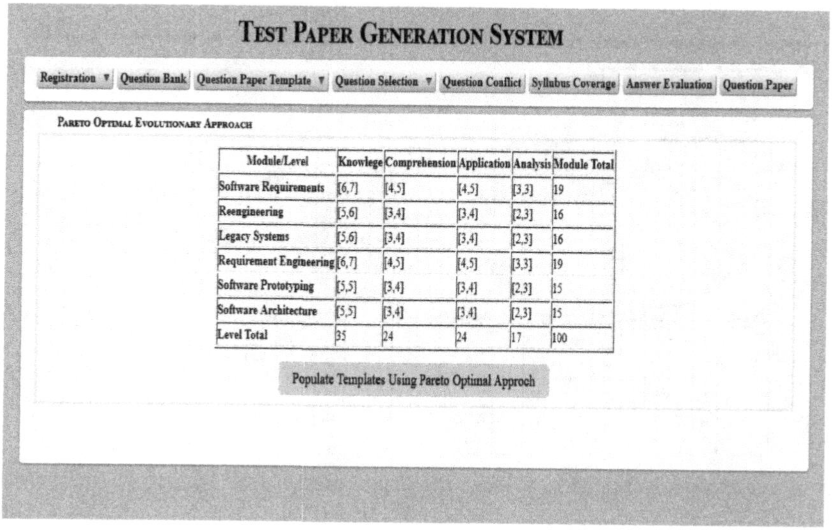

Module/Level	Knowlege	Comprehension	Application	Analysis	Module Total
Software Requirements	[6,7]	[4,5]	[4,5]	[3,3]	19
Reengineering	[5,6]	[3,4]	[3,4]	[2,3]	16
Legacy Systems	[5,6]	[3,4]	[3,4]	[2,3]	16
Requirement Engineering	[6,7]	[4,5]	[4,5]	[3,3]	19
Software Prototyping	[5,5]	[3,4]	[3,4]	[2,3]	15
Software Architecture	[5,5]	[3,4]	[3,4]	[2,3]	15
Level Total	35	24	24	17	100

Figure 6. Iterative stage of pareto-optimal test paper template generation

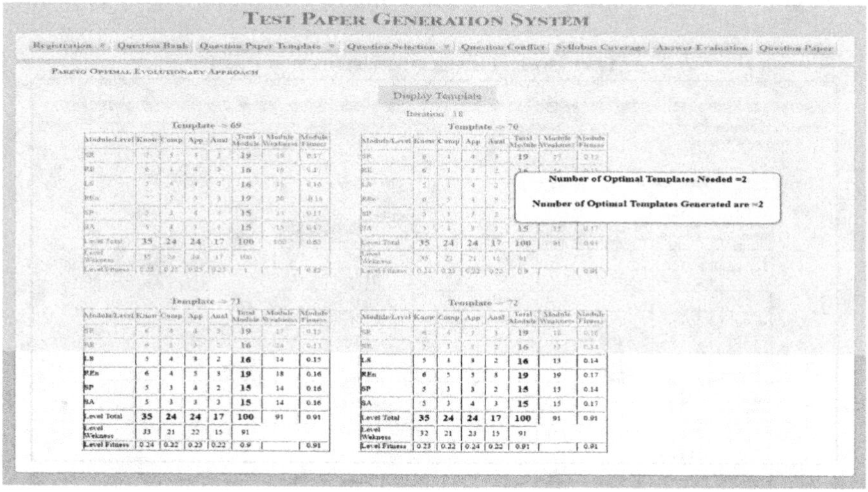

the successful generation of the two optimal templates at the end of the 15th iteration.

Figure.7 displays optimally generated two different pareto-optimal based optimal templates. Optimal templates are generated by successfully performing mutation operation on the 58th and 60th templates. Mutation rate assigned within

Figure 7. Stage of pareto-optimal template generation with optimal templates

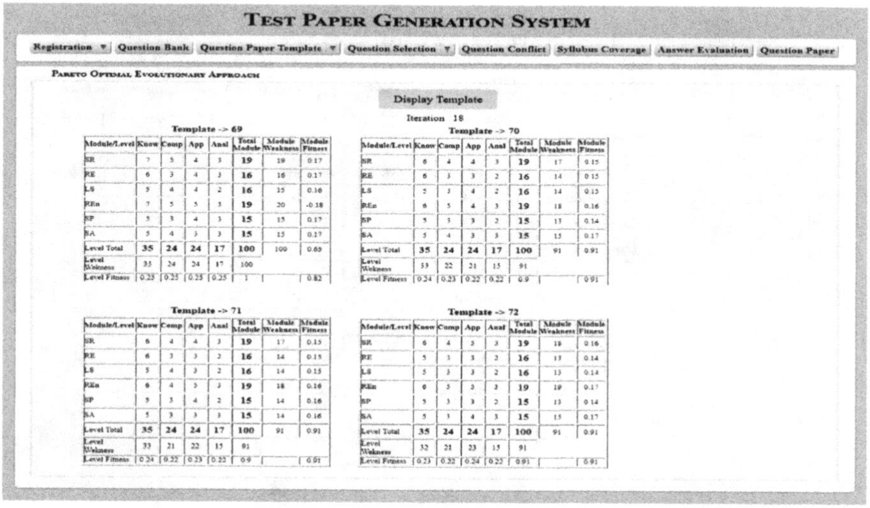

the source code is 0.2 and is carried out using the same method discussed above for evolutionary approach-based mutation operation.

Comparison of the iterative stages of evolutionary test paper template and pareto-optimal evolutionary test paper template generation is represented in Figure.8. From the results shown in Figure.8, it is experimentally found that the pareto-optimal approach has been able to successfully reduce the runtime delay of evolutionary algorithm.

We have used Bloom's taxonomy cognitive processing levels to allot difficulty levels to the test paper templates. We have generated templates with three major difficulty levels such as high, medium and low. High difficulty templates have high distribution of marks across higher/difficult levels of the taxonomy. Medium difficulty templates have proportionate distribution of marks across all levels of taxonomy and low difficulty templates have low distribution of marks across higher/difficult levels of taxonomy. Provision is made in TPGS to prepare graphs of test paper template on different difficulty levels such as low, medium and high. Figure 9 displays the three different graphs of test paper templates corresponding to low, medium and high difficulty levels.

The dynamic templates generated by the previously discussed evolutionary computational approaches such as evolutionary approach as well as pareto-optimal evolutionary approach were successful in providing the flexibility for framing many qualitatively good examination test papers using the same template. But at the same time, the iterative process of generation of population of templates encountered significant run time delay and also does not guarantee to find optimal solutions in a finite amount of time. In order to overcome these limitations, we introduced an incremental algorithm using matrix balancing technique that automatically scales and balances all entries of the template. The bi-proportional matrix balancing technique carries out iterative scaling and proportional fitting of the optimal template so as to satisfy the user specified number of modules, user specified number of levels and user specified marks requirement of each examination.

The bi-proportional matrix scaling approach accept evolutionary approach or pareto-evolutionary approach based optimal template as input and proceeds with scaling of the same Test paper Template (TPT) as per the user specified module constraints, level constraint and total marks constraint and generates a scaled test paper template. Figuure.10 shows the stage at which an optimal pareto-optimal template gets accepted to proceed with the matrix scaling

Figure 8. Comparative analysis of iterative stages of evolutionary approach and pareto-optimal approach based test paper template generation

TEST PAPER GENERATION SYSTEM

Registration ▾ | Question Bank | Question Paper Template ▾ | Question Selection ▾ | Question Conflict | Syllabus Coverage | Answer Evaluation | Question Paper

COMPARISON APPROACH

Evolutionary Approach			Pareto-Optimal Evolutionary Approach		
Template No	Iteration	Fitness	Template No	Iteration	Fitness
T1,1	1	0.6092	T1,1	1	0.5958
T1,2	1	0.6096	T1,2	1	0.6021
T1,3	1	0.6102	T1,3	1	0.6172
T1,4	1	0.6112	T1,4	1	0.6233
T2,5	2	0.6125	T2,5	2	0.6238
T2,6	2	0.6132	T2,6	2	0.6346
T2,7	2	0.6142	T2,7	2	0.6355
T2,8	2	0.6143	T2,8	2	0.6355
T3,9	3	0.6158	T3,9	3	0.6537
T3,10	3	0.6173	T3,10	3	0.6824
T3,11	3	0.6174	T3,11	3	0.6835
T3,12	3	0.6174	T3,12	3	0.6866
T4,13	4	0.6176	T4,13	4	0.6871
T4,14	4	0.6186	T4,14	4	0.6871
T4,15	4	0.6191	T4,15	4	0.6886
T4,16	4	0.6200	T4,16	4	0.6912
T5,17	5	0.6214	T5,17	5	0.6932
T5,18	5	0.6215	T5,18	5	0.7257
T5,19	5	0.6216	T5,19	5	0.7292
T5,20	5	0.6217	T5,20	5	0.7321
T6,21	6	0.6218	T6,21	6	0.7374
T6,22	6	0.6219	T6,22	6	0.7374
T6,23	6	0.6220	T6,23	6	0.7374
T6,24	6	0.6231	T6,24	6	0.7374
T7,25	7	0.6232	T7,25	7	0.7374
T7,26	7	0.6249	T7,26	7	0.7374
T7,27	7	0.6251	T7,27	7	0.7374
T7,28	7	0.6264	T7,28	7	0.7396
T8,29	8	0.6267	T8,29	8	0.7396
T8,30	8	0.6270	T8,30	8	0.8105
T8,31	8	0.6272	T8,31	8	0.8105
T8,32	8	0.6275	T8,32	8	0.8117
T9,33	9	0.6285	T9,33	9	0.8117
T9,34	9	0.6287	T9,34	9	0.8120
T9,35	9	0.6291	T9,35	9	0.8122
T9,36	9	0.6298	T9,36	9	0.8122
T10,37	10	0.6301	T10,37	10	0.8222
T10,38	10	0.6309	T10,38	10	0.8222
T10,39	10	0.6312	T10,39	10	0.8222
T10,40	10	0.6317	T10,40	10	0.8226
T11,41	11	0.6319	T11,41	11	0.8226
T11,42	11	0.6321	T11,42	11	0.8226
T11,43	11	0.6325	T11,43	11	0.8226
T11,44	11	0.6337	T11,44	11	0.8226
T12,45	12	0.6342	T12,45	12	0.8226
T12,46	12	0.6355	T12,46	12	0.8226
T12,47	12	0.6363	T12,47	12	0.8226
T12,48	12	0.6369	T12,48	12	0.8234
T13,49	13	0.6376	T13,49	13	0.8234
T13,50	13	0.6377	T13,50	13	0.8234
T13,51	13	0.6391	T13,51	13	0.8234
T13,52	13	0.6400	T13,52	13	0.8234
T14,53	14	0.6402	T14,53	14	0.8234
T14,54	14	0.6410	T14,54	14	0.8234
T14,55	14	0.6413	T14,55	14	0.8237
T14,56	14	0.6422	T14,56	14	0.9754
T15,57	15	0.6424	T15,57	15	0.9871
T15,58	15	0.6424	T15,58	15	0.9871
T15,59	15	0.6432	T15,59	15	0.9871
T15,60	15	0.6440	T15,60	15	0.9874
T16,61	16	0.6441	T16,61	16	0.9883
T16,62	16	0.6445	T16,62	16	0.9883
T16,63	16	0.6447	T16,63	16	1.0000
T16,64	16	0.6450	T16,64	16	1.0000
T17,65	17	0.6458	Terminated		
T17,66	17	0.6466	Terminated		
T17,67	17	0.6477	Terminated		
T17,68	17	0.6478	Terminated		
T18,69	18	0.6478	Terminated		
T18,70	18	0.6490	Terminated		
T18,71	18	0.6497	Terminated		
T18,72	18	0.6500	Terminated		
T19,73	19	0.6501	Terminated		
T19,74	19	0.6508	Terminated		
T19,75	19	0.6519	Terminated		
T19,76	19	0.6527	Terminated		
T20,77	20	0.6533	Terminated		
T20,78	20	0.6540	Terminated		
T20,79	20	0.6542	Terminated		
T20,80	20	0.6556	Terminated		
T21,81	21	0.6562	Terminated		
T21,82	21	0.6564	Terminated		
T21,83	21	0.6568	Terminated		
T21,84	21	0.6595	Terminated		
T22,85	22	0.6599	Terminated		
T22,86	22	0.6647	Terminated		
T22,87	22	0.6650	Terminated		
T22,88	22	0.6654	Terminated		
T23,89	23	0.6673	Terminated		
T23,90	23	0.6682	Terminated		
T23,91	23	0.6684	Terminated		
T23,92	23	0.6711	Terminated		
T24,93	24	0.6728	Terminated		
T24,94	24	0.6739	Terminated		
T24,95	24	0.6743	Terminated		
T24,96	24	0.6761	Terminated		
T25,97	25	0.6771	Terminated		
T25,98	25	0.6772	Terminated		
T25,99	25	0.6777	Terminated		
T25,100	25	0.6794	Terminated		
T26,101	26	0.6807	Terminated		
T26,102	26	0.6828	Terminated		
T26,103	26	0.6828	Terminated		
T26,104	26	0.6834	Terminated		
T27,105	27	0.6835	Terminated		
T27,106	27	0.6867	Terminated		
T27,107	27	0.6882	Terminated		
T27,108	27	0.6890	Terminated		
T28,109	28	0.6924	Terminated		
T28,110	28	0.7003	Terminated		
T28,111	28	0.7056	Terminated		

Figure 9. Evolutionary approach and pareto-optimal evolutionary approach-based test paper template with low, high and medium and high difficulty level.

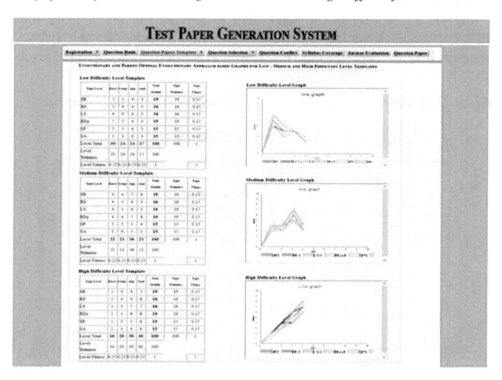

Figure 10. Accepting stage of pareto-optimal template for matrix scaling

TEST PAPER GENERATION SYSTEM

| Registration ▼ | Question Bank | Question Paper Template ▼ | Question Selection ▼ | Question Conflict | Syllabus Coverage | Answer Evaluation | Question Paper |

PARETO OPTIMAL EVOLUTIONARY APPROACH

Software Engineering Question Paper Template (SEQPT)

Module/Level	Knowlege	Comprehension	Application	Analysis	Total Module
Software Requirements	7	4	5	3	19
Reengineering	6	4	4	2	16
Legacy Systems	6	4	3	3	16
Requirement Engineering	6	5	5	3	19
Software Prototyping	5	4	3	3	15
Software Architecture	5	3	4	3	15
Level Total	35	24	24	17	100

Do you Wish to continue with Matrix Scaling Approach ?

Yes   No

approach for generating a scaled test paper template for the subject of Software Engineering (SE).

Figure. 11 represents the screenshot displaying the selection of four different modules namely software requirement, Reengineering, Legacy systems, Requirement Engineering as well as four different cognitive levels

Figure 11. Screenshot with input for matrix scaling of SE test paper template

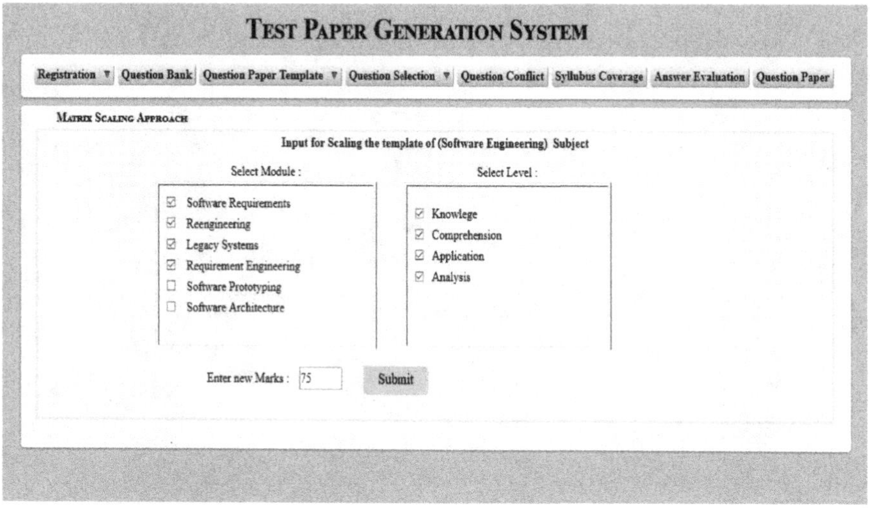

such as knowledge, comprehension, application and analysis for generating a scaled test paper template of Software Engineering (SE).

Figure.12 represent the SE-SEED-CELLS, SE-SCALED-MODULE-WEIGHTS, SE-SCALED-LEVEL-WEIGHTS as well the newly generated template for the Initial Stage of SEQPT-Seed-Cell-Scaling. The process of generation of all the sub-components of the newly generated template used for the initial stage of SEQPT-Seed-Cell-Scaling has been discussed in detail in chapter 1 under section 1.5. Also, the entire process of matrix scaling is included in the same section.

Figure.13 displays the iterative stages of SEQPT-Seed-Cell-Scaling. The result of Figure.13 shows that the row adjustments and column adjustments of matrix scaling generated a scaled-SEQPT at the end of the 3rd iteration. It is further necessary to carry out another two more steps namely the scaled SEQPT rounding and the scaled SEQPT L1-error fixing. Figure.14 shows the

Figure 12. Initial Stage of SEQPT-seed-cell-scaling of matrix scaling for SE scaled test paper template generation

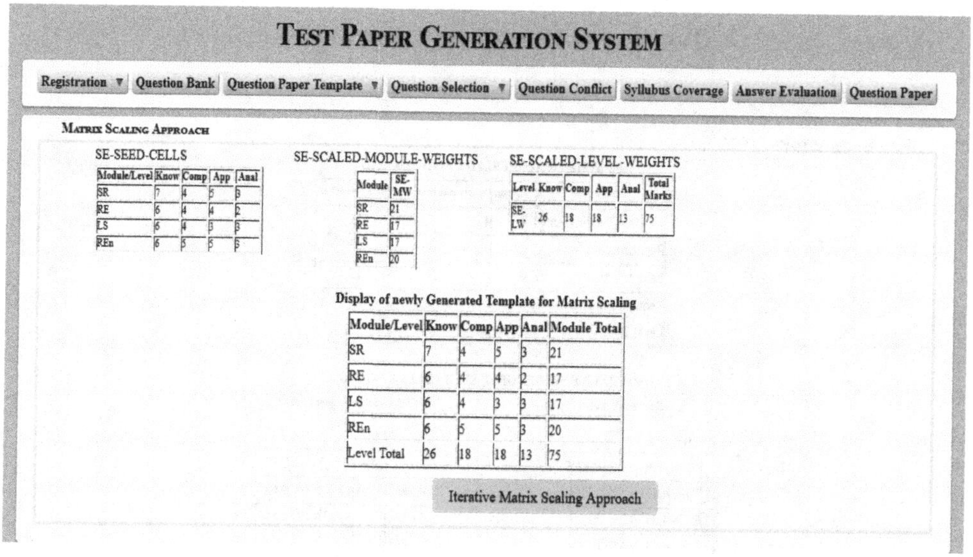

scaled SEQPT that has been generated after undergoing the scaled SEQPT rounding and the scaled SEQPT L1-error fixing operations.

Applications of Test paper Template: Continuous assessment requires generation of dynamic test papers for different examinations. Automatically generating dynamic TPTs satisfying user input number of subject-wise modules and user input number of taxonomy wise cognitive levels is very significant in situations where novice instructors wish to prepare test papers for various types of examinations. But the evolutionary approach based iterative process of generation of population of TPTs encountered significant run time delay as well as included the limitation of having no guarantee of generation of optimal solutions in a finite amount of time. In order to overcome these limitations, we introduced an incremental approach using matrix balancing technique that automatically scales and balances all entries of the TPT. The bi-proportional matrix balancing technique performs iterative scaling and proportional fitting of the TPT to satisfy the user input number of modules, user input number of levels and user input marks requirement of each examination.

Figure 13. Iterative stages of SEQPT-seed-cell-scaling of matrix scaling for SE scaled test paper template generation

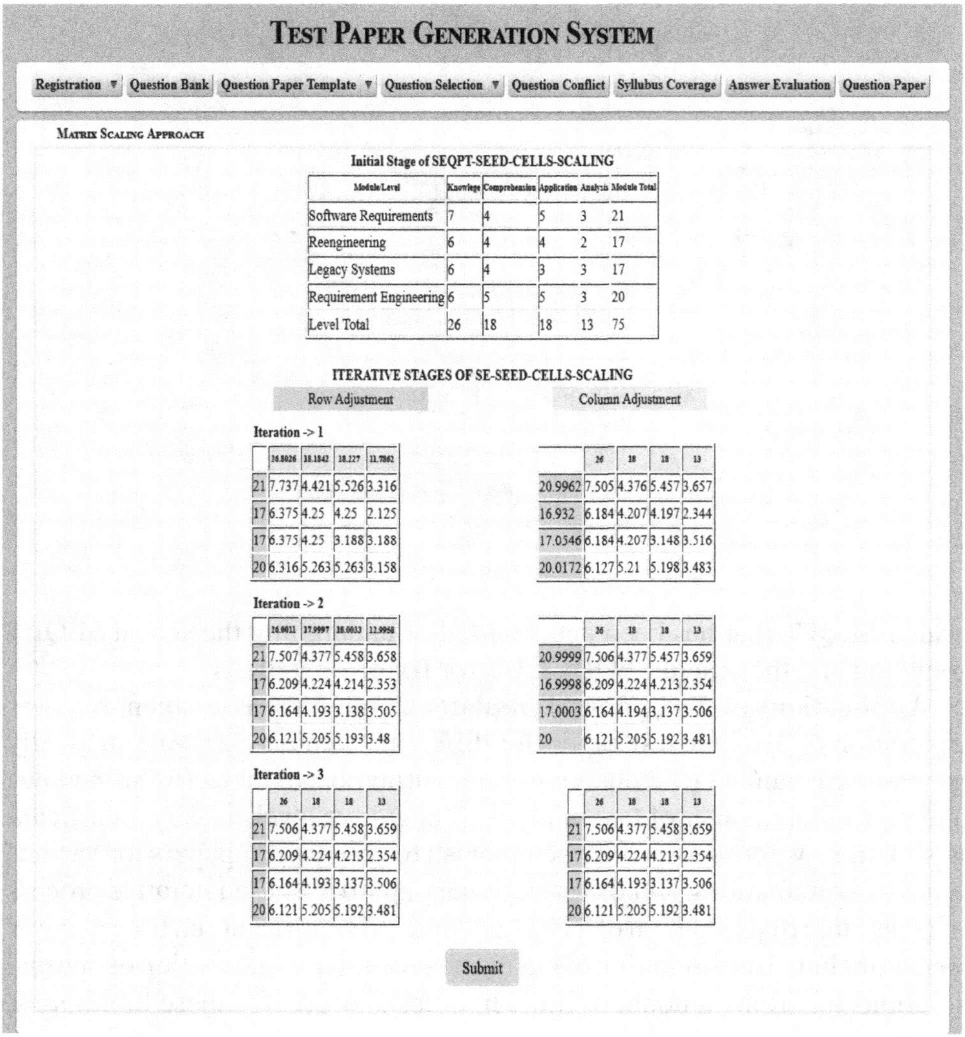

The functionalities supported by the second module named as Question Conflict Detection is as follows:

Question Conflict Detection: The grouping algorithm for clustering the questions which can also be known as the process of Question Conflict Detection is a kind of partitioning algorithm. It considers words of question vector, applies different similarity measures and computes question-similarity-matrix. During the process of computation of each row of the question-similarity-matrix, the grouping algorithm does parallel generation of question clusters by selecting the set of questions satisfying the input similarity threshold value. Hence, it does not require the initial specification of the number of clusters as well as the iterative stages of cluster formulation. Similarity matrix of a set of questions in a Question Bank (QB) is a two-dimensional matrix representing the pair-wise similarity of module-wise questions. Pair-wise similarity computation can be performed using cosine similarity and jaccard similarity coefficient which assign a similarity score to each pair of compared questions. Cosine of the angle is generally 1.0 for identical vectors and is in the range of 0.0 to 1.0 for non-similar or partially similar vectors. The performance efficiency of cosine in detecting the similarity of questions in a QB has been confirmed by tallying its results with jaccard coefficient. Jaccard coefficient is a statistical measure for comparing the similarity and diversity of documents. The jaccard similarity coefficient ranges between

Figure 14. Scaled SEQPT generated as an output template of SE matrix scaling

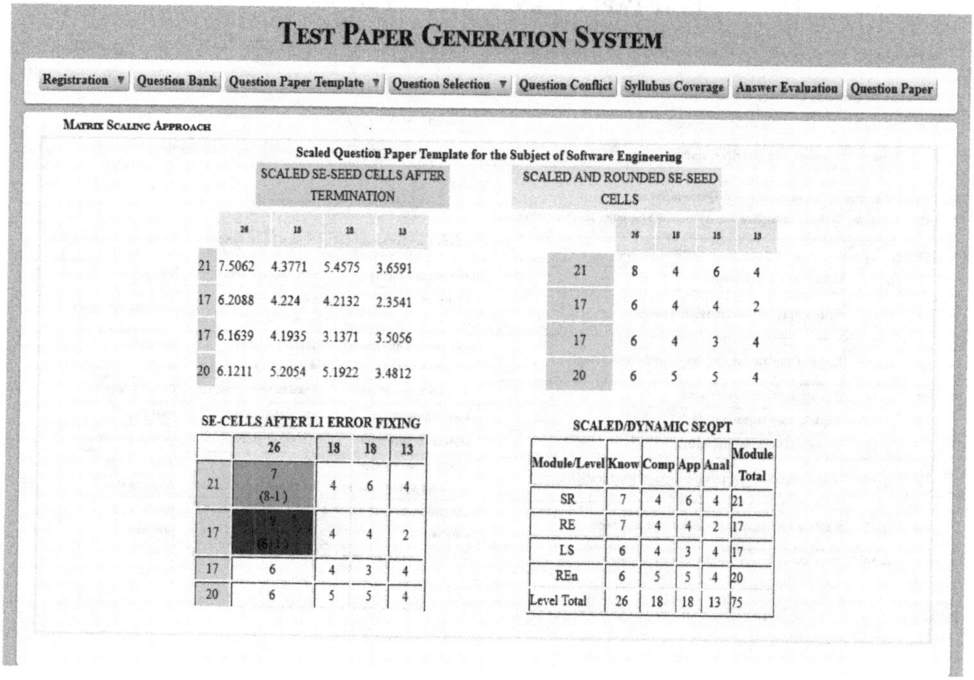

0 and 1. It is 1 when two question vectors are identical and zero when they are disjoint.

Figure.15. displays the input for Question Conflict Identification as well as the Question Bank (QB) pre-processing. User is allowed to select any course, choose any subject under the selected course and specify the module of the subject. The questions in the QB of the specified module undergo question conflict detection. The initial stage of question conflict detection performs the operation of module-wise questions' pre-processing. Extraction of the question terms during the pre-processing stage is carried out using the four different pre-processing stages such as tokenization, stop-word-removal, stemming and normalization. Details of pre-processing stage are explained in chapter 2 under section2.2. Figure.15 presents the pre-processed terms of

Figure 15. The extracted list of terms under software requirements module of software engineering (SE) subject

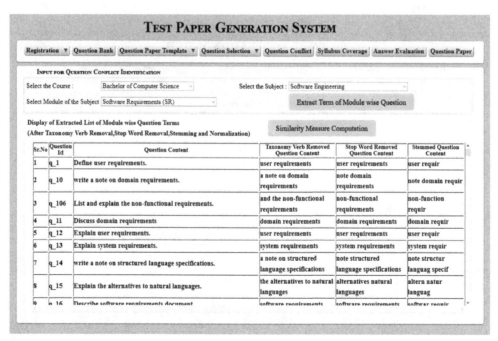

questions under the Software Requirement module of Software Engineering subject offered for Bachelor of Computer Science course.

Figure 16. Td-idf score of question terms under software requirements module of SE

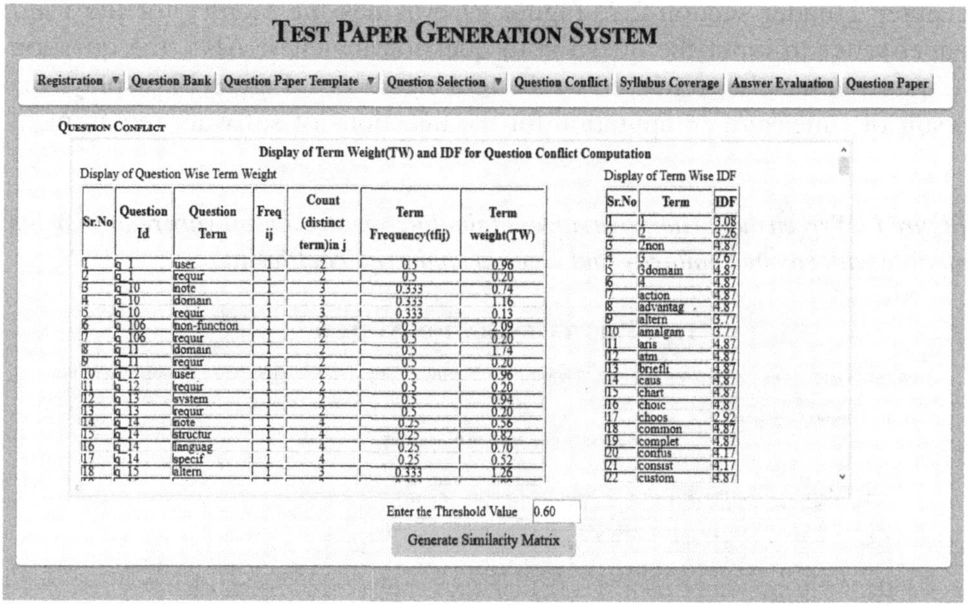

TEST PAPER GENERATION SYSTEM

Registration ▼ | Question Bank | Question Paper Template ▼ | Question Selection ▼ | Question Conflict | Syllubus Coverage | Answer Evaluation | Question Paper

QUESTION CONFLICT

Display of Term Weight(TW) and IDF for Question Conflict Computation

Display of Question Wise Term Weight

Sr.No	Question Id	Question Term	Freq ij	Count (distinct term)in j	Term Frequency(tfij)	Term weight(TW)
1	q_1	user	1	2	0.5	0.96
2	q_1	requir	1	2	0.5	0.20
3	q_10	note	1	3	0.333	0.74
4	q_10	domain	1	3	0.333	1.16
5	q_10	requir	1	3	0.333	0.13
6	q_106	non-function	1	2	0.5	2.09
7	q_106	requir	1	2	0.5	0.20
8	q_11	domain	1	2	0.5	1.74
9	q_11	requir	1	2	0.5	0.20
10	q_12	user	1	2	0.5	0.96
11	q_12	requir	1	2	0.5	0.20
12	q_13	system	1	2	0.5	0.94
13	q_13	requir	1	2	0.5	0.20
14	q_14	note	1	4	0.25	0.56
15	q_14	structur	1	4	0.25	0.82
16	q_14	languag	1	4	0.25	0.70
17	q_14	specif	1	4	0.25	0.52
18	q_15	altern	1	3	0.333	1.26

Display of Term Wise IDF

Sr.No	Term	IDF
1	1	3.08
2	2	6.26
3	2non	4.87
4	3	2.67
5	3domain	4.87
6	4	4.87
7	action	4.87
8	advantag	4.87
9	altern	5.77
10	amalgam	5.77
11	ans	4.87s
12	atm	4.87
13	briefli	4.87
14	caus	4.87
15	chart	4.87
16	choic	4.87
17	choos	5.92
18	common	4.87
19	complet	4.87
20	confus	4.17
21	consist	4.17
22	custom	4.87

Enter the Threshold Value 0.60

Generate Similarity Matrix

Figure.16 represents the term weight scores of question terms for cosine similarity measure using tf-idf weighting method. Detail description of tf-idf calculation is discussed in chapter 2 under Table 1.

The second stage of question conflict detection carries out the generation of the similarity matrix for the questions of Software Requirement module. Figure.16 displays the threshold value specified by user as 0.60 for similarity matrix computation. Figure.17 shows the cosine similarity matrix as well as the jaccard similarity matrix computed for the selected set of questions. The formula used for cosine similarity and jaccard similarity are discussed in detail in chapter 2 under section 2.2.

The third stage of question conflict detection performs the formulation of the clusters of similar questions. Figure.A.18 displays the upper part of it with the cluster representations and the down part of it with the details of the question contents of the respective clusters. From the displayed output, it is generalized that the cosine similarity-based clusters are more accurate than the jaccard similarity-based clusters.

The precision, recall and f-measure values are computed to compare the performance of cosine similarity with jaccard coefficient while formulating question clusters for the questions in Question Bank (QB) of SE. The detail explanation of precision, recall and f-measure computations are done in chapter 2 under section 2.2. Figure.19 provides the facility for the user/ paper-setter to input the question to question matches. Also, the question to question matches retrieved by the tool are shown. Figure.19 displays the result of f-measure computation for the questions of software requirement

Figure 17. Screenshot of iterative stages of similarity matrix of software requirements module with cosine similarity and jaccard similarity coefficient

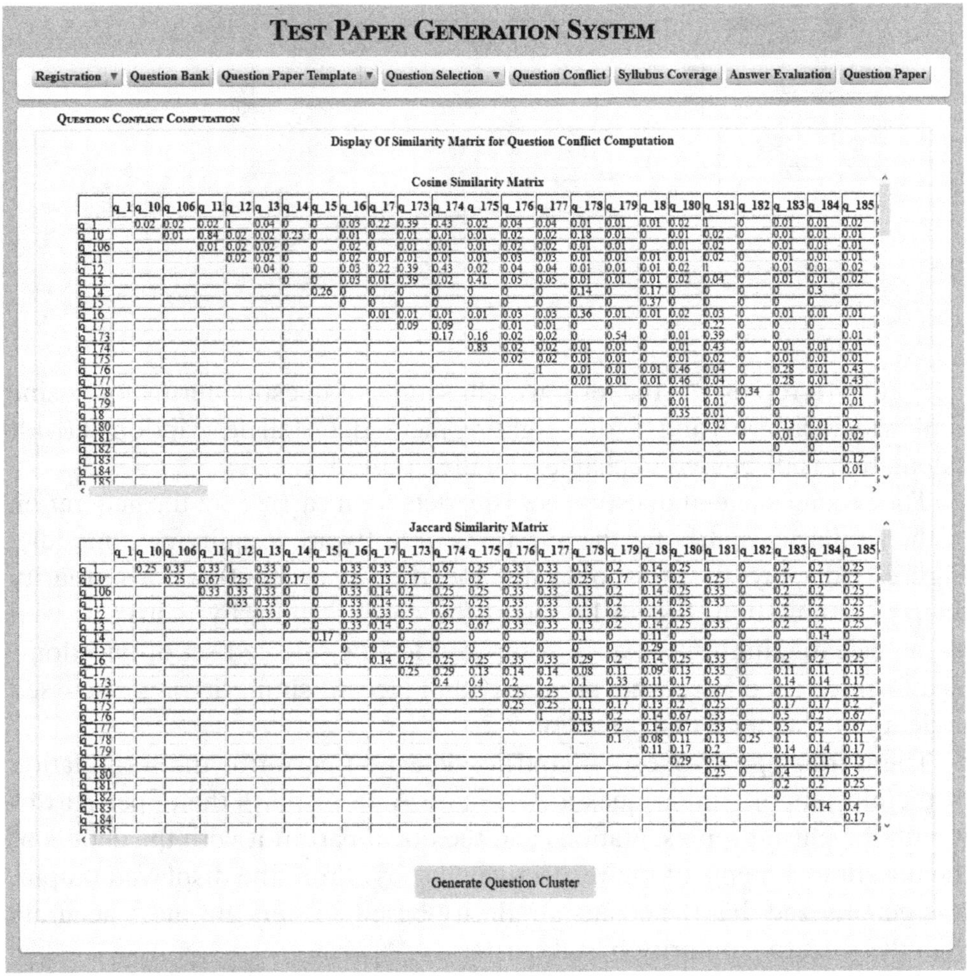

TEST PAPER GENERATION SYSTEM

Registration ▼ | Question Bank | Question Paper Template ▼ | Question Selection ▼ | Question Conflict | Syllabus Coverage | Answer Evaluation | Question Paper

QUESTION CONFLICT COMPUTATION

Display Of Similarity Matrix for Question Conflict Computation

Cosine Similarity Matrix

Jaccard Similarity Matrix

Generate Question Cluster

module. As the f-measure value of cosine similarity is 0.86 as compared to

Figure 18. The extracted clusters of similar questions using cosine similarity and jaccard similarity coefficient

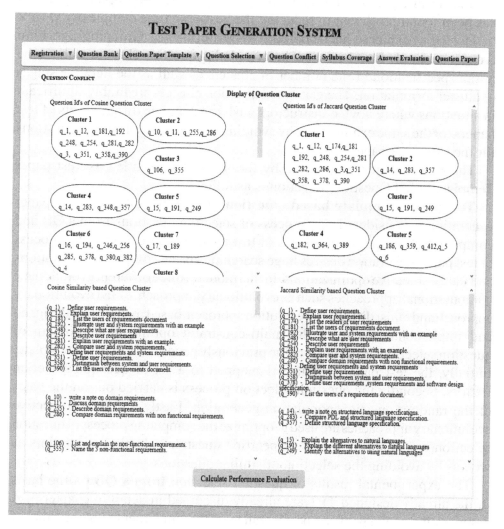

jaccard similarity which is only 0.66, cosine similarity is experimentally found to be more accurate for question cluster formulation.

Applications of Question Conflict Detection: Grouping algorithms are widely used in document similarity and feature extraction applications. Our partition-based grouping algorithm has undergone its experimentation in three different application areas. The first application, presented in this module, is in the area of clustering questions in a Question Bank. It consists of a new approach of computing the question similarity matrix and use of the matrix in clustering the questions. Partition-based grouping algorithm has been found proficient in reducing the best-case time complexity O (n × (n-1)/2 log n) of hierarchical approach to O (n× (n-1)/2). Grouping algorithm is experimentally found efficient in formulating question clusters without the initial specification of the number of clusters as well as the iterative stages of cluster formulation. The generated question clusters are highly significant in situations where novice Instructors wish to formulate different sets of test papers for the same examination by avoiding the selection of similar questions for the same test paper.

The functionalities supported by the third module titled as Test paper Template based Question Selection is as follows:

Test paper Template based Question Selection: Automatic test paper generation is considered as a process of selecting questions from a QB and composing the paper on the basis of test paper specifications. The process of test paper generation desires huge searching space, complex computations and multi-objective optimizations. In this module, three different evolutionary computational approaches such as evolutionary approach, elitist evolutionary approach and elitist differential evolution approach-based methods are designed and implemented to solve the multi-constraint optimization problem of question selection on the basis of the previously generated test paper template. Initially, the test paper template is mapped to a set of question selection vectors. Secondly the question selection process is carried out on the basis of the random question population generation. Lastly, the multi-objective evolutionary approaches are used to optimize the computing process of question selection by satisfying the user specified question selection constraints as well as by avoiding the selection of similar questions.

The experimental results of question selection from a QB on the basis of the already designed TPT are already discussed in detail in chapter 3. A comparative analysis of the performance of the implemented algorithms of

Figure 19. The Precision, recall and F-measure computation using cosine similarity and jaccard similarity coefficient for the questions of software requirement module.

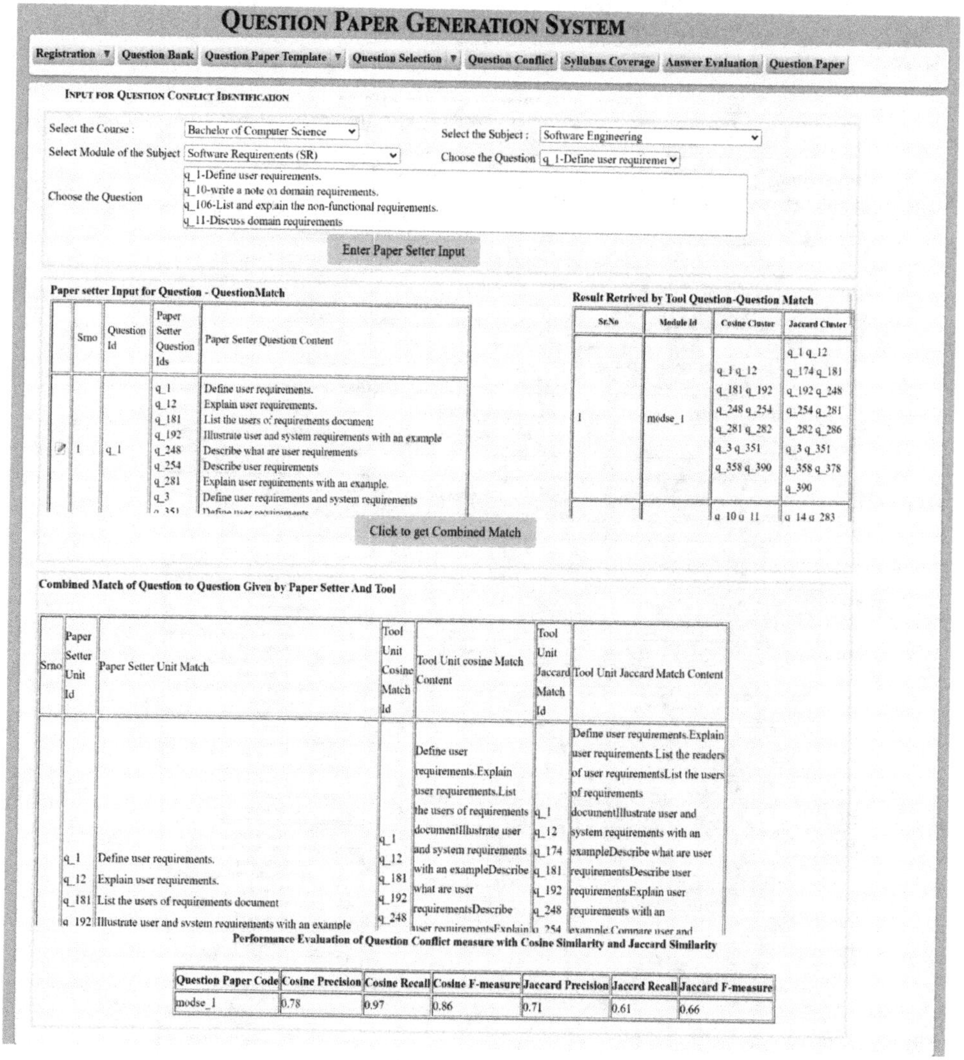

Figure 20. A comparative analysis of the performance of evolutionary approach, elitist evolutionary approach and elitist differential evolutionary approach

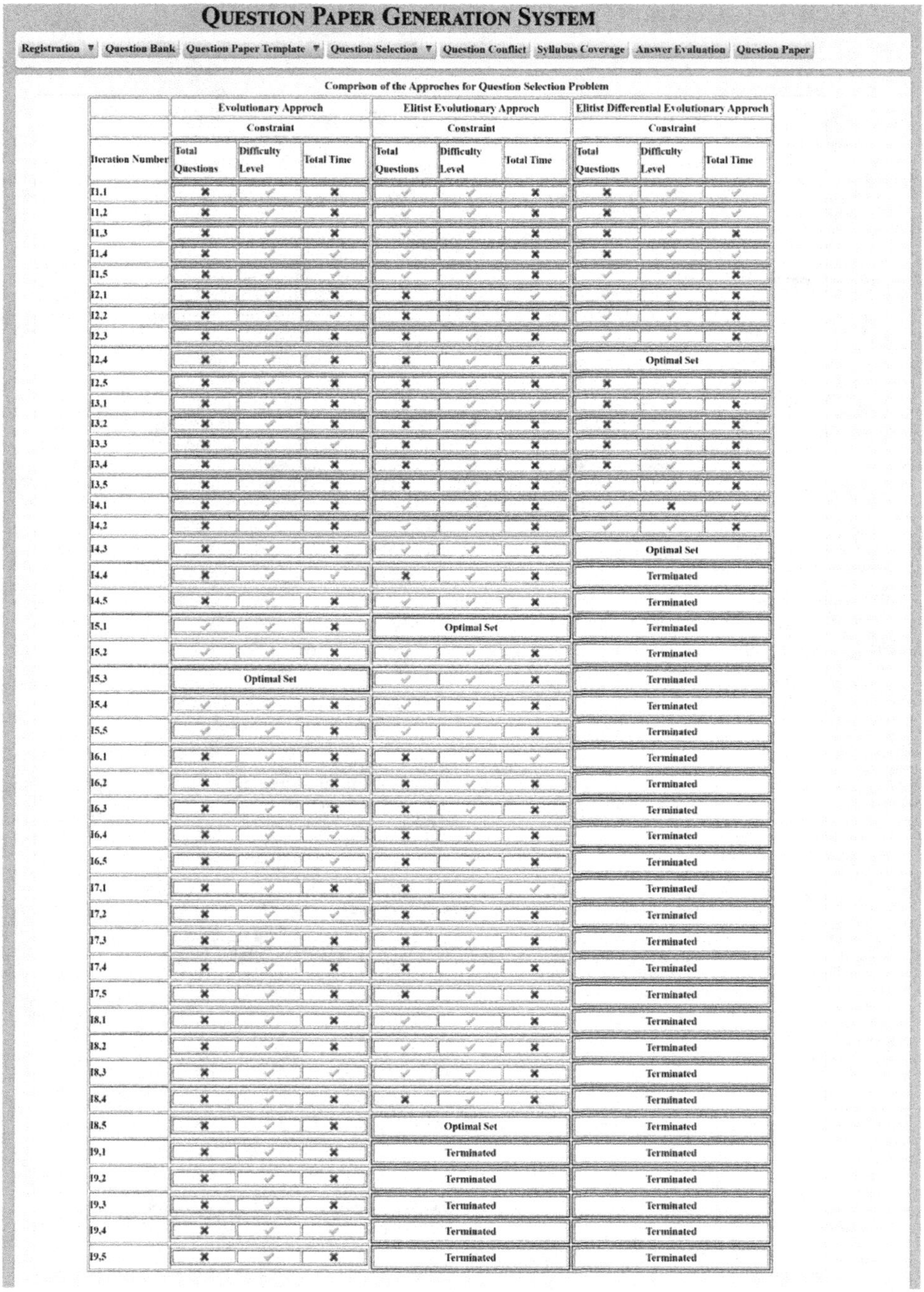

QUESTION PAPER GENERATION SYSTEM

| Registration ▼ | Question Bank | Question Paper Template ▼ | Question Selection ▼ | Question Conflict | Syllabus Coverage | Answer Evaluation | Question Paper |

Comparison of the Approches for Question Selection Problem

Iteration Number	Evolutionary Approch			Elitist Evolutionary Approch			Elitist Differential Evolutionary Approch		
	Constraint			Constraint			Constraint		
	Total Questions	Difficulty Level	Total Time	Total Questions	Difficulty Level	Total Time	Total Questions	Difficulty Level	Total Time
I1.1	✗	✓	✗	✓	✓	✗	✗	✓	✓
I1.2	✗	✓	✗	✗	✓	✗	✗	✓	✓
I1.3	✗	✓	✗	✓	✓	✗	✗	✓	✗
I1.4	✗	✓	✓	✓	✓	✗	✗	✓	✓
I1.5	✗	✓	✓	✓	✓	✗	✓	✓	✗
I2.1	✗	✓	✗	✗	✓	✓	✓	✓	✗
I2.2	✗	✓	✓	✗	✓	✗	✓	✓	✗
I2.3	✗	✓	✗	✗	✓	✓	✓	✓	✗
I2.4	✗	✓	✗	✗	✓	✗	Optimal Set		
I2.5	✗	✓	✗	✗	✓	✗	✗	✓	✓
I3.1	✗	✓	✗	✗	✓	✓	✗	✓	✗
I3.2	✗	✓	✗	✗	✓	✗	✗	✓	✗
I3.3	✗	✓	✓	✗	✓	✗	✗	✓	✗
I3.4	✗	✓	✗	✗	✓	✗	✗	✓	✗
I3.5	✗	✓	✗	✗	✓	✗	✓	✓	✗
I4.1	✗	✓	✗	✓	✓	✗	✓	✗	✓
I4.2	✗	✓	✗	✓	✓	✗	✓	✓	✗
I4.3	✗	✓	✗	✓	✓	✗	Optimal Set		
I4.4	✗	✓	✓	✗	✓	✓	Terminated		
I4.5	✗	✓	✗			✗	Terminated		
I5.1	✓	✓	✗	Optimal Set			Terminated		
I5.2	✓	✓	✗	✓	✓	✗	Terminated		
I5.3	Optimal Set			✓	✓	✗	Terminated		
I5.4	✓	✓	✗	✓	✓	✗	Terminated		
I5.5	✓	✓	✗	✓	✓	✗	Terminated		
I6.1	✗	✓	✗	✗	✓	✓	Terminated		
I6.2	✗	✓	✗	✗	✓	✗	Terminated		
I6.3	✗	✓	✗	✗	✓	✗	Terminated		
I6.4	✗	✓	✓	✗	✓	✗	Terminated		
I6.5	✗	✓	✓	✗	✓	✗	Terminated		
I7.1	✗	✓	✗	✗	✓	✓	Terminated		
I7.2	✗	✓	✓	✗	✓	✗	Terminated		
I7.3	✗	✓	✗	✗	✓	✗	Terminated		
I7.4	✗	✓	✗	✗	✓	✗	Terminated		
I7.5	✗	✓	✗	✗	✓	✗	Terminated		
I8.1	✗	✓	✗	✓	✓	✗	Terminated		
I8.2	✗	✓	✗	✓	✓	✗	Terminated		
I8.3	✗	✓	✓	✓	✓	✗	Terminated		
I8.4	✗	✓	✗	✗	✓	✗	Terminated		
I8.5	✗	✓	✗	Optimal Set			Terminated		
I9.1	✗	✓	✗	Terminated			Terminated		
I9.2	✗	✓	✗	Terminated			Terminated		
I9.3	✗	✓	✗	Terminated			Terminated		
I9.4	✗	✓	✓	Terminated			Terminated		
I9.5	✗	✓	✗	Terminated			Terminated		

evolutionary approach, elitist evolutionary approach and elitist differential evolutionary approach-based methods are displayed in Figure.20.

Applications of Test paper Template-based Question Selection: Question selection problem has been modeled as a multi-constraint optimization problem that aims at generating test papers satisfying many constraints projected by the user. In order to assure many constraints while generating a mathematical model, we have de-signed and implemented multi-objective evolutionary computations such as evolutionary approach, elitist evolutionary approach and elitist differential evolution approach. Differential evolution approach implements global parallel search and also applies its genetic operators such as mutation, crossing and selection to generate optimal solution during the search process. Experimental result shows that differential evolution approach can solve the issue of intelligent generation of test papers satisfying multiple constraints. Another significance of this module is the added advantage of solving the Multi-Objective Parallel Test Paper Com- position (MPQPC) problem using differential evolution method which involves satisfying a set of complex constraints in parallel. This work is one of the best attempts to search for the pareto-optimal set in the do- main of test paper composition. It is of high practical importance as the user is able to experiment the generation of a set of parallel test papers of high quality than just a single test paper even though the difficulty of the problem is certainly dependent on the complexity of the constraints.

The functionalities supported by the fourth module named as Syllabus Coverage Evaluator for a Test paper is as follows:

Syllabus Coverage Evaluator for a Test paper: The existing work in evaluating the syllabus coverage of a test paper has been in-effective in assigning precedence to the unit-weightages while computing the syllabus coverage. Hence, we designed and implemented a grouping algorithm for evaluating the syllabus coverage of questions of an examination test paper by analyzing the questions on different criteria such as the unit-weightages, Bloom's taxonomy, leaning outcomes etc. Cosine similarity and word-order similarity measures are used to compute the similarity between question content and syllabus content. Similarity measure is found by computing the similarity matrix between question vectors and syllabus vectors. The similarity matrix is used as a baseline in grouping the unit-wise questions; matching its weightage against syllabus content and evaluating the syllabus coverage of the test paper.

During the syllabus coverage evaluation, as shown in Figure.20, user is allowed to select any course, choose any subject under the selected course and specify the required test paper of the subject. The selected test paper undergoes its syllabus coverage evaluation. The initial stage of syllabus coverage evaluation performs the operation of pre- processing of the question content of Information Technology test paper with its corresponding syllabus content. Extraction of the question terms and syllabus terms during the pre-processing stage is carried out using the four different pre-processing stages such as tokenization, stop-word-removal, stemming and normalization. Detail discussion of the pre-processing done on question content and syllabus content is presented in chapter 4 under section 4.2. Also, the entire process of syllabus coverage evaluation is explained in detail within chapter 4. Figure.21 displays

Figure 21. Extracted list of terms of syllabus file and test paper

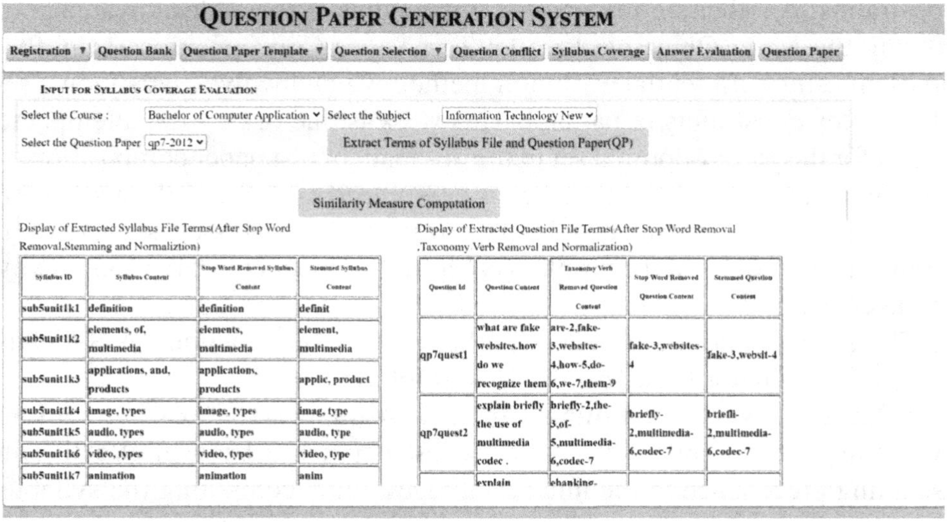

the initial stage of syllabus coverage evaluation generating the pre-processed terms of Information Technology test paper content and its syllabus content.

The second stage of syllabus coverage evaluation carries out the generation of the question Vs syllabus similarity matrix using cosine similarity and word-order similarity measures. Figure.22 represents the term weight scores of question terms as well as syllabus terms for cosine similarity measure using tf-idf weighting method. Detail description of tf-idf calculation is discussed

Figure 22. Cosine similarity computation of question to syllabus match

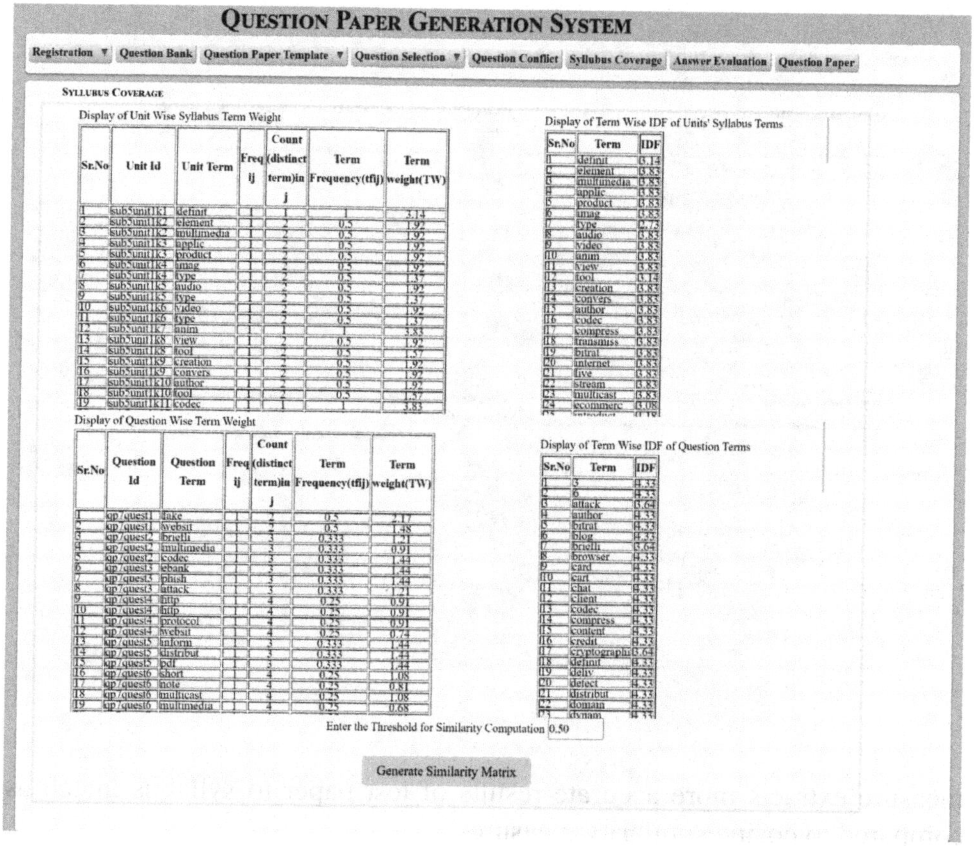

QUESTION PAPER GENERATION SYSTEM

| Registration ▼ | Question Bank | Question Paper Template ▼ | Question Selection ▼ | Question Conflict | Syllabus Coverage | Answer Evaluation | Question Paper |

SYLLABUS COVERAGE

Display of Unit Wise Syllabus Term Weight

Sr.No	Unit Id	Unit Term	Freq ij	Count (distinct term)in j	Term Frequency(tfij)	Term weight(TW)
1	sub5unit1k1	definit	1	1	1	3.14
2	sub5unit1k2	element	1	2	0.5	1.92
3	sub5unit1k2	multimedia	1	2	0.5	1.92
4	sub5unit1k3	applic	1	2	0.5	1.92
5	sub5unit1k3	product	1	2	0.5	1.92
6	sub5unit1k4	imag	1	2	0.5	1.92
7	sub5unit1k4	type	1	2	0.5	1.37
8	sub5unit1k5	audio	1	2	0.5	1.92
9	sub5unit1k5	type	1	2	0.5	1.37
10	sub5unit1k6	video	1	2	0.5	1.92
11	sub5unit1k6	type	1	2	0.5	1.37
12	sub5unit1k7	anim	1	1	1	3.83
13	sub5unit1k8	view	1	2	0.5	1.92
14	sub5unit1k8	tool	1	2	0.5	1.37
15	sub5unit1k9	creation	1	2	0.5	1.92
16	sub5unit1k9	convers	1	2	0.5	1.92
17	sub5unit1k10	author	1	2	0.5	1.92
18	sub5unit1k10	tool	1	2	0.5	1.37
19	sub5unit1k11	codec	1	1	1	3.83

Display of Question Wise Term Weight

Sr.No	Question Id	Question Term	Freq ij	Count (distinct term)in j	Term Frequency(tfij)	Term weight(TW)
1	up /quest1	take	1	2	0.5	2.17
2	up /quest1	websit	1	2	0.5	1.48
3	up /quest2	brietli	1	3	0.333	1.21
4	up /quest2	multimedia	1	3	0.333	0.91
5	up /quest2	codec	1	3	0.333	1.44
6	up /quest3	ebank	1	3	0.333	1.44
7	up /quest3	phish	1	3	0.333	1.44
8	up /quest3	attack	1	3	0.333	1.21
9	up /quest4	http	1	4	0.25	0.91
10	up /quest4	http	1	4	0.25	0.91
11	up /quest4	protocol	1	4	0.25	0.91
12	up /quest4	websit	1	4	0.25	0.74
13	up /quest5	inform	1	3	0.333	1.44
14	up /quest5	distribut	1	3	0.333	1.44
15	up /quest5	pdf	1	3	0.333	1.44
16	up /quest5	short	1	3	0.333	1.44
17	up /quest6	note	1	4	0.25	0.81
18	up /quest6	multicast	1	4	0.25	1.08
19	up /quest6	multimedia	1	4	0.25	0.68

Display of Term Wise IDF of Units' Syllabus Terms

Sr.No	Term	IDF
1	definit	3.14
2	element	3.83
3	multimedia	3.83
4	applic	3.83
5	product	3.83
6	imag	3.83
7	type	2.74
8	audio	3.83
9	video	3.83
10	anim	3.83
11	view	3.83
12	tool	3.14
13	creation	3.83
14	convers	3.83
15	author	3.83
16	codec	3.83
17	compress	3.83
18	transmiss	3.83
19	bitrat	3.83
20	internet	3.83
21	live	3.83
22	stream	3.83
23	multicast	3.83
24	ecommerce	3.08

Display of Term Wise IDF of Question Terms

Sr.No	Term	IDF
1	5	4.33
2	6	4.33
3	attack	3.64
4	author	4.33
5	bitrat	4.33
6	blog	4.33
7	brietli	3.64
8	browser	4.33
9	card	4.33
10	cart	4.33
11	chat	4.33
12	client	4.33
13	codec	4.33
14	compress	4.33
15	content	4.33
16	credit	4.33
17	cryptographi	3.64
18	definit	4.33
19	deliv	4.33
20	detect	4.33
21	distribut	4.33
22	domain	4.33
23	dynam	4.33

Enter the Threshold for Similarity Computation 0.50

[Generate Similarity Matrix]

in chapter 4 under Table 1(a) and table 1 (b). Also, Figure. 22 displays the threshold value specified by user as 0.50 for similarity matrix computation.

Figure.23 shows the cosine similarity matrix as well as the word-order similarity matrix computed for the selected set of questions. The formula used for cosine similarity and word-order similarity are discussed in detail in chapter 4 under section 4.2. The cosine similarity of question- vector and syllabus-vector, qv and sv is calculated by performing the dot product of question-vector terms and syllabus-vector terms. The word order similarity between question vector and syllabus vector, qv and sv is computed as the normalized difference of the common word order pairs in qv and sv. The experimental result of Figure.23 generalizes that the word-order similarity

Figure 23. Cosine similarity and word order similarity of question to syllabus match

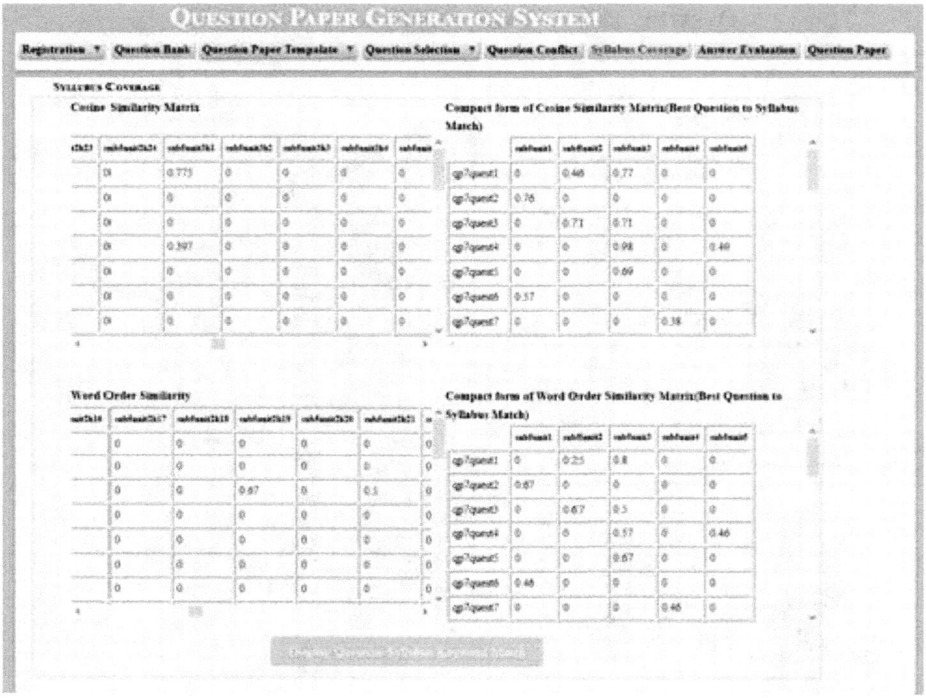

measure extracts more accurate results of test paper to syllabus match as compared to cosine similarity measure.

Figure.24 and Figure.25 represents the syllabus coverage evaluation performed with cosine similarity and word-order similarity for Information Technology subject's Test paper and its Syllabus Match. For the given test paper, word-order similarity shows 77% of questions to be directly from the syllabus and the rest 23% questions to be application-oriented questions and are not directly matching with the syllabus contents. On the other hand, cosine similarity finds 65% of questions to be directly from the syllabus and the rest 35% questions to be indirectly from the syllabus contents.

The precision, recall and f-measure values are computed to compare the performance of cosine similarity with word-order similarity while evaluating the syllabus coverage of information technology test paper. The detail explanation of precision, recall and f-measure computations are done in chapter 4 under section 4.4. Figure.25 provides the facility for the user/paper-setter to input the question to syllabus matches. Also, the question to syllabus matches retrieved by the tool is shown. Figure.25 displays the result of f-measure computation for the questions of Information technology with its respective syllabus content. The f-measure value of word-order similarity is 0.64 as compared to cosine similarity which is only 0.38. Word-order

Figure 24. Syllabus coverage evaluation performed with cosine and word order similarity of question to syllabus match

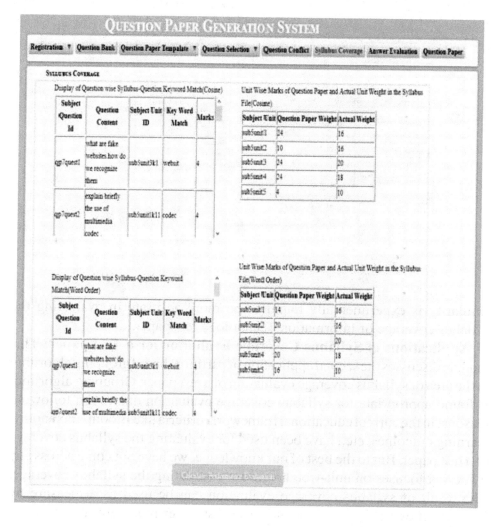

Figure 25. Syllabus coverage evaluation performed with cosine similarity and word order similarity of question to syllabus match

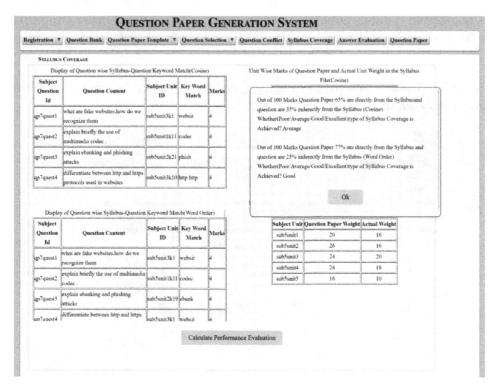

similarity is experimentally found to be more accurate in evaluating the syllabus coverage of Information Technology test paper.

Applications of Syllabus Coverage Evaluator for a Test paper: This module discusses the second application of partition-based grouping algorithm in the area of syllabus coverage evaluation of a test paper. Grouping algorithm is found appropriate for syllabus coverage evaluation due to the following reasons: In the current educational framework, criteria like Bloom's taxonomy, learning outcomes, etc., have been used for evaluating the syllabus coverage of a test paper. But to the best of our knowledge, we have not come across any work that focuses on unit-weightages for computing the syllabus coverage. The result of syllabus coverage evaluation can be used as a measure by the subject expert or test paper-setter or test paper moderator to revise the questions of examination test paper accordingly.

The functionalities supported by the fifth module titled as Answer Paper Evaluator is as follows:

Answer Paper Evaluator: The assessment of descriptive answers is found to be tiresome and time consuming by users due to the increase in number of examinations in continuous assessment system. Here we design and implement a grouping algorithm that assist in computing the similarity measure of common word pair vectors of student answer content and question solution content, supports in representing the similarity measures of student answer to question solution in the form of a similarity matrix and speed up the parallel operation of finding the marks obtained under each question in the subject examination along with the generation of the similarity matrix. Latent Semantic Analysis (LSA) is a generally used technique for automatic determination of document similarity. While computing the similarity between text documents, LSA s accuracy improves with the size of the documents. Unfortunately, it does not take into account the word-order and hence very short documents may not be able to accept the benefit of LSA. Taking a look at the functionality of cosine, cosine similarity is expected to encounter a major disadvantage of term independence while comparing sequential terms in answer content and solution content. In the tf-idf representation of cosine similarity, the term frequency of each term is normalized by the inverse document frequency (idf). The idf normalization has been expected to reduce the weight of terms which occur more frequently in the collection of answer content or solution content. This is a major issue in the answer content, as a single answer normally includes many similar answers or otherwise does include similar answer terms. Also, in the solution content, most of the terms are expected to repeat across the solution sub-contents, as a specific solution explains mostly similar and associated concepts. This majorly is expected to deteriorate the entire tf-idf score of terms of answer content as well as solution content. Hence, the similarity matrix generation has been carried out with Word Order similarity measure. The experimental results of Answer Paper Evaluation on the basis of Solution Key Content are already discussed in detail in chapter 5.

Applications of Answer Paper Evaluator: This work focused on the third application of partition-based grouping algorithm for descriptive answer evaluation. Grouping algorithm has been found efficient in computing question-wise-marks along with the generation of the similarity matrix of every question. Word Order based syntactic similarity measure act as a good measure in evaluating the short descriptive answer papers of internal examinations having the answers in the form of definitions and expansions where in the order of words has more significance.

Figure 26. Performance evaluation of cosine similarity and word order similarity of question to syllabus match

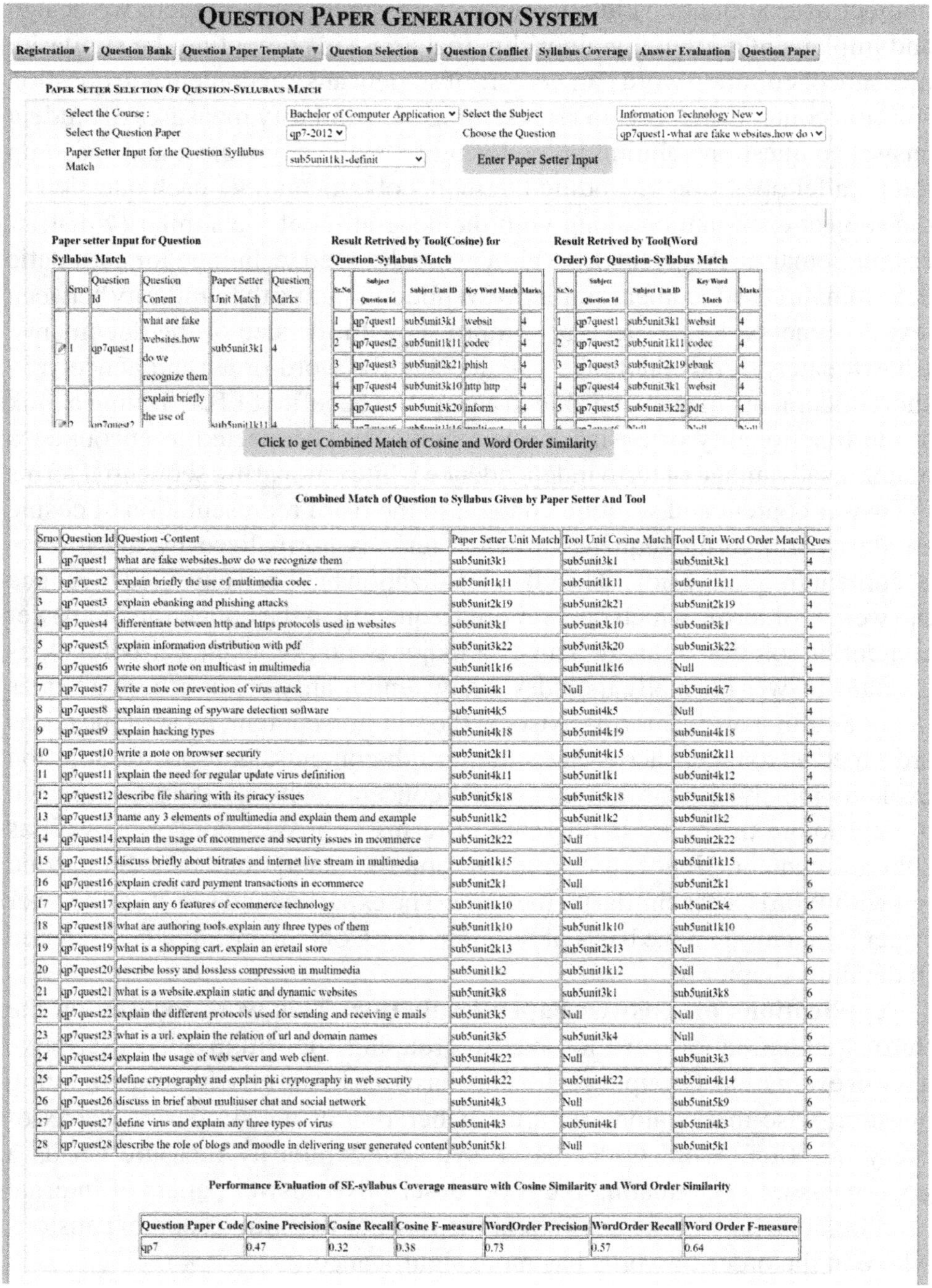

Srno	Question Id	Question Content	Paper Setter Unit Match	Question Marks
1	qp7quest1	what are fake websites.how do we recognize them	sub5unit3k1	4
2		explain briefly the use of	sub5unit1k11	4

Sr.No	Subject Question Id	Subject Unit ID	Key Word Match	Marks
1	qp7quest1	sub5unit3k1	websit	4
2	qp7quest2	sub5unit1k11	codec	4
3	qp7quest3	sub5unit2k21	phish	4
4	qp7quest4	sub5unit3k10	http http	4
5	qp7quest5	sub5unit3k20	inform	4

Sr.No	Subject Question Id	Subject Unit ID	Key Word Match	Marks
1	qp7quest1	sub5unit3k1	websit	4
2	qp7quest2	sub5unit1k11	codec	4
3	qp7quest3	sub5unit2k19	ebank	4
4	qp7quest4	sub5unit3k1	websit	4
5	qp7quest5	sub5unit3k22	pdf	4

Combined Match of Question to Syllabus Given by Paper Setter And Tool

Srno	Question Id	Question -Content	Paper Setter Unit Match	Tool Unit Cosine Match	Tool Unit Word Order Match	Ques
1	qp7quest1	what are fake websites.how do we recognize them	sub5unit3k1	sub5unit3k1	sub5unit3k1	4
2	qp7quest2	explain briefly the use of multimedia codec .	sub5unit1k11	sub5unit1k11	sub5unit1k11	4
3	qp7quest3	explain ebanking and phishing attacks	sub5unit2k19	sub5unit2k21	sub5unit2k19	4
4	qp7quest4	differentiate between http and https protocols used in websites	sub5unit3k1	sub5unit3k10	sub5unit3k1	4
5	qp7quest5	explain information distribution with pdf	sub5unit3k22	sub5unit3k20	sub5unit3k22	4
6	qp7quest6	write short note on multicast in multimedia	sub5unit1k16	sub5unit1k16	Null	4
7	qp7quest7	write a note on prevention of virus attack	sub5unit4k1	Null	sub5unit4k7	4
8	qp7quest8	explain meaning of spyware detection software	sub5unit4k5	sub5unit4k5	Null	4
9	qp7quest9	explain hacking types	sub5unit4k18	sub5unit4k19	sub5unit4k18	4
10	qp7quest10	write a note on browser security	sub5unit2k11	sub5unit4k15	sub5unit2k11	4
11	qp7quest11	explain the need for regular update virus definition	sub5unit4k11	sub5unit1k1	sub5unit4k12	4
12	qp7quest12	describe file sharing with its piracy issues	sub5unit5k18	sub5unit5k18	sub5unit5k18	4
13	qp7quest13	name any 3 elements of multimedia and explain them and example	sub5unit1k2	sub5unit1k2	sub5unit1k2	6
14	qp7quest14	explain the usage of mcommerce and security issues in mcommerce	sub5unit2k22	Null	sub5unit2k22	6
15	qp7quest15	discuss briefly about bitrates and internet live stream in multimedia	sub5unit1k15	Null	sub5unit1k15	4
16	qp7quest16	explain credit card payment transactions in ecommerce	sub5unit2k1	Null	sub5unit2k1	6
17	qp7quest17	explain any 6 features of ecommerce technology	sub5unit1k10	Null	sub5unit2k4	6
18	qp7quest18	what are authoring tools.explain any three types of them	sub5unit1k10	sub5unit1k10	sub5unit1k10	6
19	qp7quest19	what is a shopping cart. explain an eretail store	sub5unit2k13	sub5unit2k13	Null	6
20	qp7quest20	describe lossy and lossless compression in multimedia	sub5unit1k2	sub5unit1k12	Null	6
21	qp7quest21	what is a website.explain static and dynamic websites	sub5unit3k8	sub5unit3k1	sub5unit3k8	6
22	qp7quest22	explain the different protocols used for sending and receiving e mails	sub5unit3k5	Null	Null	6
23	qp7quest23	what is a url. explain the relation of url and domain names	sub5unit3k5	sub5unit3k4	Null	6
24	qp7quest24	explain the usage of web server and web client.	sub5unit4k22	Null	sub5unit3k3	6
25	qp7quest25	define cryptography and explain pki cryptography in web security	sub5unit4k22	sub5unit4k22	sub5unit4k14	6
26	qp7quest26	discuss in brief about multiuser chat and social network	sub5unit4k3	Null	sub5unit5k9	6
27	qp7quest27	define virus and explain any three types of virus	sub5unit4k3	sub5unit4k1	sub5unit4k3	6
28	qp7quest28	describe the role of blogs and moodle in delivering user generated content	sub5unit5k1	Null	sub5unit5k1	6

Performance Evaluation of SE-syllabus Coverage measure with Cosine Similarity and Word Order Similarity

Question Paper Code	Cosine Precision	Cosine Recall	Cosine F-measure	WordOrder Precision	WordOrder Recall	Word Order F-measure
qp7	0.47	0.32	0.38	0.73	0.57	0.64

Conclusion

This book mainly discussed the application of multi-objective algorithms in Test paper Modeling. Five different types of problems addressed were, Dynamic Template Generation using Multi-Objective Optimization, Grouping of Questions from a Question Bank using Partition Based Clustering, Multi-Objective Optimization for Question Selection in Tem- plate Based Test paper Models, Syllabus Coverage Evaluation in Test paper Models and Answer Evaluation of Short Descriptive Questions. The improved solutions of evolutionary algorithms greatly enhance the globalized search and ensure the optimal generation of multiple sets of test papers. The success of evolutionary algorithms is experimentally proved by efficiently generating dynamic test paper templates as well as optimally selecting questions from the given question bank. The simplicity of partition-based grouping algorithms makes it easy for the formulation of conflicting question groups, evaluation of syllabus coverage as well as evaluation of question-answer of the generated test papers. All the above designed and implemented algorithms were experimented for Test paper Modeling with the real datasets from courses offered at Goa University. The findings from the application of multi-objective algorithms and grouping algorithms in these problems are:

1. **Multi-Objective Optimization Problem of Dynamic Template Generation:** Three different approaches namely Evolutionary Approach, Pareto-optimal Evolutionary Approach and Bi- proportional Matrix Scaling Approach were attempted and algorithms were designed under this class. The algorithms were implemented and tested on real data. These findings have been published in (Paul et al, 2013; Paul et al, 2013b; Paul et al, 2012; Paul et al, 2011; Paul et al, 2011b, Paul et al, 2011c). The generated templates can be applied in modeling the test papers of elementary schools, higher secondary schools or even university-based examinations with minor alterations in the objectives and constraint functions.

2. **Grouping Problem of Document Clustering via Matrix Representation:** Different approaches such as cosine similarity and jaccard similarity were attempted and algorithms were designed under this class too. The grouping algorithm was implemented and tested on real data. Experimental result has been published in (Paul et al 2014).. The implemented Partition-based Grouping algorithm reduced the time complexity $O(n \times (n-1)/2 \log n)$ of the generally used hierarchical approaches to $O(n \times (n-1)/2)$.

3. **Multi-Objective Optimization Problem of Question Selection in Template Based Test Paper Models:** Three different approaches namely Evolutionary Approach, Elitist Evolutionary Approach and Elitist Differential Evolution Approach were attempted and algorithms were designed under this class. The algorithms were implemented and tested on real data. These findings have been published in (Paul et al, 2014; Paul et al, 2014b, Paul et al 2014c). It was identified that the Question Selection model is dependent on the user-defined values of mutation probability, crossover probability as well as the generated initial solutions. The dependency on user-defined mutation probabilities has been sorted out to some extent, by using evolving/self- adapted mutation probabilities in Differential Evolution Approach.

Grouping Problem of Syllabus-Coverage Evaluation in Test paper Models: Different approaches such as cosine similarity approach and word-order based similarity approach were attempted and grouping algorithms were designed under this class. The partition-based grouping algorithms were implemented and tested on real data. Results obtained indicate that word-order similarity is a better measure than cosine similarity in evaluating the syntactic similarity of short documents. The findings have been published in (Paul et al, 2014).

4. **Grouping Problem of Question-Answer Evaluation in Test Paper Models:** Word-order based syntactic similarity approach was attempted and partition-based grouping algorithm was designed under this class. The algorithm was implemented and tested on real data. Results obtained indicate that word-order similarity is a good and better measure in evaluating the syntactic similarity of short documents. The findings have been published in (Paul et al, 2014).

Another significant area covered in the book was focusing on extracting keywords from text's collection in order to use them as attributes for text classification. As the amount of unstructured data in our world continues to increase, text-mining tools that allow us to sift through this information with ease will become more and more valuable. Text mining tools are beginning to be readily applied in the biomedical field, where the volume of information on a particular topic makes it impossible for a researcher to cover all the material. Text mining methods can also be used by the government's intelligence and security agencies to try to piece together terrorist warnings and other security threats. Another area that is already benefiting from text mining tools is education. Students and educators can find more information relating to their topics at faster speeds, than using traditional adhoc searching.

The largest target for text mining developers right now is the business world. There are many businesses today with overwhelming amounts of information that they don't use, because they have no reasonable way of analyzing it. Text mining tools can help these businesses analyze their competition, customer base and marketing strategies, thereby allowing them to financially profit from the text mining software purchase.

One of the challenging areas of text mining is the problem of extracting keywords from text's collection in order to use them as attributes for text classification. Keyword extraction techniques seem to be maturing rapidly, with new techniques arising concurrently. Classification is a costly and time-consuming process, requiring highly trained individuals to consume a large amount of information and summarize it. Automatic keyword extraction is a process, by which representative terms are systematically extracted from a text with either minimal or no human intervention, depending on the model used. The goal of automatic extraction is to apply the power and speed of computation to the problems of access and discoverability, adding value to information organization and retrieval without the significant costs and drawbacks associated with human indexers. Research is taking place in numerous fields across the globe, and there is no clear frontrunner among the technologies and algorithms.

This research work has presented a system for information retrieval using stemming, keyword extraction and categorization, which leads to the creation of an automatic keyword extractor and classifier. Many changes can be proposed in order to make the system more efficient.

Our goal is to create an information extraction mechanism that will be able to process many kinds of inputs, realize the type of text and understand the percentage of the keywords that has to be stored. The use of this mechanism, as already mentioned, is its support for information extraction and information categorization mechanisms. This keyword extraction mechanism is actually a module of a complete mechanism, starting from information retrieval and finalization. In our work, this module is used in order to support a text summarization mechanism, which leads – with the help of the Keyword Extraction module- to text categorization. More specifically, we use the extracted keywords in order to determine the category of our retrieved texts and additionally create a summary of the text in order to present to the users a part of the text and not the whole text. The most commonly used keyphrase extraction Algorithm, known as KEA, limits keywords to three-token phrases (or trigrams), and applies the Lovins stemming technique to arrive at its keywords. In our work, there is no limit for the width of the keyword and it is applying the Porter Stemming Algorithm.

FUTURE WORK

We have briefly presented directions of research for automatic classification of documents based on information retrieval and knowledge discovery in databases. This approach is based on the extraction of keywords automatically and to use these keywords for text classification. Hence, the construction of the keyword list is considered as an important and useful research subject in the domain of document classification. We have presented an algorithm that is based on the idea that the appropriate keywords for text classification are those that are frequent within the document set. This algorithm reduces the search space by building larger keywords from already extracted smaller ones. Moreover, it is significant to add a new feature that would calculate differently the weight of the keywords in a text and not just the frequency count of keywords. We also propose to proceed with some experimentation on cross language text collections, especially for medical texts. We have designed an algorithm to use bit maps to speed up the process of finding the frequency count of the candidate phrases, which will be used in the next version of this software. We also have plans of using the maximal frequent itemset concept used in finding frequent itemsets to identify keywords in a depth-first manner.

Text classification is an active and important area of research where machine learning and information retrieval research intersect. Automatic classification schemes can greatly facilitate the process of categorization. Categorization of documents is challenging, as the number of discriminating words can be very large. A possible approach to overcome this problem is to learn weights for different features (or words in document data sets). In this approach, each feature has a weight associated with it. A higher weight for a feature implies that this feature is more important in the classification task. The use of association patterns for text categorization has attracted great interest and a variety of useful methods can be developed. Prime focus can be on what kind of association patterns are the best candidate for pattern-based text categorization and what is the most desirable way to use patterns for text categorization.

The results obtained will continue to motivate us to further develop more advanced and powerful algorithms in this research area. One among the noticeable limitation which can be considered for future research is the identification of conceptual similarity between the text documents. In our implementations, we focused only on the syntactic similarity of short documents which can be extended to incorporate more of semantic similarity measures.

REFERENCES

Paul, Naik, Rane, & Pawar. (2011b). Dynamic Test paper Template Generation using GA Approach. *Proceedings of Academic Demo, The 17th International Conference on Management of Data (COMAD)*.

Paul, D. V., Naik, S. B., & Pawar, J. D. (2012). Use of an Evolutionary Approach for Test paper Template Generation. *Proceedings of 4th IEEE International Conference on Technology for Education (T4E)*, 144-148.

Paul, D. V., Naik, S. B., Rane, P., & Pawar, J. D. (2011a). Dynamic Examination Test paper Generation System using Template, Genetic Algorithm and Educational Taxonomy. *Proceedings of Work-In-Progress Track, The 17th International Conference on Management of Data (COMAD)*.

Paul, D. V., & Pawar, J. D. (2014a). An Evolutionary Approach for Question Selection from a Question Bank: A Case Study. *International Journal of ICT Research and Development in Africa*, 4(1), 61–75. doi:10.4018/ijictrda.2014010104

Paul, D. V., & Pawar, J. D. (2014b). Elitist-Multi-Objective Differential Evolution for Multiple Test paper Generation. *International Journal of Web Applications*, 6(2), 43–56.

Paul, D. V., & Pawar, J. D. (2014c). Use of Common-Word Order Syntactic Similarity Metric for Evaluating Syllabus Coverage of a Test paper. *International Journal of Web Applications*, *6*(2), 68–81.

Paul, D. V., & Pawar, J. D. (2014d). A Grouping Strategy based Partition Algorithm for Clustering Questions in a Question Bank. *Journal of Convergence Information Technology*, *9*(2), 70.

Paul, D. V., & Pawar, J. D. (2014e). A Syllabus-Fairness Measure for Evaluating Open-Ended Questions. In Advances in Signal Processing and Intelligent Recognition Systems. Springer International Publishing.

Paul, D. V., & Pawar, J. D. (2014f). Use of Syntactic Similarity based Similarity Matrix for Evaluating Descriptive Answer. *Proceedings of 6th IEEE International Conference on Technology for Education (T4E)*, 253-256. 10.1109/T4E.2014.60

Paul, D. V., & Pawar, J. D. (2014g). Multi-Objective Differential Evolution Approach for Question Selection Problem. *Proceedings of Fifth IEEE International Conference on the Applications of Digital Information and Web Technologies (ICADIWT)*, 240-246. 10.1109/ICADIWT.2014.6814673

Paul, D. V., & Pawar, J. D. (2013a). Dynamic Test paper Tem- plate Generation using Bi-proportional Scaling Method. *Proceedings of 5th IEEE International Conference on Technology for Education (T4E)*, 80-83.

Paul, D. V., & Pawar, J. D. (2013b). Pareto-optimal Solutions for Test paper Template Generation. *Proceedings of IEEE International Conference on Advances in Computing, Communication and Informatics, (ICACCI)*, 747-751.

Paul, D. V., & Pawar, J. D. (2011). Application of Text Mining Techniques for Evaluating Examination Test paper. *Proceedings of International Conference on Database and Data Mining (ICDDM)*, 74-78.

Related Readings

To continue IGI Global's long-standing tradition of advancing innovation through emerging research, please find below a compiled list of recommended IGI Global book chapters and journal articles in the areas of document classification, text categorization and performance measures. These related readings will provide additional information and guidance to further enrich your knowledge and assist you with your own research.

Abdelkoui, F., & Kholladi, M. (2017). Extracting Criminal-Related Events from Arabic Tweets. *Journal of Information Technology Research*, *10*(3), 34–47. doi:10.4018/JITR.2017070103

Abdo, A. S., Salem, R. K., & Abdul-Kader, H. M. (2017). Enhancement of Data Quality in Health Care Industry. In A. E. Hassanien & T. Gaber (Eds.), *Handbook of Research on Machine Learning Innovations and Trends* (pp. 230–250). IGI Global. doi:10.4018/978-1-5225-2229-4.ch011

Agarwal, R. (2018). Ordering Policy and Inventory Classification Using Temporal Association Rule Mining. *International Journal of Productivity Management and Assessment Technologies*, *6*(1), 37–49. doi:10.4018/ IJPMAT.2018010103

Agarwal, R. & Mittal, M. (2018). Optimal Ordering Policy With Inventory Classification Using Data Mining Techniques. In Handbook of Research on Promoting Business Process Improvement Through Inventory Control Techniques (pp. 305-326). IGI Global. http://doi:10.4018/978-1-5225-3232-3.ch017

Agrawal, D., & Bonde, P. (2017). Improving Classification Accuracy on Imbalanced Data by Ensembling Technique. *Journal of Cases on Information Technology, 19*(1), 42–49. doi:10.4018/jcit.2017010104

Agrawal, R., & Gupta, N. (2017). Educational Data Mining Review. In S. Tamane, V. K. Solanki, & N. Dey (Eds.), *Privacy and Security Policies in Big Data* (pp. 149–165). IGI Global. doi:10.4018/978-1-5225-2486-1.ch007

Ahmed, S., Gaber, T., & Hassanien, A. E. (2017). Telemetry Data Mining Techniques, Applications, and Challenges. In A. E. Hassanien & T. Gaber (Eds.), *Handbook of Research on Machine Learning Innovations and Trends* (pp. 915–924). IGI Global. doi:10.4018/978-1-5225-2229-4.ch040

Akhtar, N., & Ahamad, M. V. (2018). Graph Tools for Social Network Analysis. In N. Meghanathan (Ed.), *Graph Theoretic Approaches for Analyzing Large-Scale Social Networks* (pp. 18–33). IGI Global. doi:10.4018/978-1-5225-2814-2.ch002

Akremi, A., Sallay, H., & Rouached, M. (2018). Intrusion Detection Systems Alerts Reduction. In Y. Maleh (Ed.), *Security and Privacy Management, Techniques, and Protocols* (pp. 255–275). IGI Global. doi:10.4018/978-1-5225-5583-4.ch010

Al-Khasawneh, A. M. (2018). Decision Support System for Diabetes Classification Using Data Mining Techniques. In J. Tan (Ed.), *Handbook of Research on Emerging Perspectives on Healthcare Information Systems and Informatics* (pp. 281–303). IGI Global. doi:10.4018/978-1-5225-5460-8.ch012

Al Mazari, A. (2018). Computational and Data Mining Perspectives on HIV/AIDS in Big Data Era. In A. Al Mazari (Ed.), *Big Data Analytics in HIV/AIDS Research* (pp. 81–116). IGI Global. doi:10.4018/978-1-5225-3203-3.ch004

Alsukhni, E., AlEroud, A., & Saifan, A. A. (2019). A Hybrid Pre-Post Constraint-Based Framework for Discovering Multi-Dimensional Association Rules Using Ontologies. *International Journal of Information Technology and Web Engineering, 14*(1), 112–131. doi:10.4018/IJITWE.2019010106

Alsukhni, E., Saifan, A. A., & Alawneh, H. (2017). A New Data Mining-Based Framework to Test Case Prioritization Using Software Defect Prediction. *International Journal of Open Source Software and Processes, 8*(1), 21–41. doi:10.4018/IJOSSP.2017010102

Ameri, H., Alizadeh, S., & Noughabi, E. A. (2017). Application of Data Mining Techniques in Clinical Decision Making. In E. A. Noughabi, B. Raahemi, A. Albadvi, & B. H. Far (Eds.), *Handbook of Research on Data Science for Effective Healthcare Practice and Administration* (pp. 257–295). IGI Global. doi:10.4018/978-1-5225-2515-8.ch012

Arora, S., & Kumar, D. (2017). Hybridization of SOM and PSO for Detecting Fraud in Credit Card. *International Journal of Information Systems in the Service Sector*, 9(3), 17–36. doi:10.4018/IJISSS.2017070102

Badhe, V., Singh, S., & Arvind, T. S. (2019). Ideating a Recommender System for Business Growth Using Profit Pattern Mining and Uncertainty Theory. In D. S. Rajput, R. S. Thakur, & S. M. Basha (Eds.), *Sentiment Analysis and Knowledge Discovery in Contemporary Business* (pp. 223–249). IGI Global. doi:10.4018/978-1-5225-4999-4.ch013

Bala, K. Choubey, D. K. Paul, S. & Lala, M. G. (2018). Classification Techniques for Thunderstorms and Lightning Prediction. In Soft-Computing-Based Nonlinear Control Systems Design (pp. 1-17). IGI Global. http://doi:10.4018/978-1-5225-3531-7.ch001

Batra, M., & Jyoti, V. (2019). Feature Based Opinion Mining. In R. Agrawal & N. Gupta (Eds.), *Extracting Knowledge From Opinion Mining* (pp. 20–39). IGI Global. doi:10.4018/978-1-5225-6117-0.ch002

Bay, Ä. (2017). Determination of Voting Tendencies in Turkey through Data Mining Algorithms. *International Journal of E-Adoption*, 9(1), 50–58. doi:10.4018/IJEA.2017010105

Bershadsky, A., & Berezin, A. (2019). Theoretical and Technological Perspectives on Development of Information Monitoring System for Solving Complex Problems. In U. G. Benna (Ed.), *Optimizing Regional Development Through Transformative Urbanization* (pp. 288–306). IGI Global. doi:10.4018/978-1-5225-5448-6.ch014

Bhatnagar, V., Goyal, M., & Hussain, M. A. (2018). A Novel Aspect Based Framework for Tourism Sector with Improvised Aspect and Opinion Mining Algorithm. *International Journal of Rough Sets and Data Analysis*, 5(2), 119–130. doi:10.4018/IJRSDA.2018040106

Bimonte, S., Sautot, L., Journaux, L., & Faivre, B. (2017). Multidimensional Model Design using Data Mining. *International Journal of Data Warehousing and Mining*, 13(1), 1–35. doi:10.4018/IJDWM.2017010101

Biswas, S. K., Devi, D., & Chakraborty, M. (2018). A Hybrid Case Based Reasoning Model for Classification in Internet of Things (IoT) Environment. *Journal of Organizational and End User Computing*, 30(4), 104–122. doi:10.4018/JOEUC.2018100107

Boulaaba, A., & Faiz, S. (2018). Towards Big GeoData Mining and Processing. *International Journal of Organizational and Collective Intelligence*, 8(2), 60–73. doi:10.4018/IJOCI.2018040104

Byty, Ã., §i, E. Sejdiu, B. Avdiu, A. & Ahmedi, L. (2019). A Semantic Sensor Web Architecture in the Internet of Things. In Semantic Web Science and Real-World Applications (pp. 75-97). IGI Global. http://doi:10.4018/978-1-5225-7186-5.ch004

C. J. P. (2017). An Overview of Text Information Extraction from Images. In Advanced Image Processing Techniques and Applications (pp. 32-60). IGI Global. http://doi:10.4018/978-1-5225-2053-5.ch002

C. S. & S. V. (2018). Promoting Business Activities Using Utility Mining Techniques. In *Handbook of Research on Promoting Business Process Improvement Through Inventory Control Techniques* (pp. 520-533). IGI Global. http://doi:10.4018/978-1-5225-3232-3.ch027

Canbolat, Z. N., & Pinarbasi, F. (2020). Augmented Reality and Mobile Consumers. In S. M. Loureiro (Ed.), *Managerial Challenges and Social Impacts of Virtual and Augmented Reality* (pp. 76–94). IGI Global. doi:10.4018/978-1-7998-2874-7.ch005

Canbolat, Z. N., & Pinarbasi, F. (2020). Using Sentiment Analysis for Evaluating e-WOM. In S. M. Loureiro & H. R. Kaufmann (Eds.), *Exploring the Power of Electronic Word-of-Mouth in the Services Industry* (pp. 101–123). IGI Global. doi:10.4018/978-1-5225-8575-6.ch007

Chadha, A. (2018). Efficient Clustering Algorithms in Educational Data Mining. In Handbook of Research on Knowledge Management for Contemporary Business Environments (pp. 279-312). IGI Global. http://doi:10.4018/978-1-5225-3725-0.ch015

Chang, A., Trappey, C. V., Trappey, A. J., & Chen, L. W. (2020). Web Mining Customer Perceptions to Define Product Positions and Design Preferences. *International Journal on Semantic Web and Information Systems*, 16(2), 42–58. doi:10.4018/IJSWIS.2020040103

Chantrapornchai, C., Kaegjing, A., Srakaew, S., Piyanuntcharatsr, W., & Krakhaeng, S. (2017). Utilizing Architecture Aspects for in Data Mining for Computer System Design. In S. Bhattacharyya, S. De, I. Pan, & P. Dutta (Eds.), *Intelligent Multidimensional Data Clustering and Analysis* (pp. 225–252). IGI Global. doi:10.4018/978-1-5225-1776-4.ch009

Chellamuthu, G., Kannimuthu, S., & Premalatha, K. (2019). Data Mining and Machine Learning Approaches in Breast Cancer Biomedical Research. In D. S. Rajput, R. S. Thakur, & S. M. Basha (Eds.), *Sentiment Analysis and Knowledge Discovery in Contemporary Business* (pp. 175–204). IGI Global. doi:10.4018/978-1-5225-4999-4.ch011

Cheng, L. C., Wu, C., & Chen, C. (2019). Behavior Analysis of Customer Churn for a Customer Relationship System. *Journal of Global Information Management*, 27(1), 111–127. doi:10.4018/JGIM.2019010106

Darabi, S. A., & Teimourpour, B. (2017). A Case-Based-Reasoning System for Feature Selection and Diagnosing Asthma. In E. A. Noughabi, B. Raahemi, A. Albadvi, & B. H. Far (Eds.), *Handbook of Research on Data Science for Effective Healthcare Practice and Administration* (pp. 444–459). IGI Global. doi:10.4018/978-1-5225-2515-8.ch019

Das, N., & Kundu, A. (2018). Multi-Agent-Based Analysis and Design of Decision-Support System for Real-Time Environment Control. *International Journal of Green Computing*, 9(1), 1–19. doi:10.4018/IJGC.2018010101

Dasgupta, H. (2017). Data Mining and Statistics. In S. K. Trivedi, S. Dey, A. Kumar, & T. K. Panda (Eds.), *Handbook of Research on Advanced Data Mining Techniques and Applications for Business Intelligence* (pp. 15–33). IGI Global. doi:10.4018/978-1-5225-2031-3.ch002

Dasgupta, H. (2017). Data Mining Techniques in Knowledge Management. In D. S. Deshpande, N. Bhosale, & R. J. Londhe (Eds.), *Enhancing Academic Research With Knowledge Management Principles* (pp. 200–232). IGI Global. doi:10.4018/978-1-5225-2489-2.ch008

Dasgupta, S., Saha, S., & Das, S. K. (2017). Malware Detection in Android Using Data Mining. *International Journal of Natural Computing Research*, 6(2), 1–17. doi:10.4018/IJNCR.2017070101

Dass, S. & Prabhu, J. (2018). Amelioration of Big Data Analytics by Employing Big Data Tools and Techniques. In Applications of Security, Mobile, Analytic, and Cloud (SMAC) Technologies for Effective Information Processing and Management (pp. 212-232). IGI Global. http://doi:10.4018/978-1-5225-4044-1.ch011

David, S. K., Saeb, A. T., Rafiullah, M., & Rubeaan, K. (2019). Classification Techniques and Data Mining Tools Used in Medical Bioinformatics. In S. K. Strydom & M. Strydom (Eds.), *Big Data Governance and Perspectives in Knowledge Management* (pp. 105–126). IGI Global. doi:10.4018/978-1-5225-7077-6.ch005

De Guzman, F., Abaya, S., Benito, V., & Chua, I. M. (2017). Academics Mining for Information Analytics as a Method in Improving Student Performance Through Effective Learning Strategies. In P. Tripathi & S. Mukerji (Eds.), *Handbook of Research on Technology-Centric Strategies for Higher Education Administration* (pp. 73–89). IGI Global. doi:10.4018/978-1-5225-2548-6.ch005

Deisy, C., & Francis, M. (2019). Implementation of Data Mining Algorithm With R. In D. S. Rajput, R. S. Thakur, & S. M. Basha (Eds.), *Sentiment Analysis and Knowledge Discovery in Contemporary Business* (pp. 92–125). IGI Global. doi:10.4018/978-1-5225-4999-4.ch007

Desarkar, A., & Das, A. (2018). Exploration of Healthcare Using Data Mining Techniques. In B. K. Mishra & R. Kumar (Eds.), *Big Data Management and the Internet of Things for Improved Health Systems* (pp. 243–259). IGI Global. doi:10.4018/978-1-5225-5222-2.ch014

Doguc, O. (2019). Innovative Methods in Financial Risk Management. In Handbook of Research on Managerial Thinking in Global Business Economics (pp. 141-163). IGI Global. http://doi:10.4018/978-1-5225-7180-3.ch008

Dubey, R., Maurya, J. P., & Thakur, R. S. (2018). Detection Approaches for Categorization of Spam and Legitimate E-Mail. In V. Tiwari, R. S. Thakur, B. Tiwari, & S. Gupta (Eds.), *Handbook of Research on Pattern Engineering System Development for Big Data Analytics* (pp. 274–296). IGI Global. doi:10.4018/978-1-5225-3870-7.ch016

Eid, R., & Abdelkader, A. A. (2017). Customer Orientation Implementation Constructs in the Banking Sector. *International Journal of Online Marketing*, *7*(2), 1–22. doi:10.4018/IJOM.2017040101

Ekhlassi, A., & Zahedi, A. (2018). A Unique Method of Constructing Brand Perceptual Maps by the Text Mining of Multimedia Consumer Reviews. *International Journal of Mobile Computing and Multimedia Communications*, 9(3), 1–22. doi:10.4018/IJMCMC.2018070101

El Hassani, M., Falih, N., & Bouikhalene, B. (2020). Search for Information in Text Files. In M. Sarfraz (Ed.), *Critical Approaches to Information Retrieval Research* (pp. 69–77). IGI Global. doi:10.4018/978-1-7998-1021-6.ch004

Elazab, A., Mahmood, M. A., & Hefny, H. A. (2018). Social Media and Social Networking. In F. Di Virgilio (Ed.), *Social Media for Knowledge Management Applications in Modern Organizations* (pp. 144–167). IGI Global. doi:10.4018/978-1-5225-2897-5.ch007

Elhadad, M. K., Badran, K. M., & Salama, G. I. (2018). A Novel Approach for Ontology-Based Feature Vector Generation for Web Text Document Classification. *International Journal of Software Innovation*, 6(1), 1–10. doi:10.4018/IJSI.2018010101

Emamipour, S., Sali, R., & Yousefi, Z. (2017). A Multi-Objective Ensemble Method for Class Imbalance Learning. *International Journal of Big Data and Analytics in Healthcare*, 2(1), 16–34. doi:10.4018/IJBDAH.2017010102

Fernandes, B. Coimbra, C. & Abelha, A. (2018). Real-Time Healthcare Intelligence in Organ Transplantation. In Next-Generation Mobile and Pervasive Healthcare Solutions (pp. 128-152). IGI Global. http://doi:10.4018/978-1-5225-2851-7.ch009

Firoze, A., Deb, T., & Rahman, R. M. (2018). Deep Learning and Data Balancing Approaches in Mining Hospital Surveillance Data. In J. Tan (Ed.), *Handbook of Research on Emerging Perspectives on Healthcare Information Systems and Informatics* (pp. 140–212). IGI Global. doi:10.4018/978-1-5225-5460-8.ch008

Gadekallu, T., Kidwai, B., Sharma, S., Pareek, R., & Karnam, S. (2019). Application of Data Mining Techniques in Weather Forecasting. In D. S. Rajput, R. S. Thakur, & S. M. Basha (Eds.), *Sentiment Analysis and Knowledge Discovery in Contemporary Business* (pp. 162–174). IGI Global. doi:10.4018/978-1-5225-4999-4.ch010

Gallagher, C., Furey, E., & Curran, K. (2019). The Application of Sentiment Analysis and Text Analytics to Customer Experience Reviews to Understand What Customers Are Really Saying. *International Journal of Data Warehousing and Mining*, *15*(4), 21–47. doi:10.4018/IJDWM.2019100102

Guerreiro, J., & Loureiro, S. M. (2020). Unraveling E-WOM Patterns Using Text Mining and Sentiment Analysis. In S. M. Loureiro & H. R. Kaufmann (Eds.), *Exploring the Power of Electronic Word-of-Mouth in the Services Industry* (pp. 88–100). IGI Global. doi:10.4018/978-1-5225-8575-6.ch006

Guhathakurta, S., Zhang, G., Chen, G., Burnette, C., & Sepkowitz, I. (2019). Mining Social Media to Measure Neighborhood Quality in the City of Atlanta. *International Journal of E-Planning Research*, *8*(1), 1–18. doi:10.4018/IJEPR.2019010101

Gulzar, Z., & Leema, A. A. (2017). Status and Quality of E-Learning in Context of Indian Universities. In P. Tripathi & S. Mukerji (Eds.), *Handbook of Research on Technology-Centric Strategies for Higher Education Administration* (pp. 405–430). IGI Global. doi:10.4018/978-1-5225-2548-6.ch023

Hamami, D., Baghdad, A., & Shankland, C. (2017). Decision Support based on Bio-PEPA Modeling and Decision Tree Induction. *International Journal of Information Systems in the Service Sector*, *9*(2), 71–101. doi:10.4018/IJISSS.2017040104

Hamidi, H., & Hashemzadeh, E. (2017). An Approach to Improve Generation of Association Rules in Order to Be Used in Recommenders. *International Journal of Data Warehousing and Mining*, *13*(4), 1–18. doi:10.4018/IJDWM.2017100101

Hendel, R. J. (2018). A Boolean Logic Approach to Issues of Vagueness, Heuristics, Subjectivity, and Data Mining. In J. Horne (Ed.), *Philosophical Perceptions on Logic and Order* (pp. 196–217). IGI Global. doi:10.4018/978-1-5225-2443-4.ch006

Heng, S. (2017). A New Intelligent Optimization Network Online Learning Behavior in Multimedia Big Data Environment. *International Journal of Mobile Computing and Multimedia Communications*, *8*(3), 21–31. doi:10.4018/IJMCMC.2017070102

Hernandez, M. K. (2017). Survey of the Different Type of Data Analytics Algorithms. *International Journal of Strategic Information Technology and Applications*, *8*(1), 50–64. doi:10.4018/IJSITA.2017010104

Honarvar, A. R. & Sami, A. (2018). Improve Home Energy Management System by Extracting Usage Patterns From Power Usage Big Data of Homes' Appliances. In Handbook of Research on Contemporary Perspectives on Web-Based Systems (pp. 126-141). IGI Global. http://doi:10.4018/978-1-5225-5384-7.ch007

Hu, W. Kaabouch, N. Guo, H. & ElSaid, A. A. (2018). Location-Based Advertising Using Location-Aware Data Mining. In Applications of Security, Mobile, Analytic, and Cloud (SMAC) Technologies for Effective Information Processing and Management (pp. 196-211). IGI Global. http://doi:10.4018/978-1-5225-4044-1.ch010

Ibrahim, A. A., Hashad, A. I., & Shawky, N. E. (2017). A Comparison of Open Source Data Mining Tools for Breast Cancer Classification. In A. E. Hassanien & T. Gaber (Eds.), *Handbook of Research on Machine Learning Innovations and Trends* (pp. 636–651). IGI Global. doi:10.4018/978-1-5225-2229-4.ch027

Ji, C., Zhao, C., Pan, L., Liu, S., Yang, C., & Wu, L. (2017). A Fast Shapelet Discovery Algorithm Based on Important Data Points. *International Journal of Web Services Research*, *14*(2), 67–80. doi:10.4018/IJWSR.2017040104

Jiang, Y., Clarke-Midura, J., Baker, R. S., Paquette, L., & Keller, B. (2018). How Immersive Virtual Environments Foster Self-Regulated Learning. In R. Zheng (Ed.), *Digital Technologies and Instructional Design for Personalized Learning* (pp. 28–54). IGI Global. doi:10.4018/978-1-5225-3940-7.ch002

Kabli, F., Hamou, R. M., & Amine, A. (2018). Protein Classification Using N-gram Technique and Association Rules. *International Journal of Software Innovation*, *6*(2), 77–89. doi:10.4018/IJSI.2018040106

Kang, Y., & Yang, K. C. (2020). Privacy Concerns in the VR and AR Applications in Creative Cultural Industries. In S. M. Loureiro (Ed.), *Managerial Challenges and Social Impacts of Virtual and Augmented Reality* (pp. 142–164). IGI Global. doi:10.4018/978-1-7998-2874-7.ch009

Kaplesh, P., & Pang, S. K. (2020). Software Testing. In C. Pang (Ed.), *Software Engineering for Agile Application Development* (pp. 189–211). IGI Global. doi:10.4018/978-1-7998-2531-9.ch008

Karthick, G. S., & Pankajavalli, P. B. (2019). Internet of Things Testing Framework, Automation, Challenges, Solutions and Practices. In D. J. Mala (Ed.), *Integrating the Internet of Things Into Software Engineering Practices* (pp. 87–124). IGI Global. doi:10.4018/978-1-5225-7790-4.ch005

Kasemsap, K. (2017). Knowledge Discovery and Data Visualization. *International Journal of Organizational and Collective Intelligence*, 7(3), 56–69. doi:10.4018/IJOCI.2017070105

Kasemsap, K. (2018). Electronic Commerce and Decision Support Systems. In G. Sreedhar (Ed.), *Improving E-Commerce Web Applications Through Business Intelligence Techniques* (pp. 251–270). IGI Global. doi:10.4018/978-1-5225-3646-8.ch011

Kejriwal, M. (2020). Domain-Specific Search Engines for Investigating Human Trafficking and Other Illicit Activities. In Encyclopedia of Criminal Activities and the Deep Web (pp. 478-496). IGI Global. http://doi:10.4018/978-1-5225-9715-5.ch033

Kenekar, T. V., & Dani, A. R. (2017). Privacy Preserving Data Mining on Unstructured Data. In S. Tamane, V. K. Solanki, & N. Dey (Eds.), *Privacy and Security Policies in Big Data* (pp. 167–190). IGI Global. doi:10.4018/978-1-5225-2486-1.ch008

Kenekayoro, P. (2018). An Exploratory Study on the Use of Machine Learning to Predict Student Academic Performance.]. *International Journal of Knowledge-Based Organizations*, 8(4), 67–79. doi:10.4018/IJKBO.2018100104

Khamparia, A., & Pandey, B. (2018). SVM and PCA Based Learning Feature Classification Approaches for E-Learning System. *International Journal of Web-Based Learning and Teaching Technologies*, 13(2), 32–45. doi:10.4018/IJWLTT.2018040103

Khan, W., Selamat, S. A., & Ramachandran, M. (2018). Appraisal of Transactional Data Through Visualisation for SMEs. In N. Gwangwava & M. Mutingi (Eds.), *E-Manufacturing and E-Service Strategies in Contemporary Organizations* (pp. 119–153). IGI Global. doi:10.4018/978-1-5225-3628-4.ch006

Khare, A. R., & Shrivasta, P. (2018). Data Mining for the Internet of Things. In A. K. Prasad (Ed.), *Exploring the Convergence of Big Data and the Internet of Things* (pp. 181–191). IGI Global. doi:10.4018/978-1-5225-2947-7.ch013

Klepac, G. (2018). Finding Optimal Input Values for Desired Target Output by Using Particle Swarm Optimization Algorithm Within Probabilistic Models. In Incorporating Nature-Inspired Paradigms in Computational Applications (pp. 76-107). IGI Global. http://doi:10.4018/978-1-5225-5020-4.ch003

Klepac, G. (2018). Using Particle Swarm Optimization Algorithm as an Optimization Tool Within Developed Neural Networks. In Y. Shi (Ed.), *Critical Developments and Applications of Swarm Intelligence* (pp. 215–244). IGI Global. doi:10.4018/978-1-5225-5134-8.ch009

Kompalli, P. L. (2018). Knowledge Discovery Using Data Stream Mining. In H. Bansal, G. Shrivastava, G. N. Nguyen, & L. Stanciu (Eds.), *Social Network Analytics for Contemporary Business Organizations* (pp. 231–258). IGI Global. doi:10.4018/978-1-5225-5097-6.ch012

Kompalli, P. L. (2019). Knowledge Discovery From Evolving Data Streams. In Machine Learning Techniques for Improved Business Analytics (pp. 19-39). IGI Global. http://doi:10.4018/978-1-5225-3534-8.ch002

Krishna, G. (2018). Social Networking Data Analysis Tools and Services. In H. Bansal, G. Shrivastava, G. N. Nguyen, & L. Stanciu (Eds.), *Social Network Analytics for Contemporary Business Organizations* (pp. 19–34). IGI Global. doi:10.4018/978-1-5225-5097-6.ch002

Krishnamoorthy, S., Sadasivam, G. S., Rajalakshmi, M., Kowsalyaa, K., & Dhivya, M. (2017). Privacy Preserving Fuzzy Association Rule Mining in Data Clusters Using Particle Swarm Optimization. *International Journal of Intelligent Information Technologies*, *13*(2), 1–20. doi:10.4018/IJIIT.2017040101

Kumar, A., & Sarkar, B. K. (2018). Performance Assessment of Learning Algorithms on Multi-Domain Data Sets. *International Journal of Knowledge Discovery in Bioinformatics*, *8*(1), 27–41. doi:10.4018/IJKDB.2018010103

Kumar, M. & Bajeel, P. N. (2017). Introduction to System Reliability Evaluation through Bayesian Approach. In Mathematical Concepts and Applications in Mechanical Engineering and Mechatronics (pp. 130-153). IGI Global. http://doi:10.4018/978-1-5225-1639-2.ch007

Kumar, M. S. & Prabhu, J. (2018). Recent Development in Big Data Analytics. In Applications of Security, Mobile, Analytic, and Cloud (SMAC) Technologies for Effective Information Processing and Management (pp. 233-257). IGI Global. http://doi:10.4018/978-1-5225-4044-1.ch012

Kumar, R., Pandey, P., & Pattnaik, P. K. (2017). Discover Patterns from Web-Based Dataset. In G. Sreedhar (Ed.), *Web Data Mining and the Development of Knowledge-Based Decision Support Systems* (pp. 78–106). IGI Global. doi:10.4018/978-1-5225-1877-8.ch006

Kumar, R., Pattnaik, P. K., & Pandey, P. (2017). Secure Data Analysis in Clusters (Iris Database). In S. K. Trivedi, S. Dey, A. Kumar, & T. K. Panda (Eds.), *Handbook of Research on Advanced Data Mining Techniques and Applications for Business Intelligence* (pp. 52–61). IGI Global. doi:10.4018/978-1-5225-2031-3.ch004

Kumar, S., Tiwari, P., & Denis, K. V. (2018). Augmenting Classifiers Performance through Clustering. *International Journal of Information Retrieval Research*, *8*(1), 57–68. doi:10.4018/IJIRR.2018010104

Kuri-Morales, A. F. (2019). Minimum Database Determination and Preprocessing for Machine Learning. In L. Zhang & Y. Ning (Eds.), *Innovative Solutions and Applications of Web Services Technology* (pp. 94–131). IGI Global. doi:10.4018/978-1-5225-7268-8.ch005

Lachana, Z., Loutsaris, M. A., Alexopoulos, C., & Charalabidis, Y. (2020). Automated Analysis and Interrelation of Legal Elements Based on Text Mining. *International Journal of E-Services and Mobile Applications*, *12*(2), 79–96. doi:10.4018/IJESMA.2020040105

Leung, C. K., Carmichael, C. L., Johnstone, P., Xing, R. R., & Yuen, D. S. (2017). Interactive Visual Analytics of Big Data. In J. Lu & Q. Xu (Eds.), *Ontologies and Big Data Considerations for Effective Intelligence* (pp. 1–26). IGI Global. doi:10.4018/978-1-5225-2058-0.ch001

Liu, S., Ni, C., Liu, Z., Peng, X., & Cheng, H. N. (2017). Mining Individual Learning Topics in Course Reviews Based on Author Topic Model. *International Journal of Distance Education Technologies*, *15*(3), 1–14. doi:10.4018/IJDET.2017070101

Lomax, S., & Vadera, S. (2017). Case Studies in Applying Data Mining for Churn Analysis. *International Journal of Conceptual Structures and Smart Applications*, *5*(2), 22–33. doi:10.4018/IJCSSA.2017070102

Lorenzi, F. Dumer, L. C. Vernetti, R. F. Pereira, D. S. Reategui, E. B. & Epstein, D. (2019). Serious Games Tools to Support the Literacy Process. In Handbook of Research on Immersive Digital Games in Educational Environments (pp. 112-130). IGI Global. http://doi:10.4018/978-1-5225-5790-6.ch005

Lu, R., Tsao, H., Lin, H. K., Ma, Y., & Chuang, C. (2019). Sentiment Analysis of Brand Personality Positioning Through Text Mining. *Journal of Information Technology Research*, *12*(3), 93–103. doi:10.4018/JITR.2019070106

Lytras, M. D., Papadopoulou, P., Marouli, C., & Misseyanni, A. (2018). Higher Education Out-of-the-Box. In S. L. Burton (Ed.), *Engaged Scholarship and Civic Responsibility in Higher Education* (pp. 67–100). IGI Global. doi:10.4018/978-1-5225-3649-9.ch004

Mahajan, R. (2019). Introduction to Use and Analysis of Big Data in E-Learning. In L. N. Makewa, B. M. Ngussa, & J. M. Kuboja (Eds.), *Technology-Supported Teaching and Research Methods for Educators* (pp. 75–87). IGI Global. doi:10.4018/978-1-5225-5915-3.ch004

Manogaran, G., Thota, C., & Lopez, D. (2018). Human-Computer Interaction With Big Data Analytics. In D. Lopez & M. Durai (Eds.), *HCI Challenges and Privacy Preservation in Big Data Security* (pp. 1–22). IGI Global. doi:10.4018/978-1-5225-2863-0.ch001

Meddah, I. H., & Belkadi, K. (2018). Mining Patterns Using Business Process Management. In R. M. Hamou (Ed.), *Handbook of Research on Biomimicry in Information Retrieval and Knowledge Management* (pp. 78–89). IGI Global. doi:10.4018/978-1-5225-3004-6.ch005

Menad, H., & Amine, A. (2017). A Bio Inspired Approach for Cardiotocogram Data Classification. *International Journal of Organizational and Collective Intelligence*, *7*(3), 1–14. doi:10.4018/IJOCI.2017070101

Menad, H., & Amine, A. (2018). Bio-Inspired Algorithms for Medical Data Analysis. In R. M. Hamou (Ed.), *Handbook of Research on Biomimicry in Information Retrieval and Knowledge Management* (pp. 251–275). IGI Global. doi:10.4018/978-1-5225-3004-6.ch014

Mihaescu, M. C. (2018). Machine Learning Data Analysis for On-Line Education Environments. In S. Khalid (Ed.), *Applied Computational Intelligence and Soft Computing in Engineering* (pp. 277–300). IGI Global. doi:10.4018/978-1-5225-3129-6.ch012

Mohan, S. V., & Angamuthu, T. (2018). Association Rule Hiding in Privacy Preserving Data Mining. *International Journal of Information Security and Privacy*, *12*(3), 141–163. doi:10.4018/IJISP.2018070108

Mohbey, K. K. (2018). Utility Based Frequent Pattern Extraction from Mobile Web Services Sequence. *Journal of Information Technology Research, 11*(2), 31–52. doi:10.4018/JITR.2018040103

Moorthy, U., & Gandhi, U. D. (2018). A Survey of Big Data Analytics Using Machine Learning Algorithms. In D. Lopez & M. Durai (Eds.), *HCI Challenges and Privacy Preservation in Big Data Security* (pp. 95–123). IGI Global. doi:10.4018/978-1-5225-2863-0.ch005

Mukherjee, S. & Nath, A. (2017). Web Service Clustering and Data Mining in SOA System. In Exploring Enterprise Service Bus in the Service-Oriented Architecture Paradigm (pp. 157-177). IGI Global. http://doi:10.4018/978-1-5225-2157-0.ch011

Navlani, A., & Gupta, V. B. (2017). Alternative Clustering. In R. Sahu, M. Dash, & A. Kumar (Eds.), *Applying Predictive Analytics Within the Service Sector* (pp. 1–12). IGI Global. doi:10.4018/978-1-5225-2148-8.ch001

Ng, W. S. (2017). Web Data Mining in Education. In G. Sreedhar (Ed.), *Web Data Mining and the Development of Knowledge-Based Decision Support Systems* (pp. 58–77). IGI Global. doi:10.4018/978-1-5225-1877-8.ch005

Nguyen, S., Olinsky, A., Quinn, J., & Schumacher, P. (2018). Predictive Modeling for Imbalanced Big Data in SAS Enterprise Miner and R. *International Journal of Fog Computing, 1*(2), 83–108. doi:10.4018/IJFC.2018070103

Pabreja, K. (2017). Comparison of Different Classification Techniques for Educational Data. *International Journal of Information Systems in the Service Sector, 9*(1), 54–67. doi:10.4018/IJISSS.2017010104

Pal, A., & Kumar, M. (2017). Frequent Itemset Mining in Large Datasets a Survey. *International Journal of Information Retrieval Research, 7*(4), 37–49. doi:10.4018/IJIRR.2017100103

Paliwal, G., & Bunglowala, A. (2019). Ubiquitous Wearable Healthcare Monitoring System Architectural Design for Prevention, Detection, and Monitoring of Chronic Diseases. In T. Edoh, P. Pawar, & S. Mohammad (Eds.), *Pre-Screening Systems for Early Disease Prediction, Detection, and Prevention* (pp. 190–218). IGI Global. doi:10.4018/978-1-5225-7131-5.ch007

Pandey, A. & Pandey, R. (2017). Service-Oriented Framework for Advance Diagnosis of MSMEs Turning into NPAs. In Exploring Enterprise Service Bus in the Service-Oriented Architecture Paradigm (pp. 264-282). IGI Global. http://doi:10.4018/978-1-5225-2157-0.ch017

Paul, S., Mitra, A., & Dey, S. (2017). Issues and Challenges in Web Crawling for Information Extraction. In D. Acharjya & A. Mitra (Eds.), *Bio-Inspired Computing for Information Retrieval Applications* (pp. 93–121). IGI Global. doi:10.4018/978-1-5225-2375-8.ch004

Porouhan, P., & Premchaiswadi, W. (2017). Process Mining and Learners' Behavior Analytics in a Collaborative and Web-Based Multi-Tabletop Environment. *International Journal of Online Pedagogy and Course Design*, *7*(3), 29–53. doi:10.4018/IJOPCD.2017070103

Pradhan, M. (2018). Indian Healthcare Service Management Through Data Mining. In Next-Generation Mobile and Pervasive Healthcare Solutions (pp. 219-233). IGI Global. http://doi:10.4018/978-1-5225-2851-7.ch014

Prasad, A. V., & Mandhala, V. N. (2017). Mining on Social Media. In G. Sreedhar (Ed.), *Web Data Mining and the Development of Knowledge-Based Decision Support Systems* (pp. 206–222). IGI Global. doi:10.4018/978-1-5225-1877-8.ch013

Premalatha, M., Viswanathan, V., Suganya, G., Kaviya, M., & Vijaya, A. (2018). Educational Data Mining and Recommender Systems Survey. *International Journal of Web Portals*, *10*(1), 39–53. doi:10.4018/IJWP.2018010104

Pudumalar, S. Suriya, K. S. & Rohini, K. (2018). Data Classification and Prediction. In Applications of Security, Mobile, Analytic, and Cloud (SMAC) Technologies for Effective Information Processing and Management (pp. 149-173). IGI Global. http://doi:10.4018/978-1-5225-4044-1.ch008

Puri, S., & Singh, S. P. (2018). Hindi Text Document Classification System Using SVM and Fuzzy. *International Journal of Rough Sets and Data Analysis*, *5*(4), 1–31. doi:10.4018/IJRSDA.2018100101

Puri, S., & Singh, S. P. (2019). A Hybrid Hindi Printed Document Classification System Using SVM and Fuzzy. *Journal of Information Technology Research*, *12*(4), 107–131. doi:10.4018/JITR.2019100106

Puri, S., & Singh, S. P. (2020). A Fuzzy Matching based Image Classification System for Printed and Handwritten Text Documents. *Journal of Information Technology Research*, *13*(2), 155–194. doi:10.4018/JITR.2020040110

Rahman, N. (2018). Data Mining Techniques and Applications. *International Journal of Strategic Information Technology and Applications*, *9*(1), 78–97. doi:10.4018/IJSITA.2018010104

Rahmani, A. (2019). Big Data and Privacy State of the Art. In H. A. Bouarara, R. M. Hamou, & A. Rahmani (Eds.), *Advanced Metaheuristic Methods in Big Data Retrieval and Analytics* (pp. 104–158). IGI Global. doi:10.4018/978-1-5225-7338-8.ch006

Rahmani, M. E., & Amine, A. (2019). Ecological Data Exploration. In H. A. Bouarara, R. M. Hamou, & A. Rahmani (Eds.), *Advanced Metaheuristic Methods in Big Data Retrieval and Analytics* (pp. 27–62). IGI Global. doi:10.4018/978-1-5225-7338-8.ch002

Rahmani, M. E., Amine, A., & Hamou, R. M. (2018). Sonar Data Classification Using a New Algorithm Inspired from Black Holes Phenomenon. *International Journal of Information Retrieval Research*, *8*(2), 25–39. doi:10.4018/IJIRR.2018040102

Ramsey, G. W., & Bapna, S. (2019). Predicting Patient Turnover. In K. Chui & M. D. Lytras (Eds.), *Computational Methods and Algorithms for Medicine and Optimized Clinical Practice* (pp. 108–132). IGI Global. doi:10.4018/978-1-5225-8244-1.ch006

Rana, H., & Lal, M. (2017). A Comparative Study Based on Rough Set and Classification Via Clustering Approaches to Handle Incomplete Data to Predict Learning Styles. *International Journal of Decision Support System Technology*, *9*(2), 1–20. doi:10.4018/IJDSST.2017040101

Rawat, B., & Dwivedi, S. K. (2019). Discovering Learners' Characteristics Through Cluster Analysis for Recommendation of Courses in E-Learning Environment. *International Journal of Information and Communication Technology Education*, *15*(1), 42–66. doi:10.4018/IJICTE.2019010104

Reddi, S. (2017). Privacy Preserving Data Mining Using Time Series Data Aggregation. *International Journal of Strategic Information Technology and Applications*, *8*(4), 1–15. doi:10.4018/IJSITA.2017100101

Reddy, C. M. (2017). Knowledge-Based Decision Support System for Analyzing the Relevancies of Various Attributes Based on Their Characteristics. In G. Sreedhar (Ed.), *Web Data Mining and the Development of Knowledge-Based Decision Support Systems* (pp. 184–193). IGI Global. doi:10.4018/978-1-5225-1877-8.ch011

Rouhani, S., & Maryam MirSharif. (2018). Data Mining Approach for the Early Risk Assessment of Gestational Diabetes Mellitus. *International Journal of Knowledge Discovery in Bioinformatics, 8*(1), 1–11. doi:10.4018/IJKDB.2018010101

Safdari, R., Rezaei-Hachesu, P., Marjan GhaziSaeedi, Samad-Soltani, T., & Zolnoori, M. (2018). Evaluation of Classification Algorithms vs Knowledge-Based Methods for Differential Diagnosis of Asthma in Iranian Patients. *International Journal of Information Systems in the Service Sector, 10*(2), 22–35. doi:10.4018/IJISSS.2018040102

Samanta, S., & Pal, M. (2018). Link Prediction in Social Networks. In N. Meghanathan (Ed.), *Graph Theoretic Approaches for Analyzing Large-Scale Social Networks* (pp. 164–172). IGI Global. doi:10.4018/978-1-5225-2814-2.ch010

Santana-Mansilla, P., Costaguta, R., & Schiaffino, S. (2018). A Multi-Agent Model for Personalizing Learning Material for Collaborative Groups. In F. Cipolla-Ficarra (Ed.), *Optimizing Human-Computer Interaction With Emerging Technologies* (pp. 343–375). IGI Global. doi:10.4018/978-1-5225-2616-2.ch015

Saoud, M. S., Boubetra, A., & Attia, S. (2018). A Simulation Decision Support System for the Healthcare Emergency Department Optimization. In J. Tan (Ed.), *Handbook of Research on Emerging Perspectives on Healthcare Information Systems and Informatics* (pp. 347–367). IGI Global. doi:10.4018/978-1-5225-5460-8.ch015

Sarmah, S. P. & Moharana, U. C. (2018). Spare Parts Inventory Management Literature and Direction Towards the Use of Data Mining Technique. In Handbook of .Research on Promoting Business Process Improvement Through Inventory Control Techniques (pp. 534-558). IGI Global. http://doi:10.4018/978-1-5225-3232-3.ch028

Sarowar, M. G., Kamal, M. S., & Dey, N. (2019). Internet of Things and Its Impacts in Computing Intelligence. In N. Dey & S. Tamane (Eds.), *Big Data Analytics for Smart and Connected Cities* (pp. 103–136). IGI Global. doi:10.4018/978-1-5225-6207-8.ch005

Sathiyamoorthi, V. (2017). Data Mining and Data Warehousing. In G. Sreedhar (Ed.), *Web Data Mining and the Development of Knowledge-Based Decision Support Systems* (pp. 312–337). IGI Global. doi:10.4018/978-1-5225-1877-8.ch016

Sathiyamoorthi, V. (2017). Challenges and Issues in Web-Based Information Retrieval System. In N. K. Kamila (Ed.), *Advancing Cloud Database Systems and Capacity Planning With Dynamic Applications* (pp. 176–194). IGI Global. doi:10.4018/978-1-5225-2013-9.ch008

Sathiyamoorthi, V. (2017). Web Caching System. In S. Saeed, Y. A. Bamarouf, T. Ramayah, & S. Z. Iqbal (Eds.), *Design Solutions for User-Centric Information Systems* (pp. 184–204). IGI Global. doi:10.4018/978-1-5225-1944-7.ch011

Sayed, S., Ansari, S. A., & Poonia, R. (2018). Overview of Concept Drifts Detection Methodology in Data Stream. In V. Tiwari, R. S. Thakur, B. Tiwari, & S. Gupta (Eds.), *Handbook of Research on Pattern Engineering System Development for Big Data Analytics* (pp. 310–317). IGI Global. doi:10.4018/978-1-5225-3870-7.ch018

Sedkaoui, S. (2019). Investigating the Factors for Predictive Marketing Implementation in Algerian Organizations. In N. Ray (Ed.), *Managing Diversity, Innovation, and Infrastructure in Digital Business* (pp. 82–115). IGI Global. doi:10.4018/978-1-5225-5993-1.ch005

Seino, K., Enomoto, Y., & Miyazawa, S. (2018). Narrative Analysis of Employment Support for Students With Developmental Disabilities. In T. Ogata & S. Asakawa (Eds.), *Content Generation Through Narrative Communication and Simulation* (pp. 341–357). IGI Global. doi:10.4018/978-1-5225-4775-4.ch012

Sethuraman, M. S. (2017). Computational Intelligence Foundations and Principles. In V. Santhi (Ed.), *Recent Advances in Applied Thermal Imaging for Industrial Applications* (pp. 62–85). IGI Global. doi:10.4018/978-1-5225-2423-6.ch003

Shetty, C., Sowmya, B. J., Anemish, S., & Seema, S. (2019). IOT and Data Analytics Solution for Reducing Pollution, Accidents, and Its Impact on Environment. In K. Srinivasa, P. Lathar, & G. Siddesh (Eds.), *The Rise of Fog Computing in the Digital Era* (pp. 177–209). IGI Global. doi:10.4018/978-1-5225-6070-8.ch009

Shokouhyar, S., Saeidpour, P., & Otarkhani, A. (2018). Predicting Customers' Churn Using Data Mining Technique and its Effect on the Development of Marketing Applications in Value-Added Services in Telecom Industry. *International Journal of Information Systems in the Service Sector*, *10*(4), 59–72. doi:10.4018/IJISSS.2018100104

Shrivastava, S., & Pateriya, R. K. (2018). Secure Framework for E-Commerce Applications in Cloud Environment. In G. Sreedhar (Ed.), *Improving E-Commerce Web Applications Through Business Intelligence Techniques* (pp. 82–109). IGI Global. doi:10.4018/978-1-5225-3646-8.ch004

Simmonds, J., Gómez, J. A., & Ledezma, A. (2018). Statistical and Data Mining Techniques for Understanding Water Quality Profiles in a Mining-Affected River Basin. *International Journal of Agricultural and Environmental Information Systems*, *9*(2), 1–19. doi:10.4018/IJAEIS.2018040101

Singh, D. (2017). An Effort to Design an Integrated System to Extract Information Under the Domain of Metaheuristics. *International Journal of Applied Evolutionary Computation*, *8*(3), 13–52. doi:10.4018/IJAEC.2017070102

Solanki, A. & Kumar, E. (2018). Study and Analysis of Delay Factors of Delhi Metro Using Data Sciences and Social Media. In Innovative Applications of Big Data in the Railway Industry (pp. 209-223). IGI Global. http://doi:10.4018/978-1-5225-3176-0.ch009

Sreedhar, G. (2018). A Framework to Improve Performance of E-Commerce Websites. In G. Sreedhar (Ed.), *Improving E-Commerce Web Applications Through Business Intelligence Techniques* (pp. 1–15). IGI Global. doi:10.4018/978-1-5225-3646-8.ch001

Sreedhar, G., & Chari, A. A. (2017). Development of Efficient Decision Support System Using Web Data Mining. In G. Sreedhar (Ed.), *Web Data Mining and the Development of Knowledge-Based Decision Support Systems* (pp. 1–11). IGI Global. doi:10.4018/978-1-5225-1877-8.ch001

Srinivasan, S., & Chauhan, D. S. (2020). Requirement-Based Test Approach and Traceability for High-Integrity Airborne Embedded Systems. In V. Gupta (Ed.), *Crowdsourcing and Probabilistic Decision-Making in Software Engineering* (pp. 35–50). IGI Global. doi:10.4018/978-1-5225-9659-2.ch003

Subashini, B., & Mala, D. J. (2017). An Effective Approach to Test Suite Reduction and Fault Detection Using Data Mining Techniques. *International Journal of Open Source Software and Processes*, 8(4), 1–31. doi:10.4018/IJOSSP.2017100101

Sumana, M., Hareesha, K. S., & Kumar, S. (2018). Semantically Secure Classifiers for Privacy Preserving Data Mining. In Y. Maleh (Ed.), *Security and Privacy Management, Techniques, and Protocols* (pp. 66–95). IGI Global. doi:10.4018/978-1-5225-5583-4.ch003

Tandon, A. (2018). Mining Smart Meter Data. In Z. H. Gontar (Ed.), *Smart Grid Analytics for Sustainability and Urbanization* (pp. 196–214). IGI Global. doi:10.4018/978-1-5225-3996-4.ch007

Tarik, B., & Zakaria, E. (2018). Privacy Preserving Classification of Biomedical Data With Secure Removing of Duplicate Records. *International Journal of Organizational and Collective Intelligence*, 8(3), 41–58. doi:10.4018/IJOCI.2018070104

Taylor, P., Griffiths, N., Bhalerao, A., Xu, Z., Gelencser, A., & Popham, T. (2017). Investigating the Feasibility of Vehicle Telemetry Data as a Means of Predicting Driver Workload. *International Journal of Mobile Human Computer Interaction*, 9(3), 54–72. doi:10.4018/ijmhci.2017070104

Tiwari, P., & Shukla, P. K. (2019). A Review on Various Features and Techniques of Crop Yield Prediction Using Geo-Spatial Data. *International Journal of Organizational and Collective Intelligence*, 9(1), 37–50. doi:10.4018/IJOCI.2019010103

Tripathi, M., Shah, S., Bahal, P., Sharma, H., & Gupta, R. (2019). Smart MM. In M. D. Lytras, N. Aljohani, L. Daniela, & A. Visvizi (Eds.), *Cognitive Computing in Technology-Enhanced Learning* (pp. 225–251). IGI Global. doi:10.4018/978-1-5225-9031-6.ch011

Vakeel, K. A. (2017). Mining Big Data for Marketing Intelligence. In S. K. Trivedi, S. Dey, A. Kumar, & T. K. Panda (Eds.), *Handbook of Research on Advanced Data Mining Techniques and Applications for Business Intelligence* (pp. 250–258). IGI Global. doi:10.4018/978-1-5225-2031-3.ch015

Vanani, I. R., & Kheiri, M. S. (2018). Big Data Analytics and Visualization of Performance of Stock Exchange Companies Based on Balanced Scorecard Indicators. In R. S. Segall & J. S. Cook (Eds.), *Handbook of Research on Big Data Storage and Visualization Techniques* (pp. 853–872). IGI Global. doi:10.4018/978-1-5225-3142-5.ch029

Varaprasad Rao, M., & Vishnu Murthy, G. (2017). DSS for Web Mining Using Recommendation System. In G. Sreedhar (Ed.), *Web Data Mining and the Development of Knowledge-Based Decision Support Systems* (pp. 22–34). IGI Global. doi:10.4018/978-1-5225-1877-8.ch003

Vargas-Vera, M. (2018). An Analysis of Student Performance in a Digital Electronics Design Course. In M. D. Lytras, L. Daniela, & A. Visvizi (Eds.), *Enhancing Knowledge Discovery and Innovation in the Digital Era* (pp. 107–125). IGI Global. doi:10.4018/978-1-5225-4191-2.ch006

Vargas-Vera, M., Salles, C., Parot, J., & Letelier, S. (2017). A E-Business Case of Study. *International Journal of Knowledge Society Research*, 8(3), 1–20. doi:10.4018/IJKSR.2017070101

Victor, N., & Lopez, D. (2018). Privacy Preserving Big Data Publishing. In D. Lopez & M. Durai (Eds.), *HCI Challenges and Privacy Preservation in Big Data Security* (pp. 47–70). IGI Global. doi:10.4018/978-1-5225-2863-0.ch003

Vinutha, H., & Basavaraju, P. (2018). Analysis of Feature Selection and Ensemble Classifier Methods for Intrusion Detection. *International Journal of Natural Computing Research*, 7(1), 57–72. doi:10.4018/IJNCR.2018010104

Wall, J. D., & Singh, R. (2017). Contextualized Meaning Extraction. *International Journal of Organizational and Collective Intelligence*, 7(3), 15–29. doi:10.4018/IJOCI.2017070102

Wang, C., Lin, C., Hwang, G., Kung, S., & Chen, S. (2017). A Test Sheet Optimization Approach to Supporting Web-based Learning Diagnosis Using Group Testing Methods. *International Journal of Online Pedagogy and Course Design*, 7(4), 1–23. doi:10.4018/IJOPCD.2017100101

Wang, S., Zhao, Y., Shu, Y., & Shi, W. (2017). Improved Approximation Algorithm for Maximal Information Coefficient. *International Journal of Data Warehousing and Mining*, 13(1), 76–93. doi:10.4018/IJDWM.2017010104

Wani, Z. H., Giri, K. J., & Bashir, R. (2019). A Generic Data Mining Model for Software Cost Estimation Based on Novel Input Selection Procedure. *International Journal of Information Retrieval Research*, *9*(1), 16–32. doi:10.4018/IJIRR.2019010102

Wu, Q., & Yang, W. (2017). A Local Approach and Comparison with Other Data Mining Approaches in Software Application. In J. Lu & Q. Xu (Eds.), *Examining Information Retrieval and Image Processing Paradigms in Multidisciplinary Contexts* (pp. 1–26). IGI Global. doi:10.4018/978-1-5225-1884-6.ch001

Yang, J., Li, J., & Xu, Q. (2018). A Highly Efficient Big Data Mining Algorithm Based on Stock Market. *International Journal of Grid and High Performance Computing*, *10*(2), 14–33. doi:10.4018/IJGHPC.2018040102

Yang, K. C., & Kang, Y. (2020). Political Mobilization Strategies in Taiwan's Sunflower Student Movement on March 18, 2014. In M. Adria (Ed.), *Using New Media for Citizen Engagement and Participation* (pp. 256–279). IGI Global. doi:10.4018/978-1-7998-1828-1.ch014

Yang, K. C., & Kang, Y. (2020). What Can College Teachers Learn From Students' Experiential Narratives in Hybrid Courses? In L. N. Makewa (Ed.), *Theoretical and Practical Approaches to Innovation in Higher Education* (pp. 91–112). IGI Global. doi:10.4018/978-1-7998-1662-1.ch006

Yeh, H., & Chang, T. (2018). Mining Customer Shopping Behavior. *International Journal of Information Systems in the Service Sector*, *10*(1), 16–27. doi:10.4018/IJISSS.2018010102

Yu, C. H., Jannasch-Pennell, A., & DiGangi, S. (2018). Enhancement of Student Experience Management in Higher Education by Sentiment Analysis and Text Mining. *International Journal of Technology and Educational Marketing*, *8*(1), 16–33. doi:10.4018/IJTEM.2018010102

Zhou, X. Li, Y. Yuan, L. Ma, G. Tan, X. Zhang, K. Gong, L. & Jia, B. (2020). Learning Path Recommendation Method Based on Knowledge Map. In Handbook of Research on Managerial Practices and Disruptive Innovation in Asia (pp. 171-184). IGI Global. http://doi:10.4018/978-1-7998-0357-7.ch009

About the Author

Dimple Valayil Paul holds a Masters degree in Computer Application, an M. Phil and a PhD in Computer Science. She is currently associated with Dnyanprassarak Mandal's College and Research Centre as an Assistant Professor in Computer Science. DM's College and Research Centre is an Educational Conglomerate which provides education from Kindergarten to Postgraduation across multidisciplinary fields and is affiliated to Goa University, India. Goa University is one of India's few universities offering western languages and has a sprawling 400 acres campus with state-of-the-art infrastructure. Dr. Paul is a rank holder in Masters degree from Bharathiar University and has more than twenty years of teaching experience in various fields of Computer Science such as Educational Data Mining, Information Extraction, Multi-objective Optimization etc. She has more than twenty international research papers published in the field of Educational Data Mining and Text Mining. She lives in Goa, India with her husband and two children.

Index

T

W

Ensure Quality Research is Introduced to the Academic Community

Become an IGI Global Reviewer for Authored Book Projects

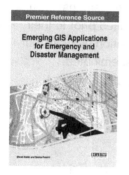

Premier Reference Source

Emerging GIS Applications for Emergency and Disaster Management

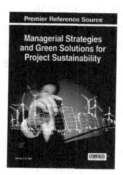

Premier Reference Source

Managerial Strategies and Green Solutions for Project Sustainability

Premier Reference Source

Comparative Approaches to Using R and Python for Statistical Data Analysis

Premier Reference Source

Solutions for High-Touch Communications in a High-Tech World

The overall success of an authored book project is dependent on quality and timely reviews.

In this competitive age of scholarly publishing, constructive and timely feedback significantly expedites the turnaround time of manuscripts from submission to acceptance, allowing the publication and discovery of forward-thinking research at a much more expeditious rate. Several IGI Global authored book projects are currently seeking highly-qualified experts in the field to fill vacancies on their respective editorial review boards:

Applications and Inquiries may be sent to:
development@igi-global.com

Applicants must have a doctorate (or an equivalent degree) as well as publishing and reviewing experience. Reviewers are asked to complete the open-ended evaluation questions with as much detail as possible in a timely, collegial, and constructive manner. All reviewers' tenures run for one-year terms on the editorial review boards and are expected to complete at least three reviews per term. Upon successful completion of this term, reviewers can be considered for an additional term.

If you have a colleague that may be interested in this opportunity, we encourage you to share this information with them.

ARE YOU READY TO PUBLISH YOUR RESEARCH?

IGI Global offers book authorship and editorship opportunities across 11 subject areas, including business, computer science, education, science and engineering, social sciences, and more!

Benefits of Publishing with IGI Global:

- Free, one-on-one editorial and promotional support.

- Expedited publishing timelines that can take your book from start to finish in less than one (1) year.

- Choose from a variety of formats including: Edited and Authored References, Handbooks of Research, Encyclopedias, and Research Insights.

- Utilize IGI Global's eEditorial Discovery® submission system in support of conducting the submission and blind review process.

- IGI Global maintains a strict adherence to ethical practices due in part to our full membership with the Committee on Publication Ethics (COPE).

- Indexing potential in prestigious indices such as Scopus®, Web of Science™, PsycINFO®, and ERIC – Education Resources Information Center.

- Ability to connect your ORCID iD to your IGI Global publications.

- Earn royalties on your publication as well as receive complimentary copies and exclusive discounts.

Get Started Today by Contacting the Acquisitions Department at:

acquisition@igi-global.com